Animation, Embodiment, and Digital Media

Animation, Embodiment, and Digital Media

Human Experience of Technological Liveliness

Kenny K. N. Chow

The Hong Kong Polytechnic University

First published 2013 by
PALGRAVE MACMILLAN

Palgrave Macmillan in the UK is an imprint of Macmillan Publishers Limited, registered in England, company number 785998, of Houndmills, Basingstoke, Hampshire RG21 6XS.

Palgrave Macmillan in the US is a division of St Martin's Press LLC, 175 Fifth Avenue, New York, NY 10010.

Palgrave Macmillan is the global academic imprint of the above companies and has companies and representatives throughout the world.

Palgrave® and Macmillan® are registered trademarks in the United States, the United Kingdom, Europe and other countries.

ISBN 978-1-349-44888-3   ISBN 978-1-137-28308-5 (ebook)
DOI 10.1057/9781137283085

This book is printed on paper suitable for recycling and made from fully managed and sustained forest sources. Logging, pulping and manufacturing processes are expected to conform to the environmental regulations of the country of origin.

A catalogue record for this book is available from the British Library.

A catalog record for this book is available from the Library of Congress.

For Ida

Contents

Figures and Tables

Figures

Tables

Acknowledgments

Some of the earliest thoughts or perspectives in this work can date back to my PhD study at the School of Literature, Media, and Communication (formerly School of Literature, Communication, and Culture), Georgia Institute of Technology. I would like to thank the faculty members I met there, including Janet Murray, Jay Bolter, Kenneth Knoespel, Nancy Nersessian, Michael Nitsche, and Qi Wang, for the diverse inspiration I gained from them. Their classes and words paved the way for the construction of my dissertation, which became the theoretical underpinning of this work.

In particular, I am much indebted to my chief advisor, Fox Harrell. I would like to express my deepest gratitude for his enduring guidance, patience, and encouragement. What I have learned from Fox is not limited to academic knowledge but is also a broadened vision of life and culture. More than an advisor, he is also my lifetime mentor and a close friend. Meanwhile, a thank you also goes to another advisor, Mark Turner, not only for his influential work and contribution to cognitive science, but also for his open attitude toward my rather unconventional area of study. His support has boosted my confidence and the feedback has stimulated my critical thinking.

Partial contents of the book have been presented at various conferences, or published in related proceedings or journals. I am grateful to all the anonymous reviewers and editors who have provided comments and suggestions to my articles. I would like to particularly mention Suzanne Buchan and Joon Yang Kim, Editor and Associate Editor of *Animation: An Interdisciplinary Journal*, as well as Maureen Furniss, Editor of *Animation Journal*. They responded to some of my previous writing with valuable advice and reflective feedback that helped sharpen my thoughts in the concept development of this work. They deserve my very special gratitude.

My thanks are also extended to all other reviewers who have reviewed the earlier proposals and the final manuscript of this book. Their opinions complement my limited thoughts in many important aspects. They have played a part in shaping my thoughts.

I would especially like to thank Felicity Plester and Chris Penfold at Palgrave Macmillan for their quick response and professional advice during the publishing process. I would also like to thank John Lee for the last-minute text-editing work.

Last but not least, I would not have been able to write this book without the support of my current serving institute, The Hong Kong Polytechnic University, as well as the former Dean of the School of Design, Lorraine Justice, the current Dean of the School of Design, Cees de Bont, and many colleagues of mine for their concrete support in my absence, including Bruce Wan, Violet Chan, and Alex Ho.

Personally, I want to thank my parents. This book is dedicated to my beloved wife, Ida Chu, for her tolerance all the time.

Abbreviations

LED	light-emitting diode
GUI	graphical user interface
HCI	human–computer interaction
NPC	non-player character
VTR	video tape recorder
AI	artificial intelligence
CGI	computer-generated images/imagery
VR	virtual reality

Part I
Introduction

Marriage of two slippery terms on a new platform

This book touches upon the concepts behind two perplexing terms, 'animation' and 'embodiment', and in particular how these concepts have evolved with the latest development of digital media.

The term 'animation' has multiple meanings. In daily usage, it refers to a medium, a form of art or entertainment, which involves a sequence of still images or cartoons shown in succession to produce an illusion of movement. Its Latin root *animare*, however, literally means 'to fill with breath' – the act of bringing something to life or the state of being full of life. As the animation theorist Alan Cholodenko puts it, the term is 'bedeviled' by two definitions, namely 'endowing with movement' and 'endowing with life'. In the former animation is considered a medium (particularly on film), whereas in the latter it is an idea (Cholodenko, 1991, p. 15). The crux here is whether movement is the sole definitive attribute of life, which is debatable. In other words, is motion itself enough to give the illusion of life? Inanimate objects, such as a vehicle or an electric fan, show movement. Natural phenomena such as lightning or snowfall appear to us as motion. Conversely, life forms like coral and plants might move at such an extremely slow speed that we can barely perceive it with the naked eye.

'Embodiment' is another equivocal term that is hard to grasp. In daily usage, it is the physical manifestation of an abstract or intangible idea, thought, or feeling. In the contexts of cognitive science and the philosophy of mind, it specifically refers to the bodily aspect of human cognition. In the latter case, the term has a double sense: 'the physical structures' of our body and 'the lived, experiential structures' that enable our sensory perception and motor action, which the phenomenologist Maurice Merleau-Ponty sees as the two sides of embodiment, namely the biological and the phenomenological (Varela et al., 1991, pp. xv–xvi). The two sides, rather than in dichotomy, are in reciprocal relation. We cannot sense or act upon the world around us without our bodies; nor can we even know the physical existence of our bodies without the sensorimotor experience of seeing, touching, or internally sensing where our body parts are; that is proprioception in physiology.

Animation and embodiment, two slippery terms, seem to meet and intertwine with each other in the digital age. With the latest advances in computer graphics and interactive multimedia technologies, digital environments including graphical user interfaces, websites, video games, or computer-based artistic works have been imbued with the illusion of life. These digital media artifacts carry visualized information or visible contents that commonly consist of interactive animated elements that bring us wonder via sensorimotor experience. We still remember the amusement when we flicked over a touchscreen, a tablet computer, or a smartphone for the very first time and saw the interface panel sliding accordingly with the inertia effect. We are amazed by interactive installations or projections in museums, galleries, or even shopping arcades that seem to 'react' to our body movements. These interactive dynamic experiences are so vivid that we almost mistake them for autonomous beings, oblivious to the computing technology at work. In fact, animation and embodiment go hand in hand to shape our experience. On one hand, we feel that the digital environment is *animated*. By 'animated', I mean the medium is 'endowed with life' rather than just 'movement'. The visible digital objects show various kinds of liveliness in phenomena such as motion, reaction, adaptation, and transformation. On the other hand, through experiencing these phenomena of liveliness we feel that our bodies are in touch with the digital objects.[1] We sense that we can move them or stop them; in other words, interact with them. We are *embodied* in the digital environment through the sensorimotor experience of touching or moving objects. To sum up, an environment endowed with life entails phenomenological embodiment in that environment; an embodying environment in turn should provide a sense of liveliness. The two ideas, animation and embodiment, unexpectedly, intriguingly work together, becoming interdependent in the new environment. Most important, the interplay between animation and embodiment in digital media hinges on perceptual phenomena of liveliness, which are actually made possible by computing technology, a kind of human invention not originally aimed at providing human experience.

From data to phenomena

A computer, as its name implies, is a machine originally made to compute. So, when and how did computing technology start to shift its focus on to human experience? When did the computer transform from a pure computing machine to an experiential one?

In the nineteenth century an Englishman, Charles Babbage, invented the mechanical computer with an initial view to getting it to do tedious arithmetic in place of humans. It was not until the mid-twentieth century that the first batch of electronic computers was developed to process large amounts of numerical data. The term 'computation' at that time seemed to mean strictly numerical data processing. In the latter half of the last century, many inquiries, attempts, and endeavors have been made to transform the object of processing from numerical data to everyday *information* familiar to humans, such as natural languages, diagrams, pictures, sounds, and moving images. These media materials have been successively encoded as numbers for processing. Today computers or computer-based devices commonly encapsulate and process these media contents, constituting a wide array of nonspecific human activities, including communication, entertainment, creative expression, persuasion, aesthetics, poetics, and others. Machines processing media content include video game consoles, personal or tablet computers, and smartphones, which are part of modern life. In other words, computational devices have become 'intimate' companions to some people. Computational media, the virtual container of aforementioned information that is familiar to humans in computational devices, have become pervasive.

Lately, the object of processing has been further transcended, aiming at human-familiar, dynamic, lively *phenomena*. The term 'phenomena' literally means things appearing for humans to view, to perceive, to experience. Many computational devices of today are intended to augment human experience. They give rise to perceptual phenomena that may evoke a sense of life among their users. These phenomena include not only the usual illusion of movement as in animated images but also other apparently biological or natural phenomena of life such as reaction to stimuli, adaptation to changes in surroundings, metamorphosis (rapid shape-shifting), growth in size or population (gradual change), and even breath (rhythmic and persistent change). For example, an application icon in the dock (a special container of user-selected application icons for easy access) of the Macintosh OS X system bounces up and down in response to a user click. In such computer platform games as *Super Mario Bros.* (1985), a player character suddenly gets transfigured after 'picking up' a special gem or treasure. A few websites dynamically display a graphical representation of social phenomena and track their changes; for example friendship establishment on social networks or exit poll results across geographical election regions. These phenomena are dynamically generated and presented by computational processes, which collectively make digital environments look lively.

Since these computer-generated dynamic phenomena are reminiscent of our everyday, worldly, and bodily experience of life, I call them 'animated phenomena'. Hence, the aforementioned digital media artifacts not only process data, information, media contents, and user input, but also generate and present animated phenomena through dynamic, responsive, and emergent visuals (and audio too). They evoke everyday experiences of life, and sometimes create unprecedented ones among users. Human users of these digital products are recurrently and concurrently engaged in sensory perception and motor action, as well as other cognitive processes such as interpretation and imagination. In other words, this is embodiment in Merleau-Ponty's phenomenological sense because animated phenomena in digital media engage with our 'lived, experiential structures'. They create a situated, perceptual, and even cognitive experience that can only be felt by the embodied user first-hand. The coupling of sensorimotor experience and human cognition particularly resonates with an emergent school of thought in cognitive science: the embodiment of mind, or embodied cognition, which proposes, in contrast to the traditional mind–body dualism, that human thinking is fundamentally inseparable from and dependent upon the physical body and the associated sensorimotor experience. This book is therefore an endeavor to articulate, based on an embodied cognition approach, the emergent kind of technology-mediated human experience, so as to generate a common vocabulary for analyzing existing digital media artifacts and, more importantly, to suggest principles for creating embodying, evocative, and affective new digital designs.

The book: Theory and design

This book is about the human experience of animated phenomena in digital media. It advocates a theoretical and design perspective that emphasizes the pursuit of animated phenomena that evoke in us the everyday experience of life and regards such pursuit as a primary objective of creating digital designs. To this end, the book is organized in three parts.

Part I introduces readers to the diverse everyday examples of animated phenomena. The single chapter in this part characterizes the phenomena, relates associated human experiences to the idea of embodied cognition, distinguishes the proposed topic of investigation, what I call 'technological liveliness', from other comparable areas of study, and establishes sensorimotor experience, cognitive processes, and computing technology as the underpinning of this research.

Part II is about theory. It delineates four interrelated perspectives on technological liveliness in four chapters, respectively discussing (1) from a spectator's viewpoint, how the user of a digital design perceives liveliness (2) how the user's body interacts with the lively digital environment (3) how one's mind makes sense of the animated phenomena, and (4) how the user acts like a performer improvising with the computational system to co-create liveliness. Each perspective brings forth a principle for the analysis and design of animated phenomena emerging in digital media.

Part III is about analysis and design. It closely examines a corpus of digital media artifacts from three major genres, namely user interfaces of systems or devices, video games, and digital art, examined in three separate chapters. Every artifact is articulated and analyzed according to the principles derived from Part II. The last chapter of this part illustrates how the proposed perspectives and principles inform new possibilities of creating more embodying, evocative, and affective forms of multimedia design objects.

Readers might be aware that Parts II and III are cross-referenced. The former is organized according to principles with illustrative examples from various genres, while the latter enumerates the corpus, with references to principles developed in Part II. After finishing Part I, readers interested in the theoretical articulation on the basis of perceptual psychology, cognitive semantics, phenomenology, and others in relation to the topic of technological liveliness may move on to Part II, while those less concerned with theories may skip the individual chapters and flip to the chapter summaries of Part II straight away, then choose any chapter in Part III to find out how animated phenomena are manifested in particular design artifacts. Since the two parts are cross-referenced, readers can always jump back and forth if at any moment they want to know more about either theoretical grounding or design thinking embedded in any artifacts.

Hence, this book is intended for multiple audiences. On one hand, for researchers, educators, and students interested in the relationship between art, technology, and philosophy in the digital context, the theory part centralizing the new technology-mediated human experience is particularly thought-provoking. Meanwhile, the related analysis part provides good references for readers to employ the proposed approach in their respective studies. On the other hand, for digital media artists, designers, or developers, the analysis and design part is inspirational and visionary. It encourages them to think critically about digital designs, using another lens focusing on embodied cognition in humans. Moreover, they can trace back to the theory related to a particular design easily and the theories are not genre-specific. Readers practicing solely in one digital media type, for example video games, might broaden their visions by referring to other comparable genres, such as digital art. This cross-referencing feature certainly adds another level of intellectual value to the book.

Finally, the work in this book is expected to serve as a bridge between two ways of thinking. For readers inclined toward humanistic concerns (e.g., art theorists or designers), the book informs possibilities of employing cognitive research results and computational approaches in analysis and creation of meaning. For those with backgrounds in technological research and development (e.g., computer science researchers or programmers), this book provides evidence supporting the vital role of human experience and also humanistic orientations for designing and developing new technologies. At the end, it will bring about an interplay of the two minds.

1
Technological Liveliness

A glance at three animated cases

Animated traffic signals

I came across an intriguing traffic light in Spain some years ago. Pedestrians are supposed to cross the road when a little 'walking' green man lights up. The green man walks at first and then runs as the light is about to turn red. The traffic light shows a matchstick man animated in a walking cycle. Images produced by a matrix of light-emitting diodes (LEDs) are displayed successively at a certain speed to achieve an illusion of movement. The green man appears to walk, then run because of the varying playback speed, a technique widely employed in creating moving images.

This case fascinated me. First, it informed me of the ubiquity of animation in today's digitally mediated environments. Similar traffic lights were installed in many other cities around the world (see Figure 1.1). This traffic light's primitive graphical form makes intertextual reference to another matchstick man in the classic computer platform game *Lode Runner*, who ran relentlessly on many Apple II computers circa 1980s. I also can't resist the temptation to think about the Incredible Hulk in comics (later on TV and Hollywood motion pictures) as the two green men run on the street in their own ways.

Second, this animated version of traffic signals provoked me into questioning its purpose. Undoubtedly, the *Lode Runner* matchstick man and the Incredible Hulk were animated to entertain the audiences. But what is the purpose of animating a traffic signal? There is no point in entertaining pedestrians. Is the animation created just for the sake of decoration, as a demonstration of advanced electronic technology, or for

Figure 1.1   An animated 'running' green man on a traffic light in Taipei. Images by Lawrence Chiu.

specific purposes with a certain meaning? Having experienced it, I would say I 'felt' a sense of warning and urgency when the little green man ran.

The genie effect

Another thought-provoking case takes place on a graphical user interface (GUI). In the Macintosh OS X system, users may enable a feature called 'genie effect' under System Preferences. A window will then elegantly shrink and twirl into the dock (a user-interface element of the system holding a list of application icons for convenient launching) when minimized, ready to be maximized at any time. As the name of the feature suggests, the effect is intended to conjure up the image of a genie, like the one in Disney's *Aladdin* (1992), who is trapped in a magical oil lamp and intermittently reveals or hides himself with a twirl (see Figure 1.2).

When first launched, this genie effect amazed many users because of its elegant animation. The mimicry of genie movement was also revolutionary in the field of human–computer interaction (HCI). The visual effect was not created for the sake of utility, because the generative process consumes extra computational power without adding any new function. From a usability perspective, it does not make the interface easier to use or learn either. What is the purpose of animating a GUI window like a genie? Is it just an embellishment, or a spectacle of computer rendering technology? In the design process of an interactive digital product, is there any agenda other than efficiency and usability? As a regular user of the OS X system, I would say the animated effect is a visual metaphor of the philosophy behind the GUI. You can open a

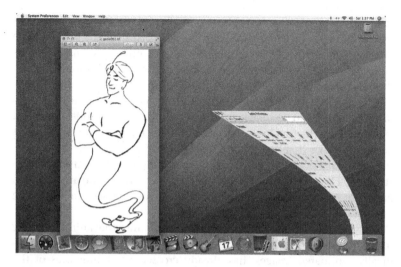

Figure 1.2 Two genies, one commonly pictured in cartoons, the other in the OS X interface environment. OS X © 2013 Apple Inc.

standby window instantly, just like summoning a genie. I 'see' the spirit of the system, and so I 'feel' the charisma of the well received technology brand as a whole.

Turning a digital page

Another case in point arises from that all-pervasive electronic device, the tablet computer. Its touchscreen allows direct operation by the fingertips without a mouse or touchpad. In an electronic book app, you can slide a finger across the screen to turn a page little by little, very much as you would with a physical book. You may also tap or flick the screen, and it will do a page flip automatically. The digital pages seem to gracefully and closely follow users' finger actions, even more so than their physical counterparts. What struck me is the way electronic books take precedence over paper books for our future generations. Infants born to a tech-savvy affluent family are more likely to be exposed to electronic books first. Such infants presented with a paper magazine are likely to think it is a broken iPad. In the YouTube video 'Baby Thinks Magazine Is a Broken iPad', the little reader flicks the magazine page expecting it to flip automatically and the 'inanimate' page inevitably disappoints him.

The touchscreen interface is commonly praised for the naturalness it affords. It epitomizes the notion of direct manipulation, which in a cursory summary means a user is able to directly affect a digital object on screen by a physical action (Murray, 2012, p. 416). With touchscreens we can directly 'turn' a digital page, but what is the value of seeing the intermediary steps of how a page turns? For efficiency and effectiveness, a system should promptly display the next page without showing the intermediaries. In fact, the animation undermines the immediacy of the experience. On the other hand, the simple tap-to-turn or flick-to-turn action and feedback are already quite easy to understand and learn, making the touchscreen highly usable. The extra animation effect does not make it more so, but instead, confuses the user as it blurs the boundary between physical reality and digital environments. Nevertheless, I believe many readers, like me, may have found an animated page turn comfortingly familiar, imbuing the reading with an immersive quality.

The little green man, the window genie, and the animated page turn show us that what people commonly call 'animation', or technically 'animated images' has already crossed the boundaries of the cinema or television and started to pervade today's digitally mediated environments, including cyberspace and even public places. In these aforementioned cases, the term 'images' does not sufficiently describe the user's perception. What one perceives and experiences are the animated phenomena, achieved by the combination of animation as an idea and embodiment via sensorimotor experience.

Characteristics of animated phenomena

The following sections focus on the animated phenomena mentioned above. As introduced at the beginning of this book, the modifier 'animated' here refers to the meaning of its Latin root. Something animated is 'instilled with life'. Meanwhile, the term 'phenomena' means occurrences for people to see, to hear, to perceive; in short, to experience. Here the occurrences themselves and the way they present themselves to the experiencers are equally important, simultaneously resonating with 'mental phenomena' and 'physical phenomena' championed by the psychologist Franz Brentano. To Brentano, the former is the 'act of presentation', such as hearing a sound or seeing an image, while the latter is the content of the occurrence, for instance, the pitch of the sound or the color of the image, acquired through perception (Brentano, 1995, pp. 79–80). In other words, the former is the way the latter presents or appears, and every phenomenon should include both. Hence, by 'animated phenomena', I mean those *technology-mediated presentations of content* that are intended for someone to experience, reminiscent of one's everyday experience of life in the world. These phenomena, which are usually generated with machines and commonly presented in interactive, dynamic digital objects, correspond to an array of biological or natural phenomena of life. They include reaction to stimuli, adaptation to changes in surroundings, autonomous motion or transformation, growth in scale or population, and even improvised or contingent behavior. They are prevalent in today's digitally mediated environments, and examples can be identified in user interfaces, video games, or computer-based artistic works.

Reaction to Stimuli

- An application icon in the dock of Macintosh OS X bounces restlessly in response to a user click when one is launching the application (Figure 1.3).
- Buttons, menus, or other widgets in some multimedia Web pages feature the rollover effect. When a user moves the mouse pointer over a button, the button responds with animated visual effects. In the application Microsoft Word for Mac, mousing over buttons triggers animated water ripples, simulating a reaction to the user's 'touch'.

Adaptation to Changes in Surroundings

- John Conway's famous computer program *Game of Life* (1970) is an exemplar demonstrating visually how cellular units in a two-dimensional grid adaptively evolve with each other.
- When an iPhone user reconfigures the home screen, he or she taps and holds an application icon until all icons start to wiggle. The icon can then be dragged across the screen while other icons move aside to make way.

Autonomous Motion or Transformation

- In the aforementioned case of traffic lights, the little green man seems to know the signal is about to turn red and so starts to walk faster and faster.
- Most non-player characters (NPCs), from alien birds in the classic arcade game *Phoenix* (1980) to computer racers in the *Gran Turismo* series (first released in 1997), are able to move autonomously. Each of them has its own internal logic.

Figure 1.3   An application icon (Fetch) bouncing in the dock of OS X. OS X ©
2013 Apple Inc. Fetch © 2000–2013 Fetch Softworks.

Growth in Scale or Population

- In many time-challenge computer games, players often
  encounter hurdles like tetrominoes in *Tetris* (1984) steadily piling up. The growing pile acts as an indicator toward the end.
  A game is over once the pile reaches the top.
- Viral websites such as *Ecotonoha* use graphical forms to represent user-submitted contents. The virtual tree in *Ecotonoha* grows
  more branches and leaves when users leave their messages.[2]

Improvised or Contingent Behavior

- To a player, competing against NPCs in computer sports games,
  just like competing against human players, is always an improvisation full of contingencies, because NPCs are programmed to
  display pseudo-randomness.
- Philip Worthington's interactive installation *Shadow Monsters*
  (2004) is a digital version of shadow puppetry, which attaches
  bizarre graphical appendages to a projection of participants'
  shadows. When a shadow moves, no matter how subtly, the
  attached appendages unexpectedly change in shapes, resulting
  in an improvised effect.

The above examples summarize the animated phenomena that engross
me, for at least three reasons. First, they are pervasive in today's digitally mediated environments. We come across animated phenomena
in everyday life across various media and platforms, including personal
computers, mobile devices, video games, computer art, and even

digital signage in public spaces. As multimedia technologies become increasingly accessible, presentation of content in an interactive and dynamic manner is now the norm.

Second, they are not oriented toward utility. At first glance it is hard to determine their practical objectives. Some of them may look similar but differ in functional terms, such as the green man on traffic lights versus the matchstick man in *Lode Runner*. Others seem to add visual interest and embellishment at best. For instance, an application window does not need to shrink and expand like a genie to be functional and usable. Nevertheless, these seemingly ornamental effects can be prominently evocative and possess value to some users. Macintosh fans might as well commend the genie effect, bouncing dock icons, and other animated effects because they add to the overall 'feel' of the acclaimed machine. The added value, which is hard to specify, is called affectivity. It is parallel to such common parameters as functionality, efficiency, and usability.

Last, but definitely not least, animated phenomena usually engage with integration of sensory and motor experiences. Not only do we visually perceive the animated phenomena, but also act with or upon the digital objects occasionally, such as crossing a road as the green man on the traffic light walks, or clicking to unhide a window on the GUI. Similarly, the digital objects sometimes respond to our actions, as the genie window twirls to minimize upon a click, or the icons on an iPhone screen make way for rearrangement. In short, users of a digital product are not passive viewers, but active participants who shape their own experiences. This perception-action-reaction link, to the users, constitutes a sensory–motor feedback loop, which reminds them of the everyday experiences of life. A bird flies away when someone approaches. The crowd disperses to make way for someone trying to cut through. Digital objects and users also interact in similar ways.

Despite these three characteristics, namely pervasiveness, affectivity, and sensorimotor engagement, such animated phenomena are commonly dismissed as peripheral concerns in the contexts of user-interface design, computer game development, and even digital art-making. This book argues that animated phenomena enabled by computing technology should be at the core of the study and creation of digital media artifacts, because they actually manifest the primal and persistent urge among humans to animate the inanimate that spans periods and cultures.

The pursuit of animated phenomena

Animated phenomena do not just take place in today's digital media context. In human history, many pre-digital or mechanical artifacts were created in pursuit of liveliness in inanimate objects, by generating an illusion of life for (and with) their audiences (and users) via mechanical means. The most widely known examples in the West include nineteenth-century optical toys/devices like the phenakistoscope and the zoetrope. Such early experimental artifacts creating moving images are considered the precursors of animation (as media) and then cinema by media theorists such as Alan Cholodenko (1991, 2007) and Lev Manovich (2001). They uncover the historical and theoretical links between these optical devices and cinematic art, via the introduction of motion. My thesis here is analogical — I aim to connect computational devices and technological liveliness, via animated phenomena. Furthermore, what I mean by 'animated phenomena', in line with Brentano's view on phenomena, is not just about the images themselves but also about the 'act of presenting' them. That is how these images are generated, perceived, and above all, experienced. Today, a person playing the video game *Super Mario Bros.* has to make the character jump at the perfect timing by 'fiddling' with the joypad. This sensorimotor experience is not unlike the way a zoetrope viewer 'fiddles' with the device to see the animated images through the slits. We will look at the similarity in the sensorimotor experiences between pre-digital artifacts and their digital counterparts in the following sections.

Optical devices

Early optical toys/devices allow a viewer to spin, flip, or illuminate pictures in succession, making them appear to move. On the surface level, playing with them seems to involve only visual perception. Yet in practice, a certain degree of motor action on the viewer's part is required, from the simplest act of leaning in to peep, to more engaging physical operations (spinning, flipping, etc.) that generate mechanical movements, and hence, moving images. A viewer moves his body parts (e.g., hands and arms) while viewing simultaneously. He detects stimuli through both visual perception and proprioception (i.e., perception within the body, such as positions and movement of arms or hands). The direction and speed of hand movement usually determine the motion of the pictures. This motor–sensory connection mobilized during the operation of these optical toys/devices lies at the core of this study. Such sensorimotor experience strikingly resembles that of some electronic media devices, such as the video tape recorder (VTR), which usually includes a control knob allowing a user to spin clockwise to jog the video forward, and anticlockwise to jog backward (see Figure 1.4). The direction and speed of spin result in the playback of the video. To the user, motor action (and the corresponding proprioception) and visual perception are tightly tied.

The nineteenth-century optical toys/devices are generally regarded as precursors of animation and even cinema in Euro-American study of the art. In fact, some mechanical artifacts from other parts of the world, particularly East Asia, also manifest the human pursuit of an illusion of life. More important, they mobilize a type of cognitive connection between motor action (through proprioception) and sensory perception on the viewer's side. These peculiar artifacts include shadow puppets, *karakuri* (Japanese mechanical doll invented in the Edo period), pacing-horse lamps and handscroll paintings.

Figure 1.4 Using a rotary knob to control VTR playback: Clockwise spin results in forward playback of the video, while anticlockwise spin results in rewind.

Shadow puppets

Shadow puppetry is a popular traditional entertainment in Asian countries such as China and Indonesia. Puppeteers use rods, instead of strings as in marionette performance, to control puppet movement. They hide behind the screen, and audiences on the floor only see the puppets' shadows projected on the screen. While moving a rod connected to the limb of a shadow puppet, a puppeteer is simultaneously a performer as well as a viewer of his own show, because he also looks at the moving puppets on the opposite side of the screen from the audience. His visual and motor apparatuses are simultaneously engaged in the control of the animated puppet shadows (see Figure 1.5). The visual–motor feedback loop is similar to the case of a computer user moving a mouse to drag an item on the GUI desktop. The puppeteer lifts the rod while the computer user drags the mouse. Both of them see an object moving in response to their action. The similarity is even more manifest in

Figure 1.5 Puppeteers being simultaneously performers and audience of their own show. Performance at Shanghai Shadowgraph Museum.

computational systems such as video games exhibiting the inertia effect. For instance, some computer platform games like *Prince of Persia* (1989) allow players to move their avatars left and right on the platforms, but players meanwhile can sense the weight due to the delayed and offset animation on screen as compared to their own action, which actually constitutes part of the dexterity challenge of such games. Another example is the inertia scrolling effect featured in the iOS system on the iPhone or iPad. When a user scrolls up or down in a window, the panel in the window moves with inertia showing follow-through and bounce-back movements. All in all, the virtual figures or digital objects in these systems are 'moved' by the computer users, just like shadow puppets moved by puppeteers.

Karakuri

Automata are medieval mechanical machines meticulously designed to 'demonstrate' self-movement, creating an illusion of autonomy. Some classic examples were built in the eighteenth century, including Jacques de Vaucanson's humanoid flute player and digesting duck (Terpak, 2001, p. 268). These artifacts were regarded as automatic performers at that time. The automation mainly relies on the clockwork mechanism and the control is largely limited to the basic on-and-off operation. So automaton performance is like playback of a movie, with primitive play-and-stop control without much audience interaction. Yet the Japanese tea-serving mechanical doll in the Edo period (Yamaguchi, 2002) is an exception. It is a specific type of *karakuri*, that is humanoid automaton, demonstrating the traditional Japanese tea ceremony in an interactive fashion (see Figure 1.6). Wearing miniature traditional costume, the doll paces with a teacup in its hands. As in an actual ceremony, it bows to offer its guest tea. When the guest picks up the teacup, it stops pacing and waits patiently. Once the teacup is returned, it lifts its head and turns back. If the guest does not do anything, the doll does not wait but just paces around and then comes back after a while. The sense of timing and contingency in the interaction resonates with that in many mini computer games. Different player actions on different occasions usually result in different outcomes. Moreover, as with some casual games whose interaction mechanisms are simulacra of human social activities (e.g., *Feel the Magic: XY/XX*), the interaction of *karakuri* reflects the ritual of the Japanese tea ceremony.

The cases of shadow puppetry and *karakuri* show that although puppets and automata may be peripheral to human actors in theatrical performance, they manifest the human pursuit of creating an illusion of life.

Figure 1.6 A contemporary reproduction of the tea-serving mechanical doll. The doll's locomotion and reaction are driven by the clockwork veiled by the costume.

Pacing-horse lamps

The Chinese pacing-horse lamp functions like a peculiar mix of mechanized zoetrope and shadow play (Needham, 1962, p. 122; Stafford & Terpak, 2001, p. 73). The special lamp, a kind of lantern widely known in Chinese folk culture, contains a rotatable cylinder with either opaque drawings on a translucent background or cutouts on its opaque wall. The candle at the center of the lantern casts shadows onto the translucent outer screen. There are vanes at the top of the cylinder so that the rising heat currents from the candle cause the cylinder to turn steadily. As a result, the shadows on the lantern shell seem to move automatically, like camera pan on the silver screen or a running marquee sign on a theater. Although the working mechanism is different from that in automata, the human operation is similar. The viewer is responsible for turning on and off the illusion of self-movement. One can also fine-tune the 'gears' of the cylinder or the vanes, like automata engineers, to adjust the running speed for an optimal viewing experience. The operation is actually echoed in today's digital media context. For instance, a programmer uses the marquee tag in HTML to animate a Web banner and control its horizontal scrolling speed. A user of a digital photo album application configures the transition effect and speed for a slideshow. The human user here takes control of the presentation of the animated effect with the support of the machine.

Handscroll paintings

Compared with pacing-horse lamps enabling user configuration, some traditional media artifacts empower their viewers with even more inter-active control. The handscroll, a distinctive format in Chinese and Japanese painting, is an exceedingly long horizontal scroll. The long for-mat not only enables the presentation of multiple points of attention distributed over the continuous canvas space, but also specifies a par-ticular order of reception structured along the horizontal composition. Classical examples include Gu Hongzhong's *The Night Entertainment of Han Xizai*, believed to have been created in tenth-century China (Wu, 1996, p. 29), and *Chojujinbutsugiga* (*Animals at Play*) created around the twelfth century in Japan (Hu, 2010, pp. 26–27). These works show a long landscape of outdoor or indoor space in which characters are involved in certain events. These events seem to unfold successively to a viewer when one scans from one end to the other of the scroll. However, the viewers should not move themselves along the scroll to scan it, but rather move the picture. The Chinese art historian Wu Hung describes the proper, and also the 'private' way of viewing a handscroll (Wu, 1996, pp. 59–61). When not in use, a handscroll is rolled up. On viewing, the spectator unrolls part of it, approximately one arm's length at a time. This length roughly defines the width of the viewing frame, and the spectator shifts this frame over the scroll every time by unrolling on one hand and rolling up on the other (see Figure 1.7).

This viewer-controlled unrolling process is strikingly similar to the act of panning the film camera. The unrolling, like panning, is coor-dinated with the viewer's eyes and hands. When the viewer's field of sight approaches the edge of the frame, the viewer gently unrolls that side of the scroll and rolls up the other end. The viewer receives stim-uli from both visual perception through the gaze and proprioception through the motor hand action, which jointly render the viewer an apparent sense of controlling a horizontal camera pan. Although the picture is undoubtedly static, the peculiar viewing process does give the beholder an experience of moving camera view in a landscape or even a narrative world. Such interaction mechanism is also common in digital media. For example, most document viewing applications in personal computers allow users to scroll pages vertically. In some versions of the

Figure 1.7 The author's hands and eyes coordinate the panning frame of a handscroll painting.

Macintosh OS X system (e.g., Leopard), users can move fingers up or down across the touchpad to 'unroll' that side of the page. The direction is the same as moving the 'thumb' in the scrollbar. Some websites feature immersive interfaces such as an interactive panorama, which lets users move the mouse pointer left or right to see the corresponding side of the scene dynamically. A user in these digital environments, like a handscroll beholder, gains a panning view, as if moving across a virtual space, because the direction of motor action runs parallel to that of the intended gaze.

All the aforementioned mechanical media artifacts resonate with the characteristics of animated phenomena enabled by computing technology. First, they present themselves on different media or platforms. The content presented can be drawings, cutouts, or three-dimensional objects. They are exhibited in different contexts, such as on stage (puppets or automata), in galleries (handscroll paintings), in domestic spaces such as sitting rooms (lanterns, handscroll paintings, or *karakuri*), or even in communal areas (lanterns or puppets). Second, these inventions do not serve a utilitarian purpose, at least initially. They were invented and designed to be toys, devices of wonder, means of entertainment, decorations, or works of art. Functionality, efficiency, and usability are not primary concerns. Last, and again most important, they represent an illusion of life involving their viewers' multiple senses. These senses not only mean aural or visual perception, but also include stimuli from touch and proprioception through motor control of the artifacts. They require viewers to spin, to flip, to raise or move items, to tune or fiddle, to unroll, and the like, while simultaneously displaying self-movement (pacing-horse lamps), reaction (puppets), or contingency (*karakuri*). Through the motor actions and perceived sensory feedback, viewers sense their bodily involvement in the generation of an illusion of life, or life-reminiscent experience. Apparently, the illusion is triggered and maintained by motor control of the artifacts, and then perceived by the viewers. Conversely, the generated illusion engrosses the viewers and incites their further bodily engagement with the artifacts. This engaging motor–sensory feedback loop characterizes the kind of embodied, life-reminiscent experience that constitutes the necessary condition of what I mean by 'animated phenomena'.

Meanwhile, different periods and origins of the above mechanical media artifacts show that the pursuit of animated phenomena is transhistorical and pan-cultural. The emergence of these artifacts spans human history, from the tenth century or earlier (handscroll paintings or shadow puppets) to the nineteenth century or later (the zoetrope or *karakuri*). Today's digital media re-creating animated phenomena definitely relay this enduring human pursuit. Moreover, the pursuit of animated phenomena is not limited to particular human cultures. There have been traditional media artifacts from the West (optical toys) and the East (pacing-horse lamps or shadow puppets). They were created in early periods when cultural exchange between different parts of the globe had yet to come into play. Although some historians like Joseph Needham suspect the striking similarity between Chinese pacing-horse lamps or shadow plays and Western magic lanterns or optical toys might have arisen from mutual knowledge, there is no evidential proof of such lineage (Needham, 1962, pp. 122–125). Even though the mechanical principles of the latter may be inspired by those of the former, this just shows that people's fascination with the illusion of life is not culturally bound.

Hence, the pursuit of animated phenomena, which spans multiple media, platforms, purposes, senses, cultures, and times, is worth more explicit theoretical investigation.

Theorizing animated phenomena

This study is about the kinds of animated phenomena presenting interactive and dynamic images enabled by computing technology, engaging users in terms of perception, action, as well as cognitive operations including interpretation and imagination. There are a few established or emergent areas of knowledge or practice in relation to this intricate topic. Regarding perception and interpretation of animated phenomena including motion and transformation presented through digital images, animation studies, an emergent field studying the unique qualities of animation as a medium in terms of aesthetics, representation, narrative, and other humanistic research interests, may provide references. There is also a corpus of literature theoretically and rigorously addressing the topic of image interpretation in general, so-called iconology or iconography, from initially linguistic approaches in visual representation, to recent cognitive approaches in understanding images. For the interaction between users and computational systems, the rising field interaction design combining industrial design practice and HCI research results may describe how a user interacts with a digital object. On the subject of digital image generation, research and development in computer graphics in the discipline of computer science may help readers to understand technological implications for user experience.

Although these fields are related to the topic of this study, a theoretical framework simply bringing together the corresponding principles, perspectives, and methodologies might not be promising or useful. As shown, animated phenomena span multiple media and platforms, with diverse purposes or meanings, and involve multiple experiential senses. The diversity and multiplicity render the problem formulation nontrivial. Consider the above areas of knowledge and practice related to the issue. Animation studies, as a field of research that largely inherited from film studies, center around issues of animated images in the context of cinema or television. Whether it is appropriate and broad enough in scope to apply cinema-based theories to the new computational media is questionable. Iconology, a niche area of study originating from art history that combines interdisciplinary approaches to understand visual images, addresses interpretation of images in a larger context than cinematics. But no major work on animated images has been conducted so far, not to mention interactive dynamic images. Interaction design, a practice heavily influenced by user evaluation-driven approaches to HCI, revolves around user action and perception but its aims are predominantly inclined toward utility and usability. These principles may not be perfectly in line with the functionally nonspecific nature of the digital media artifacts this study targets. Computer graphics research focuses on technologies of digital image generation, but seldom touches on the issue of image interpretation in digital media. All these fields provide this study with certain knowledge related to animated phenomena, but each of them has a quite distinct research agenda and perspective, different from the primary focus of this project. In fact, this project is to investigate the *human experience* of animated phenomena. As animated phenomena become pervasive in the digitally mediated environments today, the corresponding human experience also becomes everyday and mundane. Such experience is bodily, involving sensory perception and motor action. Such experience determines how meanings are made. A spectator makes sense of a digital media artifact not only through visual perception but also by interacting with it, as many aforementioned examples have shown. In other words, humans encountering animated phenomena are recurrently and concurrently engaged in sensory perception, motor action, as well as cognitive operations like meaning construction and elaboration. The coupling of sensorimotor experience and human cognition resonates with an emergent school of thought in cognitive science: embodied cognition.

Cognitive science is an interdisciplinary study of the human mind encompassing linguistics, psychology, artificial intelligence, and philosophy (Varela et al., 1991, pp. 4–5). A later perspective of the field is called embodied cognition, also known as cognitive semantics, the embodied mind, or enactive cognition, which tightly ties itself with the phenomenological tradition of philosophy. Scholars in the embodied cognition field assert that our cognition (i.e., how we think) is largely shaped by our bodily experience of the ordinary world including perception and proprioception of bodily action. As Francisco J. Varela, Evan Thompson, and Eleanor Rosch put it, cognition is 'the enactment of a world and a mind on the basis of a history of the variety of actions that a being in the world performs' (Varela et al., 1991, p. 9). In the latter part of their book, they reiterate 'cognition depends upon the kinds of experience that come from having a body with various sensorimotor capacities' (Varela et al., 1991, p. 173). George Lakoff and Mark Johnson are also congruent with such views; in their own terms, 'what we understand the world to be like is determined by many things: our sensory organs, our ability to move and to manipulate objects, the detailed structure of our brain, our culture, and our interactions in our environment'

(Lakoff & Johnson, 1999, p. 102). These statements establish a firm connection between sensorimotor experience and human cognition, both grounded in the body.

Embodied cognition is a unanimous view arising from various disciplines as an alternative to preceding dominant schools of thought in cognitive science including cognitivism and connectionism (Varela et al., 1991, pp. 7–9). In linguistics, Lakoff, Johnson, and Mark Turner respectively raised the pervasive use of metaphors in everyday languages and literary works as a departure point to argue for the bodily and experiential basis of concepts (Lakoff & Johnson, 2003; Lakoff & Turner, 1989; Turner, 1996). Gilles Fauconnier and Turner extended the ideas even to everyday practices and creative feats. In psychology, Rosch did substantial research to relate various categorical systems, including color and other perceptual qualities, to human cognition (Lakoff, 1987, pp. 42–43). In her later career, Rosch, together with Varela and Thompson, concluded that concepts of color are built upon our experiential as well as biological and cultural conditions (Varela et al., 1991, p. 172). From this, they argue that cognition is inseparable from sensory perception and motor action. There are many other researchers arriving at similar conclusions in their studies, such as in artificial intelligence (e.g., Rodney Brooks), neuroscience (e.g., Giacomo Rizzolatti), or philosophy (e.g., Hubert Dreyfus).

Among all these substantial works, application of embodied cognition theories to explaining how people experience animated phenomena in digital interactive media is still underexplored. This book is an inquiry into the relationship between the technology-enabled animated phenomena and our embodied cognition. In the following sections, I revisit the several areas of knowledge and practice related to theorizing animated phenomena. Each of them starts with a cursory overview of the influential figures, approaches, perspectives, and beliefs in the field, followed by underscoring those insightful links to the embodied cognition thought that entails bodily experience.

The study of animation

The field of animation studies represents a set of humanistic concerns for animation, including aesthetics and interpretation. Scholars in this field have predominantly drawn on two approaches, namely contextual and textual analysis (Furniss, 1998, pp. 7–12). The former looks into production contexts, including the historical, industrial, technological, and economic situations in which individual works can be understood. Some studies in this approach also review the national or cultural aspects of animated films as a film genre. For example, anime, an emerging genre, can be approached as Japanese national cinema stemming from its post-World War II economic history, just happening to be in the form of animation. Textual analysis, usually more theoretical and ahistorical than the contextual approach, draws attention to the canonical texts of the specific medium. It entails conducting close readings of works and applying theoretical models to perform analyses of the meanings, narratives, representations, or aesthetics of animation. For instance, Paul Wells's comprehensive typology of narrative strategies based on a set of canonical animated films demonstrates how this method is applied to analyzing the distinctive medium, suggesting a wealth of possibilities for animators and filmmakers to create their new works (Wells, 1998, pp. 68–126). Regarding aesthetics, Wells proposes a relational array between 'experimental' and 'orthodox' works, with a remark that animation should be inclined toward the experimental side challenging the orthodox regime of live-action movies (Wells, 1998, p. 28). Maureen Furniss meanwhile outlines a continuum of animated images in relation to two extremes, namely 'abstraction' and 'mimesis'. The continuum seems to encompass all different film styles and approaches, with the mimesis end comparable to live-action images (Furniss, 1998, pp. 5–6).

Research in film-based animation has contributed an immense and powerful corpus for the analysis of works creating an illusion of movement with sequential images. Such research related to animation narrative or aesthetics would be particularly insightful for the analysis of animated phenomena in computational media. Yet these approaches primarily centralize animated images in the context of cinema or television. The differences between these 'old' media and computational media in distribution and consumption terms render some theoretical arguments related to conventional animated films or TV shows not directly applicable to new computational animated phenomena. For example, an animated film or television show often dominantly engages with its audience's visual and aural senses for a certain period of time lasting for minutes at least. In contrast, the attention mode of a computational media consumer can be more dynamic and transient. An animated emoticon shown in an instant messaging application may draw user attention just for a second, whereas computer games of different genres, such as causal games or role-playing adventure games, may consume a player's time either intermittently or continuously. The diversity in computational media consumption modes requires quite different narrative strategies than a conventional storyline in film.

In addition, 'old' media intrinsically fall short of inciting a viewer's sensorimotor experience, because audiences of film-based animation assume a relatively passive role and so are less motivated to take motor action than the participatory and sometimes proactive consumers of computational media. Hence, analyses of perception and interpretation of animated images in 'old' media seldom consider spectators' bodily experience other than audiovisual perception. The few exceptions include Vivian Sobchack's work. Drawing upon phenomenological ideas such as those in Merleau-Ponty's work, Sobchack, extraordinarily, investigates spectators' bodily experience of film, or strictly speaking, of the cinematic culture (Sobchack, 1992, 2004). Her subject matter is the moving image but the context is still largely the cinema. As computing technology mobilizes spontaneous motor–sensory feedback loops between media consumers and the artifacts in digitally mediated environments, an account of bodily experience of animated phenomena incorporating motor action would be desirable.

The study of image interpretation

How a visual image makes meaning poses a challenge to many thinkers and researchers in the field of semiotics. Semiotics, also called semiology, is the general science of signs (Barthes, 1973a, p. 9; Gombrich, 2002, Preface) with an emphasis on the process of signification, which means how one thing 'stands for' something else (Eco, 1976, p. 8). The idea originated from Ferdinand de Saussure's linguistic work, which suggested that for any linguistic unit there is a link between its concept and its sound pattern, that is to say, a coupling of conception and perception (Saussure, 1983, p. 66). Roland Barthes reviewed and extended Saussure's idea of linguistic signs to apply to many of our everyday objects, such as fashion items and images in popular media (Barthes, 1973b). Yet Barthes and his disciples have tended to separate the material 'image' (e.g., a sound image, a graphic symbol, or a picture) from the mental 'image', which refers to concepts in our minds. Their work typically focuses on how people make and share meanings of images, resulting in a substantial volume of literature on how an internalized idea is related to the ideology shared by a group of individuals. Most such arguments rest on articulating socially or culturally established relationships, stating that any symbol, whether verbal or visual, is only conventionally linked to its meaning (Barthes, 1977c; Gombrich, 2002; Goodman, 1976). Such ideas affirm the separation of concepts and percepts.

Fortunately, there are other thinkers who dismiss the strict dichotomy between mental and material images. Ludwig Wittgenstein notably pointed out that images inside our brains (mental images) are no more abstract than images outside (material images), because we always think in terms of what we have already perceived, or even what our fingers are pointing at, whether they are verbal symbols or visual images (Mitchell, 1986, pp. 15,19). This statement resonates with the thesis in embodied cognition that concepts are structured by sensorimotor experience. Echoing Wittgenstein, W. J. T. Mitchell raised the example of a decoy: when a duck responds to a decoy, it is seeing another duck (Mitchell, 1986, p. 17). To the fooled duck, the perceived image needs to match with its mental image for it to mistake the decoy for a real duck (Mitchell, 1986, p. 90). Whether a perceptual image is interpreted as a decoy or a real duck depends on the viewer.

Another film theorist as well as perceptual psychologist, Rudolf Arnheim, also demonstrated insights suggesting a close relationship between cognition and perception. As Arnheim puts it, 'the cognitive operations called thinking are not the privilege of mental processes above and beyond perception but the essential ingredients of perception itself' (Arnheim, 1969, p. 13). He argues that in addition to the concepts of concrete objects (e.g., hat or flag, see p. 115), abstract concepts (e.g., good or bad marriage, see p. 125) also take advantage of myriad image qualities to anchor in our mind, resulting in a continuum of images of increasing degrees of abstractness, from faithful copies of percepts that replicate specific sensory experiences, to non-mimetic pure shapes that represent generic concepts (Arnheim, 1969, p. 151). Arnheim's analyses are worth comparing with Charles Sanders Peirce's trichotomy of icons (which in turn is one of the three kinds of signs; the other two are indices and symbols). Peirce categorized icons into images, diagrams, and metaphors, forming also a continuum of increasing degree of abstractness in representation based on similarity. Images deal with likeness in certain concrete perceptual qualities; diagrams work on analogies in spatial or relational structures; metaphors establish association of dissimilarities (Hiraga, 2005, pp. 31–35).

Barbara Maria Stafford also asserts that mental images are results of perception, as well as action. She quotes Merleau-Ponty: 'vision is a mirror or concentration of the universe . . . the same thing is both out there in the world and here at the heart of vision' (Stafford, 2007, p. 138). She also quotes Francis Crick and Christ of Koch: 'the information available to our eyes is not sufficient by itself . . . the brain must use past experiences to help interpret the information' (Stafford, 2007, p. 142).

Drawing upon the recent discovery of mirror neurons that tends to suggest the connection between an action we see and an action we perform, Stafford states, 'thought is an image that incites us to re-perform what we perceive' (Stafford, 2007, p. 148). To Stafford, humans understand an image by perceiving and performing it.

All these insightful works contribute to setting forth a trajectory look into the perceptual experience and cognitive operations of animated phenomena. But we still need to import other areas of knowledge about motor action in order to theorize sensorimotor experience in conjunction with cognition.

Interaction and interface design

Interaction and interface design deals with problems arising from the use of instruments or design objects. A major part of the field specializes in the design and implementation of computer interfaces originating from the fields of HCI and software engineering. The initial concerns include utility (i.e., targeting user goals), effectiveness (i.e., completeness and accuracy of results with respect to user requirements), efficiency (i.e., speed of completing a user request), and usability (i.e., how easy it is for users to learn and to use). These principles, collectively called user-centricity, are prevalently manifested in many computational systems, including the GUI of today's personal computers.

Many design conventions of today's GUIs follow Ben Shneiderman's idea of 'direct manipulation', which emphasizes spatial representation of objects (e.g., the computer desktop), physical action (e.g., the drag-and-drop mouse action), and visible feedback (e.g., change of appearance when an item is selected) (Shneiderman, 2003 [1983]). As Shneiderman puts it, the primary goal of interface design is to bring human–computer activity back to the level of early stages of Jean Piaget's theory of child development, in which children comprehend largely through physical actions. Interfaces based on this principle would be easier for children, and certainly adults too, to understand, to learn, and to use (Shneiderman, 2003 [1983]). This embodies the popular term 'user-friendliness'.

Apart from Piaget's works, many psychological principles are influential to interaction design. J. J. Gibson invented the notion 'affordance' to mean those environmental features that support what inhabitants can do. These properties in an environment, whether natural or artificial (in fact Gibson dismisses such dichotomy in an environment (Gibson, 1986, p. 130)), are usually directly perceivable, without requiring much learning (p. 143). Extending this idea of affordances, Donald Norman asserts that a good design artifact should make its clues of use, in other words its affordances, clearly visible and perceivable to users (Norman, 1988, pp. 22–23). Users should be able to map the perceptual clues to their mental models of the design and then understand how to use it. Norman's proposals, together with those of other advocates, like Jakob Nielsen's practical doctrine for website design, constitute the prevalent thought, user-centricity, in the field.

All these ideas emphasize perception and action, which align with the embodied cognition approach. They imply the use of graphical representation (although Nielsen has been a major opponent of use of graphics on the Web) for better communication between users and systems. However, user-centric approaches also tend to dismiss the use of animated visual effects, which are seen as embellishments only and do not enhance usability. For instance, Shneiderman thinks that an interface with anthropomorphic representation, which is usually presented in animated figures, 'deceives the users', 'increases anxiety', and 'reduces user control' (Shneiderman & Maes, 1997). Although Shneiderman mainly contends with Pattie Maes's agent-based approach to interface design, he also prefers excluding any kind of 'animation' from 'direct manipulation' as it might increase anxiety but not usability.

The prevalent user-centric approach inclined toward user goals does not seem to resonate with the theme of this study, in which I intend to investigate the user experience and meaning of computational media artifacts rather than their functionality and efficiency.

In this regard, Paul Dourish's 'embodied interaction' sheds light on the meaning of user action for designing interactive systems. Drawing upon thoughts in the phenomenological tradition of philosophy, particularly Martin Heidegger's 'being-in-the-world', Dourish delineates a list of high-level design principles enabling embodiment of meaning in interactive systems. The idea behind these principles is to engage users in an environment familiar to them, according to their habitual skills with physical objects and everyday practices in social activities (Dourish, 2001, p. 126). But Dourish's work mainly focuses on user engagement in the working environment. In view of this, my project is to explore how animated worldly phenomena would enhance user engagement in the experiential and lively environment of computational media artifacts (e.g., video games or entertainment applications) to make meaning more evocative of everyday life. The primary concern of this kind of computational environment or system is not functionality but rather embodiment of worldliness. Here, Merleau-Ponty's phenomenological view on intentionality and motor action, together with Gilles Deleuze's cinematic theses on perception, provides this part of the research with solid ground. Related ideas will be discussed later.

Computer graphics

In computing disciplines an area of research particularly related to the generation of animated phenomena is computer graphics, whose research agenda has primarily been about the digital synthesis of a sequence of images. Early research topics included hierarchical modeling and parametric motion in primitive graphic forms, as well as development of efficient standards and encoding for multimedia contents. These concerns have been expanded by later studies to include computer representation of physical objects and materials, photorealistic rendering (and then later stylized rendering, such as cel-shading) techniques, simulation of physical phenomena such as particle systems and spring dynamics, developing algorithmic approaches to generate organic behavior such as flocking (e.g., Craig Reynolds's *Boids*) or other self-evolving patterns such as cellular automata (e.g., John Conway's *Game of Life*), implementing artificial intelligence (AI) programs to create seemingly intelligent behavior (e.g., the Oz Project led by Joseph Bates), and so forth. Initial application domains were primarily technical, scientific, medical, architectural, and recently cinematic, yet the marvelous illusions generated by computers have spread to other communal and personal entertainment platforms, including television, digital signs and billboards, personal computers, and handheld devices.

Mainstream computing disciplines see animation as a part of computer graphics. The term 'computer animation' is narrowly understood as only computer-generated imagery (CGI) in sequence. The promising capability of generative algorithms and processes supporting interactive dynamic construction of animation has been downplayed. However, the aforementioned animated phenomena in GUIs and other computational media herald the emergence of a new animation paradigm. This interactive and dynamic form of 'computer animation' has not been addressed directly by current research in computer graphics and HCI, the agenda of which are primarily productivity- or usability- oriented, largely overlooking the potential of computational artifacts in making evocative or expressive meaning. Although a few researchers like Bates, Michael Mateas, Ken Perlin, and lately Noah Wardrip-Fruin have published works related to computer expressiveness, they have not explicitly emphasized the role of animation in computational media. This study aims to fill this knowledge gap.

The embodied cognition approach

The above sections are brief surveys of some existing approaches pertaining to animated phenomena. Some of them incorporate cognitive and experiential factors in their arguments to different extents. To focus these phenomenon-oriented thoughts on the theme of this study, the idea of embodied cognition is the crux.

On one hand, animation studies and iconology emphasize the aesthetic, expressive, and socially or even politically critical values of human artistic creations. Scholars in these areas are interested in how animation and imagery make meaning. On the other, researchers of HCI and computer graphics focus on the functional, informational, or entertainment potentials of the related designs and technologies. They are inclined to explore how people and society can pragmatically benefit from state-of-the-art technology. The two sides roughly correspond to the two aspects of human intellect, namely semantics (i.e., meaning) and pragmatics (i.e., practical uses). I believe the study and creation of animated phenomena in digital media require a perspective bridging these two aspects. Underpinning this bridge is the embodied mind. As mentioned, humans facing animated phenomena are concurrently and recurrently engaged in sensory perception, motor action, and meaning construction. Through this perceptual and bodily experience, users make use, as well as making sense, of computational media objects. As Wittgenstein puts it, 'the meaning of a word is its use in the language' (Wittgenstein, 1953, p. 43). Consumers of computational media create meaning of artifacts by putting them to use. This book is to investigate this meaning-making process taking place as an individual acts in a digital environment. This study thus resonates with the embodied cognition approach to cognitive science.

What technological liveliness is

I call the theme of this study 'technological liveliness'. It is the animated phenomena enabled by computing and related technologies. As mentioned, these animated phenomena also represent a new paradigm of computer animation emerging in today's digitally mediated environments. However, I do not straightforwardly name them as 'computer animation' or 'digital animation', because these terms are misleading.

As mentioned in the Introduction, the word 'animation' might mean slightly different things to different people. To general audiences, it is a form of entertainment, such as animated cartoons. To producers, animators, or programmers, it is the technique of creating an illusion of movement by presenting successive images at a flickering speed. To artists, animation is a singular form of moving image art enabling them to explore meaning in unprecedented and expressive ways as opposed to those directly recorded through camera lens. Although all these views sound equivocal, animation seems to be about movement. As the celebrated animator Norman McLaren puts it,

> Animation is the art of movements that are drawn; what happens between each frame is much more important than what exists on each frame (Furniss, 1998, p. 3).

This well known dictum marks movement as the essence of animation, rendering the word inappropriate and inadequate to encompass the multiplicity of senses entailed in what I mean by animated phenomena.

Moreover, the phrases 'computer animation' and 'digital animation' seem to mean just animated images generated by computers, which are commonly called computer-generated images or CGI. They definitely do not capture the distinct nature of the subject matter in this study, which is the illusion of life and its corresponding user sensory experiences. Although the kinds of animated phenomena this study centralizes are often presented in animated images generated by computers, they differ drastically from CGI in that they foreground users' sensorimotor experience through real-time, on-the-fly generation of images. First, the images in animated phenomena are generated, composed, and presented on the fly by a computational system. Different occasions can result in different instances of images. This is dynamism in a computing sense. Second, the different instances, because of real-time rendering techniques, can be immediately presented in response to user input or intervention. This responsiveness enables real-time interactivity. The two properties, namely dynamism and interactivity, of generative processes supported by today's computing and related technologies jointly render possible various characteristics of animated phenomena described earlier in this chapter, including reactive, adaptive, transformative, contingent, and improvised. More examples include the player character Mario having different appearances at different times passing the same passageway, and application icons of the dock in Macintosh OS X spontaneously scaling up or down in response to the mouse motion. Not only do users see the animated images in these scenarios, but also act upon them, move them, scale them, or set them off. The sensorimotor experience evokes everyday encounters of life in them. In other words, the essence of animated phenomena lies not in movement but in liveliness, distinguishing the subject matter of this study from conventional CGI.

In contrast to 'animation' I prefer the term 'liveliness', because the latter word has not been loaded with connotations by any communities of practice, fields of academic study, or social groups. Literally, liveliness is simply a perceptual and experiential quality. It does not assume any particular physical material, media type, presentation context, target audience group, or purpose of use. The purity and non-specificity of the word make it perfect for matching the nature of the animated phenomena I have been describing. Hence, technological liveliness primarily refers to the kind of interactive dynamic experience of animated phenomena enabled by computing and related technologies.

On a secondary level, technological liveliness also refers to the theoretical and design perspectives I intend to argue in this book. As introduced earlier, the pursuit of an illusion of life has existed across different cultures throughout history. In the past, people including craftsmen, engineers, and scientists made use of various materials and mechanics in an attempt to create this illusion. Today with the computer, artists, designers, programmers, and other users also join the enduring mission. So, technological liveliness symbolizes the creative impulses, endeavors, and feats of today's cross-disciplinary practitioners and participants who continue to pursue an illusion of life in the new media arena. In other words, the term means a primary objective in creating digital media artifacts.

Finally, I hope this term can serve another more progressive agenda, bridging the humanistic mind and technological mind. Through the manifestation of technological liveliness, artists or designers will be inspired by computational and cognitive approaches to meaning creation and humanistic interpretation. This book introduces them with more high-level frameworks of computation or cognitive models than technical details of implementation. They do not need to struggle with codes, yet will become aware of the capabilities of generative processes. Technological liveliness opens up new possibilities for them to 'animate' their ideas. On the other hand, programmers or developers will appreciate expressive potentials of computational systems. The discussion of technological liveliness shifts their focus from functional aspects to humanistic concerns. Through articulation of human experience, this book lets programmers and developers become sensitive to the user perspective on a system. Hopefully they will weigh their technological development strategies in line with our everyday life experience as well as productivity and efficiency.

All in all, my ambitious wish is to make this new vocabulary a bridge between parallel yet related disciplines.

What technological liveliness is not

The term 'technological liveliness', however, to some readers, might be easily confused with other apparently overlapping areas of study. For example, the study of artificial life includes topics such as philosophical, historical, or technological investigation into human attempts to understand life by reproducing it, at least in part, artificially (Riskin, 2007). AI, a niche research area in computer science, aims at proving (or disproving) the statement 'machines can think'. Its technical application to computational media like computer games is called game AI, supporting perception of autonomous entities in a game world by means of codes (Mateas, 2003). Moreover, there is a philosophical view, what N. Katherine Hayles calls the Computational Universe, claiming that the universe is generated through computational processes running on a vast computer underlying both human behavior and natural reality (Hayles, 2005, p. 3). In fact, a brief review of my interpretation of animated phenomena mentioned above will show nuances differentiating technological liveliness from these related yet divergent visions.

Artificial life is a persistent and also challenging endeavor of humans, covering a wide array of artifacts and technologies invented in human history to imitate some aspects of life, for instance self-movement or evolution. Examples range from early mechanical devices demonstrating simple locomotion for decorative purposes and various humanoid automata showing human or animal motion, to contemporary robots or even androids that interact with environments, complex systems emulating some essential properties of living things such as metabolism or evolution, and many others. By developing artifacts simulating biological phenomena, artificial life attempts to understand the logic of life. As Katsunori Shimohara and Chris Langton put it, artificial life should not be limited to borrowing biological principles but rather aim to influence biology (Shimohara & Langton, 1996). Technological liveliness does not follow this ambitious trajectory. Instead it investigates the illusion of life in the digital domain with emphases on how computing technology, dynamic visual imagery, and user–system interaction, come into play.

Game AI is a practical field flourishing in the past decade, thanks to the blossoming of computer games. It covers a diverse set of AI programming techniques such as path-finding strategies, models of emotional states or social situations, finite-state machines, rule-based systems, and decision-tree learning algorithms (Mateas, 2003). The function of these codes is to create a sense of autonomy in a game, making game characters or items seemingly able to act at their own will: to perceive, to react, to remember, and to search for goals. Similar algorithms could certainly be used to achieve technological liveliness, making a computational media object reactive to stimuli or adaptive to changes in surroundings. In designing and implementing technological liveliness, however, the focus is put more on the quality of perception, for example pattern, rhythm, or timing, than on the logic of behavior, such as induction or deduction.

According to Hayles, computation is 'the process that generates behavior in everything from biological organisms to human social systems' (Hayles, 2005, p. 19). It seems that liveliness, as a phenomenon in the universe, is inevitably inscribed in 'the Regime of Computation'. So, technological liveliness can be regarded as a subset of the Computational Universe. Among all processes that generate 'behavior in everything', technological liveliness focuses on technology-enabled processes that generate animated phenomena intended for humans to experience in real time. This statement ironically differentiates technological liveliness from a pure subset of the Computational Universe. In the terms 'intended', 'experience', and 'technology-enabled' lie the nuances. First, technological liveliness is intended for someone. That is to say, there is a designer arranging, programming the phenomena. Second, technological liveliness is to be experienced. In other words, there is someone perceiving and interacting with the phenomena. Third, technological liveliness is enabled by technology, rather than emerging naturally like biological or social phenomena. In fact, the notion of the Computational Universe is immense; in this notion the 'computer' is comparable to Mother Nature who governs everything in the world (Hayles, 2005, p. 19). On the contrary, technological liveliness is always manifested in real machines, usually computers, not the 'motherboard of Nature'. Computers are colleagues of humans, not the origin of us all. They work with us, collaborate with us, and improvise with us to pursue an illusion of life. In short, technological liveliness emphasizes the cognitive and experiential bases underpinning the connection between the illusion of life, humans, and computers.

Method and organization

The topic of this book is the human experience of animated phenomena in today's digitally mediated environments. Grounded in the embodied mind, humans encountering animated phenomena are engaged in sensory perception and bodily action, meanwhile making meaning of their sensorimotor experience. With computing and related technologies, these phenomena are generated on the fly and presented in real time. Their dynamic and interactive characteristics render a digital product spontaneous and contingent. Following phenomenologist ideas, human bodies are able to develop motor habits through practice and open up possibilities for sophisticated abilities in a familiar environment (Russon, 2003, pp. 29–30). Human users, after developing habitual skills, become fluent and ready to improvise with a computational media system, like playing a musical instrument in a group. It follows that four major aspects envelop the human experience of computer-based animated phenomena, namely perception, action, interpretation, and improvisation. These four aspects also correspond to the four different perspectives which a user adopts while using computational media artifacts, respectively as the observer, the body, the mind, and the performer. They jointly explain many common animated phenomena of today.

The discussion on each aspect is the core of the following four chapters, which make up Part II of this book. Each of these chapters in the meantime problematizes some predominant concepts of binary opposition in the related area. Each chapter concludes by proposing a new theoretical and design principle on the study and manifestation of technological liveliness. Each principle is also encapsulated in a qualitative variable as part of the analytical tools.

The observer perspective (Chapter 2) looks into the perception of animated phenomena. The chapter addresses the general question: what kinds of phenomena make things 'look lively' to a spectator? Instead of assuming the conventional view that pits organic behavior against mechanical motion, the chapter, after reviewing ideas from Rudolf Arnheim, Daniel Dennett, and latest perceptual or cognitive psychology research results, proposes a new typology of liveliness. It delineates two types of liveliness, namely primary liveliness that focuses viewers' eyes on certain progressive actions, and secondary liveliness that spreads one's attention over a transforming whole. The former is clear and goal-directed while the latter is complex and ambiguous. Two types of liveliness, instead of having a major–minor relationship, complement each other and jointly expand the class of animacy (i.e., conceptual categorization from animate to inanimate) toward what I call 'holistic animacy'. It echoes traditional East Asian holistic thoughts including notions of Dao and Shinto, foregrounding the balance and spread of two types of liveliness in today's digitally mediated environments. The new idea suggests that digital environments, which are comparable to natural and physical environments, are imbued with liveliness.

At the end of the chapter, the qualitative variable *variety of liveliness* and its possible values are introduced to reflect the holistic animacy of an artifact.

The body perspective (Chapter 3) articulates how a user is bodily and affectively engaged in a digital environment. The chapter first reviews early concepts regarding interaction between animate beings and their physical or machine-mediated environments, followed by recent phenomenological accounts of affectivity. While these influential thoughts underpin the notion of embodiment in interaction design, this section suggests centralizing continuous bodily motion and simultaneous perception of changes as the foundation of creating bodily and affectively engaging experience. It also delineates two temporal forms of engagement, which focus on how an object changes over time in response to use during both active and inactive moments. Drawing upon Merleau-Ponty's proposition that motion embodies intention, Deleuze's cinematic philosophy informing the perception of time, and Murray's idea of agency in digital environments, the author argues for motion-based motor input from the user side, and a constantly changing environment on the system side, in contrast to the conventional 'request-response' interaction found in many utility applications. The two qualities jointly condition 'enduring interaction', which renders the user experience engaging and intimate.

Another qualitative variable *temporal pattern of engagement* and its possible values are introduced at the end of this chapter.

The mind perspective (Chapter 4) reviews the cognitive processes of making sense of animated phenomena. Drawing upon insights from cognitive semantics, the distributed cognition idea, and recent neuroscience findings, all from the field of cognitive science, the chapter argues that animated phenomena, whose understanding relies on both our perceptual and motor apparatuses, constitutes an embodied kind of cognitive process. With examples like shadow plays and real-time animation authoring, this chapter shows that meaning construction and elaboration take place through successive conceptual blends between interactive dynamic images and mental images in the viewer's mind. Interactive dynamic images in these cases act as 'elastic' material anchors for conceptual blends, which not only 'hold' information but also 'embody' sensation or meaning in sensorimotor experience for users to elaborate imagination. This kind of imagination, which I call 'material-based', is pervasive in technological liveliness, conjoining the *material* and the *mental* in our cognition. Lastly, the chapter introduces another qualitative variable *level of understanding* and its possible values to describe different levels of conceptual blends triggered by animated images.

The performer perspective (Chapter 5) looks at improvisation between users and computational media systems. This chapter posits animated phenomena as a digitally mediated form of improvisation between users and computational media systems. It starts with an analogy between animated phenomena and live puppet performance in terms of participants' sensorimotor experience, which open up possibilities for the users of a digital environment to act not just as *spectators* but also as *performers*. This phenomenologist and post-structuralist perspective suggests the user–system interaction in animated phenomena is an improvisation between users/spectators/performers and computers in pursuit of an illusion of life. The chapter then introduces the idea of 'puppeteerly animation', which empowers users to manifest animated phenomena like puppeteers, as opposed to the traditional playback of stored 'viewerly animation'. Drawing upon Philip Auslander's notion of liveness and Steve Dixon's view on improvisation in digital media context, the chapter argues that a close look at the liveness of animated phenomena provides a theoretical device to investigate how a computational media system complements user intervention, manifesting the improvised and contingent nature of life and characterizing technological liveliness.

Finally, the chapter introduces the idea of a qualitative variable *degree of liveness* to measure the contingency of life embodied in a computational media system.

To sum up, the following four chapters aim to provoke thoughts on the entrenched relationships in the production and consumption of the illusion of life, namely animate–inanimate, stimulus–response, material–mental, and spectator–performer respectively. Meanwhile, they also construct design principles on technological liveliness and provide a set of qualitative variables for related analyses.

After Part II, the theoretical construction of design principles and analytical tools, the third part proceeds to give detailed analyses of a corpus of computational media artifacts. Each artifact will be described and articulated with a profile of values in terms of the said qualitative variables. Explication of such values with respect to the artifact then follows.

The corpus consists of computational system and website interfaces, video games, and computer-based art. According to Lakoff's description of basic-level categorization, I argue that this collection of basic-level digital media artifacts altogether defines the new concept of technological liveliness. The variety of media types reflects the ubiquity of animated phenomena in today's digitally mediated environment, and the vast differences in creators' intentions show that the phenomena are independent of purpose, meaning, and context, spanning both the mainstream and the alternatives.

The next three chapters conduct close reading of the corpus. The first basic-level category is user interfaces. This category refers to interfaces of machines, computer systems, consumer electronic devices, websites, interactive kiosks, and the like. This kind of digital environment is conventionally productivity- and usability- oriented. However, with improving accessibility of multimedia technology, increasingly more interfaces demonstrate expressiveness and affectivity in addition to basic functionality. The second basic-level category is video games, which provides us with quite a few good examples of technological liveliness, because they show many graphic elements in motion that are reactive in real time and transformative on the fly. The category here generally includes those computational media artifacts intended for entertainment, including arcade games, interactive visual novels, and entertainment applications. The third basic-level category is computer-based art. Computer-based art here refers to those works of art whose discourse processes inevitably entail the use of computing technology. The group includes interactive installations, websites, mini computer games, interactive dramas, and the like.

With the analyses of different digital media artifacts in terms of the four qualitative variables, the final chapter transforms the results into a conceptual terrain. It conceptualizes a multidimensional space in which each dimension denotes one variable and the corresponding possible values distribute along the axis. Each analyzed artifact is then positioned in the space according to its value profile. Each basic-level category, which consists of a number of artifacts, spreads across the space, and all of them form a terrain. The terrain shows the inclination of computational media, and also characterizes technological liveliness exemplified by the corpus. Hence, for designers and developers, the variables work as an index informing the position of a particular artifact with respect to the whole existing terrain. Based on this relative positioning, designers or developers can set adaptive and situational benchmarks for evaluation. Meanwhile, the multidimensional space not yet covered by the terrain also reminds them of new possibilities for creating more embodied and evocative forms of design artifacts, as well as new orientation for developing human-centered technologies.

Notes

1. Here the term digital 'objects' may draw skepticism from some readers from an ontological perspective, because these digital graphics are not made of matter but just composed of pixels that are volatile and transient. In answer to this, I contend that in today's digital environments they can be seen and touched. They are objects in phenomenological terms. In fact, many digital theorists have argued for the materiality of the digital (Chow, 2009; Hayles, 2002; Kittler, 1997; Knoespel & Zhu, 2008). Readers interested in or skeptical about this stance may refer to the related literature.
   Please also note that digital objects here are different from the abstract object in computer science, such as object-oriented programming. The digital objects I refer to are always visible, 'touchable' (through touch-based input devices), and likely moveable.
2. Unfortunately the website Ecotonoha is no longer live because the campaign has closed. But readers can easily find its traces in the form of images or videos on the Internet.

Part II
Theory

Human experience is a convoluted topic of study. Not only does it include a variety of feelings and thoughts that we sometimes talk about, but it also refers to those senses we have which are too spontaneous, continuous, and simultaneous for us to be aware of, let alone describe or articulate. The psychologist John Dewey in his influential work *Art as Experience* profoundly differentiates 'experience' from 'an experience' (Dewey, 1980, pp. 35–36). The former is uncountable, because it is a collective reference to the general phenomena continuously felt by every human at every moment. Every day when we travel between home and work, we see the streets and people, hear different sounds or overhear conversations, notice the change in temperature from the shade to under the sun, or sense the ground beneath our feet, but we seldom bother to attend to this general stream of everyday experience and consciously organize the bits and pieces into 'an experience', unless we come across something extraordinary. For example, if on a particular weekday you witness a pickpocket incident in the metro and call the police, you will remember this incident as an experience, and may even tie the loose ends together into a narrative with a beginning, middle, and end when telling others about it. In Dewey's words, an experience is characterized by 'consummation' that we extract and organize from our everyday experience (Dewey, 1980, p. 38).

This part of the book endeavors to theoretically articulate the human experience of technological liveliness in intricate ways. By experience here I mean both the mundane observations, encounters, or events a person undergoes every day as well as the events that are extraordinary and complete enough to be distilled as memorable incidents, as mentioned above. In fact, experience is the accumulation of every moment of our lives, when we see, hear, perceive, and become aware of something; when we move our bodies, act, and feel; when we interpret, remember, and imagine; when we play, practice, improvise, and create. These various streams of experience are definitely interwoven, but for the sake of articulation and analysis in the following chapters, I disentangle them into four major threads that form the skeleton of human experience. These four threads, in contrast to those in John McCarthy and Peter Wright's *Technology as Experience*, which are more like different layers of experience (McCarthy & Wright, 2004, pp. 79–94), here correspond to four different perspectives toward technological liveliness grounded in phenomenology and embodied cognition, namely perception, action, interpretation, and improvisation, which will be delineated in the following four chapters. First, Chapter 2 (the observer perspective) articulates what kinds of animated phenomena there are and why they seem reminiscent of our experiences of life. Second, Chapter 3 (the body perspective) focuses on how we act upon visible objects in a digital environment and how we feel about the bodily engagement. Third, Chapter 4 (the mind perspective) looks into our cognitive processes, including interpretation and imagination, when we encounter animated phenomena. Fourth, Chapter 5 (the performer perspective) extends the user–system relationship to a new technology-mediated form of improvisation in which the user acts not simply as a passive observer but rather an active performer. Each of these four threads brings

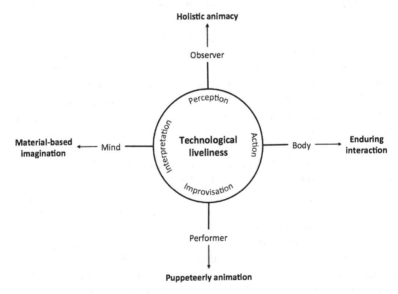

Figure II.1 The four threads of experience enveloping technological liveliness.

forth a principle for analyzing and pursuing technological liveliness, namely *holistic animacy, enduring interaction, material-based imagination,* and *puppeteerly animation* (see Figure II.1). More important, these major ideas are in the end encapsulated in four qualitative variables. Readers who are more interested in the application of the theory in digital media can jump to the summaries of the four chapters and familiarize themselves with the four qualitative variables and their possible values, and then proceed to Part III of this book. On the other hand, readers who look into Part II will find it interestingly thought-provoking.

2
The Observer: We Perceive, We Become Aware

As mentioned in Chapter 1, animated phenomena are technology-mediated presentations of digital objects reminiscent of our everyday experiences of life, including spontaneous reactions to stimuli (e.g., the fight-or-flight response in case of threats), recurrent behaviors (e.g., breathing), gradual changes (e.g., growth), and even quick shape-shifting (e.g., metamorphosis). For instance, an application icon bouncing restlessly in response to a user click demonstrates reactivity. Many screensaver programs on personal computers display animated graphical patterns, which seem to vary and repeat themselves indefinitely. A few video games use gradually extending graphical objects, such as a 'growing' pile of dirty dishes awaiting the players, to be an indicator counting down to the end of the game. A user-controlled character in a computer platform game like *Super Mario Bros.* might intermittently change its appearance. When an observer perceives similar signals in the digital environment, to what degree is one reminded of life or living things? Would one consider the restlessly bouncing application icon to be performing just a mechanical springboard effect? Or is it a funny character attending to a user's needs? How do you feel when a graphical dog silhouette runs on the computer screen during file transfer? When an iPhone user drags an app icon across the screen and other icons make way for it, does it conjure up the idea of a person making his or her way through a crowd? When vertical lines sway on the screen of an interactive installation, would one immediately think of a breeze in the virtual space, a puppet master behind the screen, or instead, the swaying lines assuming a soul, an autonomous will of their own?

In fact, every dynamic presentation reminds us of life to a certain extent. There is a spectrum of animated phenomena with subtle differences in liveliness. It extends from human-like intention-driven behaviors like chasing or avoiding, through organic motions commonly exhibited by animals such as schooling of fish, to natural phenomena not involving living things like tidal movement. This chapter examines the nuances across the spectrum and proposes a typology of liveliness for understanding the relationship between perception of animated phenomena and evocation of life. This typology, echoing with traditional East Asian holistic thought, emphasizes the balance and spread of liveliness in today's digitally mediated environments, and represents a holistic sense of life overarching the natural, physical world and even the digital domain. Such an inclusive approach to digital design gives an immersive quality for its users to indulge themselves in a familiar environment not unlike the natural world.

Liveliness, of two kinds

By 'liveliness', I mean a quality in animated phenomena that makes us think of life or living things in the real world. Yet this reminiscence is not equivalent to actual aliveness, because the former is only a spontaneous impression, which alone cannot confirm if something is alive. There is a subtle difference between liveliness and aliveness since the latter also hinges on our common knowledge (e.g., someone might be in a coma, but still alive). In other words, I am not aiming to inquire into the natural sciences of life, but instead to characterize the illusion of life. To this end, I draw upon perceptual and cognitive psychology, together with East Asian holistic views of life, to delineate liveliness as two kinds, which I call primary and secondary liveliness. The former focuses an observer's attention on a particular process that reveals an unambiguous tendency toward a result, while the latter distracts a viewer's attention over a complex transforming whole that lacks a clear direction but changes back and forth. In other words, primary liveliness is more obvious in showing intentionality as an illusion of life, while secondary liveliness is relatively ambiguous in this sense but still prominent by means of complex transformation.

In order to better illustrate this idea for readers from different disciplinary backgrounds, Table 2.1 summarizes the terminology related to movement, action, visual components, happening, animation, and film, which could be useful to our discussion.

I admit that the labels 'primary' and 'secondary' here might connote an order of importance. In fact, the two types of liveliness differ not in prominence but in nature. They represent the two 'sides' of the same coin, with unambiguous tendency or intention on one end and convoluted or cyclical complexity on the other. An observer may clearly

Table 2.1 Terminology of primary versus secondary liveliness

Primary Liveliness (obvious, directional, clear)	Secondary Liveliness (ambiguous, cyclical, complex)
Translating in space (e.g., flight)	Transforming in shape (e.g., metamorphosis)
Chasing	Wandering
Fencing	Dancing
Directional motion in tug of war	Collective emergent motion of flocks of birds
Throwing spears, shooting arrows	Raining, rippling, water splashing
Body motion of a running girl	Wiggling motion of a running girl's ponytail
Character animation	Motion graphics
Narrative film	Abstract (nonrepresentational) film

identify the intention in primary liveliness like chasing, avoiding, fighting, or dashing away. The same observer may just be equally amazed by complex transformations of secondary liveliness like dancing, schooling of fish, or even snowing. Primary liveliness, due to its intrinsic linearity and humans' inherent preference for clear direction as explained by neurobiology, has initially drawn more viewer eyeballs in traditional media. Secondary liveliness, however, with recent advances in computer graphics and multimedia technologies, has started to gain more exposure and attention in the digital arena. The following sections will further elaborate on the two kinds of liveliness and explain how they complement each other.

The ground of primary liveliness

What reminds someone of life? It has long been a major topic of study in psychology. From the 1920s onwards, the Swiss psychologist and philosopher Jean Piaget studied the conceptions of life and soul among children by conducting in-depth interviews. He concluded in his theory of child development that children have different criteria in telling the animate from the inanimate through different stages of their development. In the first stage, they consider nearly everything as alive. In the second stage, movement differentiates the animate from the inanimate.

In the third stage, they think something that generates its own movement is alive, while something moved by others is not (Arnheim, 1974, p. 400; Turkle, 1984, p. 30). His findings explain why an infant is engrossed by the hanging mobile above the crib, and why kids love the anthropomorphic sun and moon. This theory about child psychology seems to suggest the 'primitive' view that movement instills life. However, one should not hastily think that this view only applies to infants or children, just as some people see animation as cartoons only for kids. In fact, this view of early childhood psychology is still a valid part of our immediate perception after we grow up.

After Piaget, many researchers in psychology continued to investigate empirically how dynamic phenomena like movement influence people's spontaneous judgments on the animacy of an object. Fritz Heider and Marianne Simmel are among the first, creating short films of moving geometric figures and asking observers for their immediate feedback (Heider & Simmel, 1944). They found that observers projected personalities and emotions on the figures because of their temporal contiguity and spatial proximity in the films (Scholl & Tremoulet, 2000). Their findings have called attention to how observers respond to various qualities of motion, like speed, timing, direction, trajectory, and so on. For example, in order to investigate what makes a motion seem to be intentional, Winand Dittrich and Stephen Lea presented observers with films of moving letters among which there are both chasers and targets. They found that the perception of intentionality depends primarily on the motion of the chaser rather than the target. The more directly and quickly the chaser moves, the more intentional the movement seems (Dittrich & Lea, 1994). In other words, a chaser that moves prominently to its goal is more likely considered animate. Lately, Patrice Tremoulet and Jacob Feldman have demonstrated that a change in direction and speed alone, even without any target or obstacle, can produce an impression of animacy (Tremoulet & Feldman, 2000). Judith Ann Stewart also conducted similar experiments by presenting a type of motion that seemingly violates Newtonian laws; that is, it shows unexpected motion. The experiments show that an object abruptly changing direction to avoid an obstacle or suddenly accelerating toward a target is perceived to be more animate (Stewart, 1982). To sum up, prominent, solo, and unexpected movement seems lively. In these experiments, all movements are presented in primitive geometric shapes that are supposed to minimize the influence of contextual knowledge. The responses of mature human subjects show that adults' detection of animate behavior is not very different from that of infants or children.

Based on a substantial number of studies on child cognitive development, Jean M. Mandler has summarized the conceptual model, which she thinks has already been entrenched in infancy, of how people pre-reflectively tell the animate from the inanimate (Mandler, 1992). The model defines animacy by the following criteria:

1. Something starts to move on its own (i.e., self-motion).
2. The trajectory of the motion has certain rhythmic but unpredictable characteristics (i.e., an irregular trajectory).
3. There is a dependence of motion, which can be one-way or two-way (i.e., interactive motion).
4. The object not only moves, but also causes others to move (i.e., turning the animate into agents).

Mandler's model aligns with major findings from the aforementioned empirical studies of perception, that is, solo and unpredictable motion yields remind people of life. In addition, Mandler's proposal extends to consider the aspects of interactivity and agency. These aspects, especially agency, draw our attention to the issue of intentionality, that is, whether something mindfully moves itself or others. We certainly cannot scientifically verify if a certain object has a mind of its own, but what matters here is whether it seems to have one.

Daniel C. Dennett's (1987) theory of the intentional stance takes us to the viewer's perspective in order to differentiate intentional behavior from other phenomena. Dennett's theory describes three levels of abstraction one may adopt when viewing the behavior of an object. On the most concrete level (the physical stance), one uses one's knowledge of the laws of physics to predict the outcome of a behavior. For example, a flying baseball will break a window. On the next level (the design stance), one assumes there is an engineered or biological system governing the outcome and ignores the mechanics. For instance, one predicts the alarm on a clock is about to go off when the preset time comes, or a deer is about to die after being shot. On the most abstract level (the intentional stance), viewers see an object as having an intention toward a goal (Dennett, 1987, pp. 16–17). When we see several ponies fleeing the forest, we guess they may be driven by a predator (cf. Points 3 and 4 in Mandler's model). The intentional stance also applies to plants or artifacts (Dennett, 1987, pp. 16–22), which are commonly seen as inanimate. I hereby add that Dennett's model is also applicable to the way we view animated movies. When we watch an animated pendulum, we take the physical stance to predict the swing. In case the pendulum suddenly swings past the highest point and spins around, we would imagine that it gains 'celestial' energy that acts against the gravitational force, which would keep it in an orbit. The unanticipated movement (cf. Point 2 in Mandler's model) would incite us to speculate upon the intent behind it and to switch to the intentional stance, according to which we are not much concerned with how the pendulum possesses the energy (as we know it is an animation), but rather wonder what happens next. We are engaged in perceiving this kind of intentional behavior, which I call 'primary liveliness', when watching animated movies.

Mandler's model and Dennett's intentional stance jointly describe what I mean by primary liveliness. When a viewer perceives a self-movement, according to Mandler (1992) and Dennett (1987, p. 22), one pre-reflectively detects the animate motion, and habitually and effortlessly speculates on the intention behind it. The viewer concentrates on the motion and spontaneously becomes aware of the intention (although it is only a speculation). To general spectators of animation, primary liveliness is appealing because it contains comforting elements of unambiguous meaning and linear narrative. Hence, the illusion of life presented in traditional drawn and inked animated films is largely dominated by primary liveliness. This idea is best demonstrated by the classical animation principles advocated by Disney animators Frank Thomas and Ollie Johnston (1984, p. 53), such as staging and appeal. These principles state that presentation of liveliness should be 'completely and unmistakably' clear to the audience. In other words, Disney and its followers mainly pursue primary liveliness.

Where is secondary liveliness?

In animation production, primary liveliness corresponds to the primary ways of animating, like a combination of the straight-ahead and pose-to-pose methods (Williams, 2001, pp. 61–63). Animators start to create key drawings, or to set key frames in the case of computer animation, so as to drive the plots forward. Examples include the intentional eye movement of Donald Duck, or the action and reaction between Coyote and Road Runner. Conversely, secondary liveliness arises in secondary action (Blair, 1994, pp. 144–145), such as Superman's cape blowing in the air, the wiggling motion of a running girl's ponytail, or long grass fluttering in the breeze. This 'secondary' liveliness is usually accompanied by repetitive rhythmic patterns, such as waving, orbiting, and cycling. Occasionally, it involve stochastic components such as irregularity and noises. Although these elements may not contribute to the main narrative, they are integral to the illusion of real life. In practice, this kind of animation is called 'secondary' by animators because secondary motion is usually animated *after* primary action has been completed in production, but the order in which scenes are animated does not imply the order of importance. On the contrary, this secondary motion is an indispensable foundation upon which the narrative of primary action builds. Hence, secondary liveliness plays a role very different from primary liveliness. What we need to emphasize here is not the difference in degree of liveliness, but the difference in kind.

The rise of secondary liveliness

As mentioned at the beginning of this chapter, liveliness is based on spontaneous perception. The perceptual psychologist and film theorist Rudolf Arnheim argues against the purely 'intentional' approach to separating the inanimate from the animate, especially from an artistic point of view (Arnheim, 1974, p. 401). He raises a few examples like pitting 'a thunderstorm' against 'impassive passengers' from the viewpoint of a film director to argue that perceptual experience is very direct and may not involve reflective analysis. We may find something, say the thunderstorm, very lively on the basis of spontaneous perception but, on second thoughts, may not think it is alive. For Arnheim, what counts in perceiving liveliness is not whether there is a conscious/intentional mind or soul (Arnheim, 1974, p. 400), but rather the level of complexity in the observed behavior of forces at work. He describes liveliness at different levels of complexity, from simple movement to complex behavior (Arnheim, 1974, p. 401), as shown in the following list:

1. Something that moves is livelier than something that does not.
2. Movement involving internal change (i.e., change in properties like shape or size) is at a higher level of complexity than rigid object displacement in the whole.
3. The thing moving by its own force (i.e., self-initiated movement) is higher in degree of liveliness than that physically moved by others.
4. Those self-movements initiated by internal impulses are livelier than those driven by external forces.

Apparently, Arnheim's criteria of liveliness seem to overlap with Mandler's model (apart from the former's internal change that is absent from the latter, a crucial concept to be revisited later in this section). In fact, Arnheim emphasizes perceivable interplay of forces rather than perceptual evidence of intention. The more complex the interplay, the livelier a phenomenon is. In my view, the first three points cover many natural phenomena and everyday physical interactions between agents and objects, such as a falling leaf, a balloon being deflated, or a racquet hitting a tennis ball. The last point about self-movement with internal impulse corresponds to numerous intentional actions such as chasing, escaping, searching, avoiding, hesitating, and so on. In other words, Arnheim seems to regard primary liveliness as more complex than secondary liveliness. It is true *only if* what he means by internal impulse is the same thing as 'intention'. On the contrary, impulse, in Arnheim's words, can exist on a preconscious and perceptual level.

Arnheim touches upon complex behaviors without strong connection to intention, such as dancing, which is more about secondary than primary liveliness. He sees dance performance as the 'dynamics conveyed to the audience visually' (Arnheim, 1974, p. 408). Any movement of body parts must be generated by a 'narrow local impulse', which spreads over all the body and visibly brings about the posture. I believe, to the audience, these dynamics are so intricate that the interactions among various impulses can only be perceived collectively. The final images presented to observers are still prominent and full of energy, but it is definitely not a simple interactive or intentional behavior. It is a kind of highly complex secondary liveliness.

Such a dynamic phenomenon also resonates with the emergent motion of a flock of birds or school of fish, in which each animal is steering simultaneously toward local members of the flock and away from overcrowding. Viewers cannot tell where an impulse emerges because every individual motion is leading others and being led by others simultaneously, just like every muscle movement and articulation of joint a dancer exhibits. Since there are too many simultaneous interactions, no single action-and-reaction link can be separately perceived by a general observer. What one can appreciate is a dance performance in stark contrast with the obviously directional or intentional movements in primary liveliness, but nonetheless lively. Dennett's theory of the intentional stance may not apply here either, because an audience of a dance performance and a beholder of a flock of birds seem not to take any of the three stances. One just takes pleasure in looking at such dynamically complex transformations without contemplating the physical, design, or intentional implications of such phenomena.

Hence, the two kinds of liveliness differ in how they direct audience attention. While primary liveliness concentrates viewers' attention on a particular progressive center of action, secondary liveliness distracts viewers with a complex transforming whole. The former steers a viewer's gaze toward the linear unfolding of a narrative or event, while the latter distracts one's gaze with many changes that lack any apparent focus. Figure 2.1 is a visual representation showing the relation between the two types of liveliness.

Complex emergent behavior

With the latest advances in computer graphics technology, complex emergent behavior that is prevalent in natural environments has been readily replicated in the digital domain. For example, Craig Reynolds's computational model *Boids* (1986) simulates the kind of complex and emergent behavior found in flocks of birds or schools of fish. The model takes into account three different steering mechanisms: (i) to avoid crowding local members of the flock (separation); (ii) to align with the average direction of local members of the flock (alignment); and (iii) to keep close to the center of local members of the flock (cohesion) (Reynolds, 1986). It suggests the framework of computer-generated flock animation, not just constituting major visual effects of crowd animation in such spectacular movies as *Jurassic Park* (1993) and *Starship Troopers* (1997), but also providing ambience in digital environments reminiscent of real-life experience, such as those emergent patterns seen in many screensavers, or the iPhone application *Koi Pond*, a beautifully rendered computer simulation of a pond of koi fish.

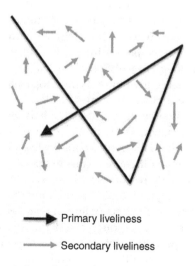

➤ Primary liveliness

➤ Secondary liveliness

Figure 2.1 A representation of the relation between primary and secondary liveliness.

Digital morphing

In secondary liveliness, emergent motion is also comparable to morphing in digital animation, a special effect showing seamless changes from one form to another. The changes usually take place in a distributed and simultaneous fashion, and so distract the audience from any obvious linear development. The audience often cannot focus on a particular part of the transformation. Nor can they fully grasp any obvious chronological or causal order of happening. As Vivian Sobchack (2000, p. 137) suggests, compared with Soviet montage and mise-en-scène, morphing presents a new 'reversible temporality' in cinema. She raises examples of digital morphing, like the 'liquid metal' robot in *Terminator 2* (1991) and the malleable bounded city in *Dark City* (1998), to illustrate how the audience are amazed by the seemingly reversible and effortless transformation of these supposedly solid materials (i.e., metal and concrete) into fluid, like 'playful cartoon physics of animated films'. This notion of 'playful cartoon physics' also parallels Norman Klein's (1993) view on shape-shifting commonly seen in Fleischer Studios' animation, as opposed to that of Disney. For instance, in Betty Boop's *Snow-White* (1933), we cannot easily find an example of anticipation or squash and stretch (both of which are Disney's principles of animation; see Thomas & Johnston, 1984, p. 47) that follows the laws of physics, but instead we see many rhythmic animation cycles and metamorphoses. Klein has repeatedly juxtaposed Disney and Fleischer in terms of metamorphosis. Disney required animators to keep a character's volume constant, whereas the Fleischer animators were free to transform their characters' bodies into any form. For example, when the clown in Betty Boop's *Snow-White* is turned into a ghost by the evil queen, he keeps dancing involuntarily in 'loops' and morphing without limits, even into a chain on a medal. Klein describes this type of morphing event as hesitation or lapse, for it is always unstable and seemingly reversible (Klein, 1993, p. 254). These seemingly reversible events demonstrate what I mean by secondary liveliness, and Klein's use of the term 'lapse', which literally means temporary loss of concentration, and that particularly resonates with my idea of distraction among the audience. Hence, digital morphing and hand-drawn shape-shifting, like emergent motions such as schooling of fish, constitute the majority of secondary liveliness. Although the digital morphing of a liquid metal robot and shape-shifting of a character may seem unnatural to our common sense, we can still relate to and make sense of these visual effects as they resemble our real-life experience of emergent motion of organisms.

Natural phenomena

In addition to complex emergent motion and metamorphosis (morphing), natural phenomena are also mirrored in digital environments. In the past, stochastic processes such as the rain, snow, lightning, falling leaves, and splashing water were considered difficult to approximate in animation production. But with the advances in computer technology, they can be realized by various heuristic algorithms incorporating an appropriate component of noise, as seen on many multimedia websites or CGI-based movies. For instance, the instant messaging website SnowDays (snowdays.me) displays an animated snowing scene with falling flakes of various size and shape created by Web users (please see Figure 6.2). In disaster movies such as *The Perfect Storm* (2000), the sounds of waves, water splashing, and rain are mostly computer-generated.

Motion graphics

If character animation is considered to display primary liveliness, motion graphics are definitely representative of secondary liveliness. Motion graphics arguably stemmed from movie title sequences by John Whitney and Saul Bass. Whitney first produced abstract geometric animation with his peculiar analog computers and then Bass, the graphic designer, added animated patterns to Whitney's animation. Their most notable collaborative work is the motion titles in Alfred Hitchcock's *Vertigo* (1958). In the said sequence, swirling patterns superimposed on a woman's eye distract the audience, symbolizing mental instability while framing the plot of the movie. Today, as related authoring tools have become increasingly accessible, motion graphics have been widely used in television program titles, commercials, music videos, rich media websites, and even motion art and electronic literature. The motion graphics in these digital creations show a creative agenda different from that of Disney-style character animation. Motion graphics do not aim at convincing the audience that an animated object assumes an autonomous mind or an intention. Instead, they present secondary liveliness to distract the audience, immersing them in certain desired atmospheres via dynamically complex motions. All these animated phenomena demonstrate the ubiquity of secondary liveliness in today's digitally mediated environments.

Holistic animacy and East Asian perspectives of life

With the rise of secondary liveliness in digital environments, the two types of liveliness described above work together to re-create our real-life experience in a holistic sense. We always encounter primary liveliness as embedded in and underpinned by secondary liveliness. Sometimes, the former captivates a person's attention, like seeing a predator chasing its prey, or watching a dog nosing around for something. Occasionally, one is perceptually engrossed in the latter, like watching the tidal movements, or people dancing a graceful waltz. These perceptual experiences illustrate what I call holistic animacy.

In perceptual psychology and cognitive science, animacy is interpreted as a perceptual property associated with cognitive processing to classify objects into qualities of animate and inanimate in an environment (Scholl & Tremoulet, 2000). As the cognitive scientist Mark Turner (1996, p. 21) puts it, people detect animacy when recognizing a complex sequence of self-initiated movements not caused by external forces. So, Turner's animacy, echoing Mandler's model, roughly overlaps with Arnheim's complexity of liveliness in that they all consider self-initiated but not necessarily intent-specific and goal-directed movement. Examples of these movements include dancing and wandering. Meanwhile, I have shown that a myriad of natural phenomena showing highly complex dynamics are also worth being considered lively from the observer's pre-reflective viewpoint. Hence by taking into account 'holistic animacy', I intend to expand the class of the animate, or to blur the boundary of animacy, to include secondary liveliness – complex movements understandably not self-initiated. Examples include grasses fluttering (or figuratively 'dancing') in the breeze or raindrops falling in a puddle causing ripples to spread. So, holistic animacy covers both primary and secondary liveliness to form a larger set of dynamic phenomena that are reminiscent of everyday life.

Animacy is also a term commonly used in linguistics. It refers to a category of nouns that differentiate whether the referent of a noun is animate or inanimate. Different languages have different systems of animacy (Woolford, 1999). For example, in English the pronouns 'he', 'she', and 'it', which refer to male, female, and generally nonhuman respectively, are distinct in their spoken and written forms. In Chinese, four pronouns indicating the two genders, the nonhuman animal, and the inanimate, although written differently, are all pronounced 'ta'. In Japanese, both inanimate objects and human can be referred to as 'mono' (although written differently). The compound term 'mononoke' is used to describe animate mythical beings, including demons, ghosts, spirits, and elves, as in the title of *Princess Mononoke* (1997). It seems that the East Asian cultures, compared with their Western counterparts, have a relatively loose classification of nouns in terms of animacy.

According to cognitive scientist George Lakoff (1987, p. 6), entrenched categorization, including linguistic classification, reveals how humans think. It follows that, to a certain extent, the classification system of animacy in a culture reflects the corresponding conception of life. In fact, the inclusive notion of holistic animacy I am proposing resonates with some historical East Asian philosophies about life and living things in the world, such as the notion of Dao in China and Shinto in Japan.

Daoist philosophy is based on Dao, a way of life, which engenders and supports the growth and development of all things, what the Chinese call the 'ten thousand things', *wanwu*, meaning all living things (Henricks, 1999, pp. 161–162). Dao 'brought all things into existence and governs their every action' (Needham, 1956, p. 37). All things are governed in such a way that they have specific characteristics, not brought about artificially but just by being different from one another naturally. The Daoist classic *Zhuangzi* has a well-known parable. A giant bird can fly thousands of miles, while a small bird struggles to even fly between adjacent trees. But both can find pleasure in flying in their own particular ways (Feng & Bodde, 1948, p. 105). The 'ten thousand things' are different in nature, but all can achieve happiness through their natural abilities. In other words, Dao is about the natural order of the whole universe, which maintains functional balance between humans, organisms, environments, and everything else, while preserving individual characteristics. This corresponds to the holistic balance between the two types of liveliness that I have been explaining.

While Dao maintains balance, the notion of Shinto suggests spread. Shintoism, a folk religion-based philosophy in Japan, prescribes the existence of 'spirit' not only in organisms but also in their living environments. This ubiquitous view of spirit is conceptualized as kami, literally anything that has 'inspired a sense of awe in man because of its power or beauty', whether it is a 'rock, a mountain, a man, or a phenomenon of nature' (Wargo, 1990). Everything can have a spirit, and these collective spirits are known as kami. As Wargo puts it, 'there is an essential oneness about the universe', in which man, nature, and even the gods, impartially constitute the whole. This holistic view of life permeates artifacts too. Yusuke Suzumura, drawing upon ideas of Wargo and other Shinto theorists, further argues that the concept of kami is demonstrated in many Japanese animations and comics, including Hayao Miyazaki's *Princess Mononoke* and Akira Toriyama's *Dragon Ball* (1985–1995), without any significant religious affiliation (Yusuke, 2011). I propose that this ubiquitous and secular spirituality also spreads from natural or cultural environments to today's digitally mediated environments. As I have shown, the two types of liveliness are prevalent in computer interfaces and video games, and also mirror our experiences of life – including a sense of wonder – from the material world to the digital world. It follows that holistic animacy covers not only organic and natural phenomena from the physical domain but also animated phenomena from the digital domain.

Implication: Spectrum of animacy – human-organism-natural-virtual

In summary, with the notions of balance and spread, holistic animacy suggests an inclusive spectrum of animacy ranging from the domains of human beings and other organisms like animals and plants, through the ever-changing natural environment, even to today's animation-laden virtual environments. It is not a binary logic between having and not having a soul, but rather about whether there is both primary and secondary liveliness, which jointly render a digital environment as immersive as its natural counterpart.

Illustrative digital objects

To illustrate the extent of holistic animacy in today's digital media context, the following sections discuss several East Asian creative works, namely animated movies, time-based installations, and video games, highlighting how they present a balance of liveliness with the aid of computing technology. Their common East Asian origin is less due to my intention than coincidence. As mentioned in the previous section, the relative ambiguous classification of animacy in some East Asian languages resonates with the holistic conception of life in those East Asian thoughts. Interestingly, East Asians also manifest such perspectives in many of their cultural creations.

A montage sequence in an anime movie

Japanese popular animation (called anime in the Western context) seems to present a balance of the two types of liveliness, both featured prominently from scene to scene. While major scenes in anime inevitably focus on action and reaction between characters and objects in order to unfold their narratives, others are able to tell a story at a slower pace. This is when the surrounding environments take the lead and display secondary liveliness. For instance, grasses or leaves may be blown by the breeze while the protagonist just stands still and gazes at the sunset. These common animated scenes are sometimes regarded as distinct aesthetics of anime. Compared with the Western mainstream counterparts like Disney and Warner Brothers, anime films often have frequent and sustained mood-setting scenes where the characters stay still. Animation loops and planar movements with multiple layers are juxtaposed to imitate camera motion (based on a visual phenomenon called motion parallax; see Lamarre, 2009, p. 39). Anime also seldom renders continuous and complete character actions with no cuts.

The characteristics of anime manifest the importance of secondary liveliness in animation, especially when such effects as loops and parallax are made easily accessible by digital production techniques like compositing. Consider Mamoru Oshii's animated cyberpunk film *Ghost in the Shell* (1995), one of the earliest anime productions extensively employing computer graphics technology such as compositing and image manipulation techniques alongside hand-drawn images (Cavallaro, 2006, p. 194). There is a notable three-minute montage sequence about half an hour after the film starts, featuring secondary liveliness that distracts the audience with animated 'backgrounds' all over the frame without focusing on certain particular figures. It is a montage of nostalgic images of a city with many recognizable Hong Kong elements such as flyovers, narrow streets, billboards, speeding cars, and hurrying crowds, plus imaginary 'tram-boats' and canals. In many shots, it applies digital compositing to exercise multilayer movement to the maximum, like the steady flow of canal water reflecting a moving boat, billboards moving across the foreground while people work in a commercial building in the background, pedestrians passing by a shop window reflecting some animated commercials, and so forth. Dynamics are distributed over the frame, and movements seem reversible or cyclical with their meaning intact, constituting typical secondary liveliness. Although the protagonist Kusanagi appears in some shots, she stays relatively still, with moving billboards in the background, her hair blowing in the wind, or varying window reflections in the foreground. In the latter half of the sequence, rain adds even more liveliness to the seemingly timeless city through lines, ripples, and catchlights on dripping water. All in all, the sequence seems to epitomize the emphasis of anime on a steadily changing atmosphere instead of goal-driven linear action. It is also an animated manifestation of similar inclinations to cover background settings more than the figures in Japanese comics as championed by the American comic artist and theorist Scott McCloud (1994, pp. 70–81) in his comparative analysis of comic works from the West and the East.

Disney's emphasis on character animation and the distinctive style of anime represent different approaches to the two types of liveliness. Yet they are by no means clearly separate from one another. Instead, there are growing mutual influences in the light of increasing accessibility of advanced computer graphics technology all over the world beyond the dichotomy of West and East. The computer-generated character Sulley in Pixar's *Monsters, Inc.* (2001) acting in a lively fashion with his 3 million hairs moving in a continuous rhythm, and the Forest Spirit turned headless gigantic body in Miyazaki's *Princess Mononoke* consciously searching the landscape for its head, while deadly fluid spills everywhere, are evidences that today's animation tends to manifest a co-presentation of the two types of liveliness I have defined.

Animated remake of a Chinese handscroll painting

With the aid of computer technology, digital media incorporate a wide array of liveliness in which their viewers are immersed. They present both primary and secondary liveliness. As mentioned in Chapter 1, some websites (e.g., Ecotonoha) feature virtual trees growing a new leaf every time a user submits a message. Many video games allow users to keep virtual pets or plants, which grow or even evolve in response to user action. Screensavers on computers display emergent animation, which is autonomous and persistent.

A particularly phenomenal demonstration of holistic animacy in digital media artifacts with strong connections to East Asian perspectives of life is the animated version of *Along the River During the Qingming Festival*, first exhibited at the 2010 Shanghai Expo China Pavillion and then in Hong Kong.[1] The work is a digital remake of the canonical Chinese handscroll painting of the same name. The original, produced in the Song Dynasty (about the eleventh century), is an exceedingly long horizontal scroll, depicting the capital then as a prosperous and vigorous city, showing hundreds of residents in various daily activities, such as dining, buying, selling, commuting, and moving things. The handscroll is a classic example of Chinese painting demonstrating multiple perspectives. It presents a landscape over which a myriad of foci are distributed. Someone looking at it usually takes an overview of it first and then closely examines individual details in a random order, thus demonstrating a combination of distraction and attention.

The digital version is supposed to be appreciated as a whole, with larger-than-life details to be examined up close. It is a computer-generated animated video projected onto a long mural (120 m wide by 6 m tall) approximately 30 times larger than the original scroll.

The computer rendering imitates the original painting style and the isometric, multi-perspectival composition. Hundreds of figures in the handscroll, including residents, animals, and even vehicles, are all animated to perform various activities. In addition, the digital animation outdoes the painting by including a night scene not depicted in the original. The four-minute day-and-night cycle loops continuously, and the installation can accommodate a huge audience at any one time.

To the audience, the work presents an engaging landscape imbued with micro-narratives. On average, a viewer spends about 30–60 minutes looking at the work and, during that time, can focus on any single mini-drama, for example a boy chasing a pig. Meanwhile, there are numerous concurrent happenings surrounding viewers' particular gaze and distracting them. They need to walk back and forth to pan across, or step back from it for a wider view. Their minds, and also their bodies, are divided among a myriad of points seeking their attention and at the same time they are distracted by the persistently transforming panorama. This scenario manifests holistic animacy in that dramatic actions of individual animated characters contend with each other but also combine to constitute an organic whole like a flock of birds in emergent motion. For example, a wooden ship, on which sailors are working, crosses under a wooden bridge, while children playfully imitate them, passers-by on the bridge take a casual peek, and others give a hand, in addition to many other activities taking place. Each of these small episodes unfolds in an individual linear narrative, but overall the ship gradually moves along the flowing river. This echoes how Arnheim, as mentioned earlier, describes dance performance, as well as the phenomenon of the emergent motion of a flock of birds or a school of fish. These dynamics are so intricate that spectators cannot easily identify a major direction of the impulses. Yet the collective performance is very lively.

A 'sandbox' game: Electroplankton

Regarding the types of liveliness discussed here, video games of different genres present slightly different compositions between the primary and the secondary. Primary liveliness in general works well with action or sports games because both rely on actions with a linear narrative toward a goal. Interestingly, such a category corresponds to many subgenres, including first-person shooting games such as *Halo* and *Doom* for the Microsoft Xbox console, which are highly popular in Western markets. Conversely, the non-directional nature of secondary liveliness seems to make it incongruent with goal-specific games. In fact, secondary liveliness is more commonly seen in simulation games or so-called sand-box games, which are the kinds of games with unspecified or flexible player goals. A player is engaged, not in targeting a clearly defined goal, but rather in exploring new possibilities or outcomes in the game world. These types of games, which account for a substantial volume of sales in East Asia, contrast significantly with the prevalent action genres in North America in terms of the types of liveliness they emphasize.

An exemplar of sandbox games that demonstrates how secondary liveliness engages players is *Electroplankton,*[2] designed and developed by Japanese interactive media artist Toshio Iwai. As an interactive music game, *Electroplankton* seems to inherit and also elaborate the artist's favorite concept of 'loop' animation. The game features a milieu with various types of figuratively depicted plankton and a few mini-games. Each mini-game allows players to 'fiddle' with the animated plankton with a stylus, or input sound through the microphone. The plankton play different sounds and perform certain cyclic actions in response. Players are rewarded with a plankton musical and ballet performance contingent upon their input. Although each has its own mechanics, the generated sound and motion in these mini-games share one fundamental principle: looping. When the loop continues, a player is able to tinker with the plankton in order to vary the output. The resulting animation does not prescribe a beginning or an end. Nor does it unfold in any obvious direction. It just presents continuously changing patterns.

When playing *Electroplankton,* one moves the stylus and instantaneously perceives the immediate response from the plankton. The dancing and singing of the plankton amaze the player, who in turn performs further motor input to the game. This perceptuomotor process is not unlike the creation process of surrealists' automatic drawing. It is also like Len Lye and other experimental animators' 'direct animation' technique (animation directly drawn on film celluloid), except that the motor–sensory feedback loop enabled by *Electroplankton* is much more transient and emergent. This feedback loop gives rise to highly responsive and emergent animation, which manifests holistic animacy. On one hand, the plankton seem to be autonomous and reactive, as their actions are governed by procedural and conditional loops; closely examining their movements, one notices a certain degree of primary liveliness. On the other hand, the plankton are numerous and so do not behave toward a pre-defined single goal. Each of them acts differently and reacts separately to user input. The player is distracted by numerous sequences unfolding all over the place, in other words, immersed in the secondary liveliness of the overall game milieu.

Summary: Variety of liveliness

This chapter has shown that liveliness, the perceptual quality of animated phenomena reminiscent of life, comes in two kinds. While primary liveliness, which conventionally draws more viewers' attention, foregrounds action that shows obvious intention or tendency toward a certain result, secondary liveliness, which has become increasingly prominent in digital media, presents complex transformations that do not contribute to one linear narrative. The former concentrates viewers' attention, while the latter distracts the audience. These two kinds of liveliness span an inclusive spectrum, which I call holistic animacy, echoing East Asian holistic perspectives of life and expanding the boundary of animacy to encompass not just humans and animals but also dynamic phenomena in natural as well as digital environments. With the balance and spread of liveliness, a digital environment can be as immersive as the natural environment.

The notion of holistic animacy is encapsulated in a qualitative variable, *variety of liveliness*, which can be classified as primary liveliness, secondary liveliness, or both.[3]

Notes

1. For more information about the work, please see the news and photos at http://www.hkexpo2010.gov.hk/eng/whats/news_detail_303.html
2. Please see the official website: http://electroplankton.com/
3. A shorter version of this chapter has been published as 'Toward Holistic Animacy: Digital Animated Phenomena Echoing East Asian Thoughts', in *Animation: An Interdisciplinary Journal*, edited by Suzanne Buchan, 7(2) (2012), pp. 175–187.

3
The Body: We Act, We Feel

Some animated phenomena, such as reaction to stimuli or adaptation to changes, entail interactive dynamic presentation supported by a digital environment, where one can act upon certain digital objects or react to them 'physically' via touch-based or motion-sensitive interfaces. For example, users run their finger across a touchpad to move a pointer or to pan the camera across a space. A player of a flight-simulation game on a handheld device with built-in accelerometers can tilt the device to steer the virtual jet or hang glider, dodging obstacles along the way. The audience of the interactive installation *Text Rain* (Camille Utterback & Romy Achituv, 1999) may move their body parts like their hands or head to see their own projected image catching and lifting falling letters (please see Figure 8.2). In all the above instances, the audiences engage their bodies with the digital environments. In fact, they are not only engaged bodily, but also affectively. The connection between bodily engagement and affection can be explicated by arguments from phenomenology in philosophy. Through repeated engagement our bodies are able to build motor habits, to develop a sense of familiarity with a situation or an object (Russon, 2003, pp. 29–30). Habituation makes us feel at home in a 'world', whether it is physical or digital. It frees up our cognitive power to do more sophisticated activities involving self-expression or evaluation. We gain a sense of control and satisfaction this way. Hence, through motor action and habituation we are at ease in a digital environment, which feels familiar and intimate to us. This briefly explains our affective engagement with a particular digital design.

The crux of the above argument is how to facilitate the kind of habituation that ensures intended positive (or negative) affects such as satisfaction (or anxiety), which lies at the point of integration of our action and perception. As mentioned in Chapter 1, Paul Dourish (2001) advocates that to create engaging interactive systems, one should make use of people's familiarity with the mundane everyday world. I would add that the everyday world with which people feel familiar is lively, and in this lively world we always move our bodies and are shown changes constantly. We continuously and spontaneously map perceived results of our actions, resulting in automatic evaluations of the current state. This process echoes what modern psychologists generally call 'appraisal' (Ekman, 1994) and it is suggested that it forms the core of our affects (Russell, 2003). Toward intended affects, this chapter argues that as opposed to the discrete, conversational type of human–computer interaction, interactive environments have to be able to continuously and simultaneously engage users in bodily motion and perception of changes. A computational system achieves this objective by requiring motion-based user input and presenting perceivable changes during various moments of use. This emergent paradigm of interaction, what D. Fox Harrell and I call *enduring interaction* (Chow, 2012; Chow & Harrell, 2011), emphasizes the temporal pattern of user engagement with an interactive system, which enables computational systems to better match users' extent of action with their perception. It determines user experience of varying intimacy, informing of strategies for creating more affective computational media artifacts.

Not turn-based interaction

Interaction between humans and computers is sometimes figuratively described as a conversation or dialogue between active participants (Crawford, 2005, p. 29). This conversation analogy, however, sometimes leads to the hasty assumption that the user and computer take turns to input and respond, as in the classical command-line interface in early operating systems such as MS-DOS, and even the prevalent point-and-click interaction in many GUIs. In MS-DOS, a user types in commands after the prompt, hits 'return', and then the system responds with results. The pattern is like an alternate question-and-answer conversation. In some GUI environments or websites, a user, rather than typing, usually rolls the mouse pointer over a button and clicks to issue a command. When a button labeled 'Next' is clicked, the system may respond by loading the contents of the next page. The user–system interaction still submits to an alternate request-and-response pattern. Nevertheless, with increasingly popular deployment of touch-based interfaces in systems such as mobile phones with touchscreens, and laptop computers equipped with touchpads, human–computer interaction has shifted its focus from the turn-based model to more continuous and engaging forms. Instant data processing is made possible by modern computers and the time lag between input and output is essentially shortened to none. Users can run their fingers continuously across the screens or pads to scroll a window and see the contents revealed simultaneously in a line-by-line fashion. Some e-book viewers on tablet computers even allow users to 'turn' a page from its corner continuously and clearly see how the page flips under their finger. Not to mention other clever systems utilizing such diverse technologies as infrared sensing devices, gyroscopes, or accelerometers to detect various motion parameters including orientation and acceleration in three dimensions. Users of these technologies, rather than in alternate action–reaction dialogues, are engaged continuously in motor action and simultaneously in perception of instantaneous system feedback.

Motor–sensory feedback mechanism

In fact, a continuous form of simultaneous control and feedback mechanism has been central to the seminal study of human–machine interaction initiated by Norbert Weiner dated back to the middle of the last century. Wiener coined the term 'cybernetics' from the Greek roots that mean 'steersman' to refer to the science of control and communication in animals and machines (Wiener, 1961, p. 19). To Wiener, the steering engine of ships is one of the earliest and best-developed forms of feedback mechanism. Although his interpretation of 'feedback', like his interpretation of steering, is inclined to regulating output by adjusting input (Wiener, 1961, p. 13), which is slightly different from my emphasis on spontaneous reaction from systems, his discussion of animal reaction to nature suggests that the way inhabitants interact with their environment is crucial to interactive system design. Let us look at a user using a mouse to drag a file icon onto a folder icon in a GUI environment. He or she keeps sliding the mouse while tracking the file icon moving on the display until it reaches the folder. This motor–sensory feedback phenomenon is reminiscent of, and phenomenologically comparable to our physical experience of moving a piece of paper from the desk into a tray. When continuously moving our body parts, we need to simultaneously 'see' something being 'moved' from one location to another. Through repeated engagements, our bodies are able to build habits that handle these regular tasks automatically without conscious thought. Though the GUI environment demands a certain level of attention and presents some kind of learning curve at first, a user can easily master the skill without noticing details of his or her action after many repetitions. Habitual users are quite accustomed to operating a wide array of input devices. They are able to automatically, immediately interpret sensory feedback from a system while acting upon the control, much like the way one has already adapted to the physical environment. In fact, this is a kind of habituation, and it hinges on continuous motor action and simultaneous change perception. This idea is evidenced in early stages of physical development. Esther Thelen shows that human bodies in infancy start to develop various simple motor skills, such as reaching out or grasping, through continuous processes of 'integrated acts' of moving body parts and perceiving changes in environments. These changes vary continuously and infinitesimally, and a baby incrementally learns the force required to move muscles to an appropriate extent in a particular context (Thelen, 1995, p. 90). The situation is similar to musical instrument practice. When a person moves his or her body parts, for example arm muscles in the case of the violin, he or she listens carefully to the continuous and simultaneous change of the pitch made and gradually becomes automatic in mapping motion with the desired melody. The above various motor skill developments, including the use of a mouse or other input devices, show that our bodies have the power to develop dexterity in response to both digital and physical environments, and at the heart of this lies the continuous and simultaneous motor–sensory feedback mechanism. This feedback loop is composed of bodily action and sensory perception of change. The following sections look into bodily motion first and then the perception of changes.

Bodily motion and intention

Repeated engagements in continuous motor action and simultaneous change perception enable our bodies to develop habitual skills. Thelen's work has demonstrated and explicated this phenomenon occurring in the early stages of human physical development when we acquire simple, concrete motor skills, such as grasping or reaching out for an object. In fact, the idea also applies to more abstract, imaginative bodily skills, like moving a phantom object or making a hand gesture to communicate or express. The phenomenologist Maurice Merleau-Ponty has provided a detailed explication of this bodily phenomenon in terms of both concrete and abstract movements.

To Merleau-Ponty, our bodies have the power to develop dexterity for, to 'absorb' knowledge from, the environments we inhabit. He believes that the 'body is our general medium for having a world' through motor habit (Merleau-Ponty, 1962, p. 146). Based on Gelb and Goldstein's empirical studies of brain-impaired patients, Merleau-Ponty describes two types of bodily movement, namely 'greifen', meaning 'to seize', and 'zeigen', 'to show' (Merleau-Ponty, 1962, p. 123). The former refers to concrete movements toward some existing objects, while the latter refers to abstract movements not relevant to any actual situation, but dependent upon one's imagination. For example, a brain-impaired patient may be able to touch her or his forehead because of a mosquito bite, but not able to point to it without any stimulus or context that necessitates that. A typical subject can perform a hand-to-forehead salute, but the patient cannot do so without placing himself in an actual situation that calls for it. The patient fails to just imagine it. This helps reveal the fact that unimpaired people have turned most abstract movements, like pointing or other gestures, into situated motor habits. Merleau-Ponty believes that it is our body that actually absorbs meaning, in the form of bodily experience (Merleau-Ponty, 1962, pp. 146–147). In Hubert Dreyfus's words, the body gets involved through practice and acquires bodily skills (Dreyfus, 1996). This habituation frees up our attention and facilitates our imagination in different situated context.

Merleau-Ponty posited that what is impaired in the patient is the 'power of laying out a past in order to move toward a future'. He called this the 'intentional arc', which is our disposition, attitude, and 'aboutness' toward something (Merleau-Ponty, 1962, pp. 135–136). The intentional arc exists in both space and time and works beneath the level of conscious conceptualization. Through repeated practice, we enrich our repertoires of actions within the intentional arc. It is the way we acquire bodily skills and build motor habits. Our bodies 'absorb' motor knowledge and take care of our everyday motion (Dreyfus, 1996). Therefore, a typical subject can perform seemingly imaginary abstract movements like various hand gestures based on the intentional arc as easily as concrete movements on the immediate, preconscious cognitive level. This habitual ability to move, or motility in short, as Merleau-Ponty puts it, reveals our consciousness as 'not a matter of "I think that" but "I can"' move toward something (Merleau-Ponty, 1962, p. 137). In other words, bodily motion immediately, pre-reflectively, and habitually exercised, no matter whether concrete or abstract, embodies one's intention toward a desirable future state.

Bodily motion and emotion

Immediate, pre-reflective bodily motion based on habituation embodies one's intention, which can be quite impulsive and desire-driven. From the phenomenologist point of view, such bodily motion is tied to one's emotion. Recent writers, following the phenomenologist traditions, have argued for the embodied nature of affectivity. Roberta De Monticelli painstakingly identifies the nuances between the common concepts related to affectivity, including feeling, passion, and emotion, in terms of the body. She describes feeling as the 'perception of values of things' (De Monticelli, 2006, p. 65). It can be positive or negative (De Monticelli, 2006, pp. 65–66), in physical or mental terms (De Monticelli, 2006, pp. 70–71). For example, positive feelings include love, pleasure, and enjoyment, while hatred, pain, and suffering are negative. One may feel 'exhausted' because of a demanding physical exercise or a challenging mind game. Compared with the neutral meaning of feeling, passion is more about one's inclination and disposition. Passion is a mode of volition, our 'wanting to have, to do, to be' (De Monticelli, 2006, p. 72). More importantly, it implies 'a *vector* of action' (ibid.). When this action becomes immediate and impulsive, passion is mobilized as emotion (De Monticelli, 2006, p. 74). To De Monticelli and many phenomenologists, emotion is closely tied to immediate and impulsive motor action. This view is also in line with the general psychologist thought that emotion has 'quick onset', 'unbidden occurrence', and 'distinctive physiology' among other characteristics (Ekman, 1994).

Michelle Maiese has explicated in even more details the 'visible' link between emotion and bodily action. She points out emotions are 'plainly visible in the features or gestures of the people who are experiencing them' (Maiese, 2011, p. 63). For instance, people might jump up and down when excited, or someone might throw any object at others in an outburst of anger. The 'sudden', 'unplanned' actions embody one's emotions (Maiese, 2011, p. 57). To Maiese, it follows that emotion is based on one's impulsive, spontaneous, and pre-reflective intention to move the body self-expressively (Maiese, 2011, pp. 62–63). This impulse is our first-order desire of 'wanting or not wanting things to be a certain way'. For instance, someone furious feels a strong urge to throw something. This first-order desire may be 'encouraged', or conversely 'governed', by second-order desires, volitions, or evaluative judgments, becoming wanting (or not) to want something (Maiese, 2011, pp. 63–66). He or she might impulsively throw a cell phone to the ground. He or she can move the body parts to act out that impulse based on motor habits. Habituation here provides room for higher order cognitive processing, such as wishing to appear a rational person (volition), or considering the cost incurred in replacing the phone (judgment), so that he or she might not want to throw it to the ground at last but just onto a couch. This hierarchy of desires sometimes suppresses one's behavior, but other times effectively moves one all the way to action (Maiese, 2011, p. 68). In cases where higher order cognitive processes prevail, desires stay as mere desires, just wants on a mental level. Yet when those processes fail to suppress the first-order desire, a person's motor action acts out the want and he or she moves self-expressively. Each of us is capable of moving the body in various ways according to the repertoire of both concrete and abstract movements, or in Merleau-Ponty's term, the intentional arc. When one has a felt need or want, the body readily performs the corresponding movements that constitute the presentation of an emotion.

According to De Monticelli, Maiese, and other phenomenologists, bodily motion not only embodies one's intention toward a desirable state, but also does so in a particular self-expressive way. Hence, an interactive system requiring user input in bodily motions or continuously engaging users in bodily action tends to invite user's desire-based affective elicitation and expression. As Merleau-Ponty puts it, through repeated engagements both abstract and concrete motor habits are built within the intentional arc. It follows that a user repeatedly engaged in motion-based input with the interactive system will readily develop motor habits to express affectively, much like an infant learning concrete motor skills. Yet, as posited at the beginning of this chapter, an interactive system has to integrate continuous motor actions with simultaneous perceivable changes in order for users to not only express affectively but also perform automatic appraisals. The following section focuses on how perception of changes comes into play.

Perception of changes and temporality

An interactive environment continuously engaging its users in bodily action also invites them to express felt needs and wants. In this way, one builds the affective motor habits and becomes able to express at ease. Furthermore, the environment has to show resulting changes in response to one's continuous action, that is, to facilitate what Thelen describes as the continuous process of 'integrated acts' of bodily motion and perception of changes. This idea of coupling motor action and sensory perception also resonates with Janet Murray's thoughts on affordance in digital environments that enables satisfying and pleasurable experience, or what she calls agency. Murray defines agency to be 'the satisfying power to take meaningful action and see the results of our decisions and choices', and she believes a certain amount of agency is always expected in computational designs (Murray, 1997, p. 126). When we double-click a folder icon, we expect the system to open the folder and show the content inside. When a user runs a finger across the touchpad, he or she expects the window to scroll down. The choices and actions we make are based on our expectation of having certain results, and a system aiming to provide a satisfying user experience should live up to this expectation. The matching of user expectations with actions generates 'the pleasurable experience of agency' (Murray, 2012, p. 12). This matching is comparable to the appraisal mechanism posited and agreed on by some major psychologists (Ekman, 1992). As Paul Ekman puts it, the mechanism can operate automatically at the primary level or sometimes take place more reflectively at higher cognitive levels, which is compatible with Maiese's idea of first-order and second-order desires. For example, a tablet computer user browsing a large image database to look for a recent photo starts flicking the touchscreen, and immediately sees photos 'flowing' under the fingertip and feels fine. After flicking repeatedly, the user evaluates the states of search and feels lost in the myriad of photos. The sense of hopelessness may make him or her want to leave or even throw away the device, a desire which may be governed by higher order desires (e.g., wanting to show the photo to a friend), so that he or she reluctantly keeps searching. Here, desire and appraisal work hand in hand, corresponding to one's motor action and sensory perception respectively. In other words, Murray's agency can be seen as a quality describing the work between desire and appraisal in the user when interacting with a computational design. Yet the interaction described in Murray's agency, in which decisions and actions are followed by results, seems to be turn-based. As I have been arguing, for an interactive environment to be bodily and affectively engaging, the interaction has to be more continuous, seamless, and simultaneous. I add to Murray's view on agency and propose a kind of 'enduring' agency: the pleasurable and affective experience of taking action continuously and seeing the results of our motion changing simultaneously during different moments of use. In the above photo-browsing example, desire-driven action and appraisal based on perception of changes take place continuously. This design perspective revolves around temporality in terms of motion and change, echoing with the latest well recognized school of thought in computational design.

As John Maeda puts it, 'dynamic surfaces' of computational objects divert users' perception and designers' attention from the spatial to the temporal (Maeda, 2000, p. 25). Ramia Mazé and Johan Redström further comment that 'the "surface" for expression' should include a temporal element (Mazé & Redström, 2005). By 'surface' they mean the perceptible form (usually through interfaces) of computer programs during execution. Lars Hallnäs regards the execution of programs, or in computer science terms, 'processing', as the materiality of computation – 'a new temporal material', because it appears only in runtime, or in Hallnäs's words, only when the computational things are 'in use' (Hallnäs, 2011). Using a computational object means perceiving and experiencing its temporal material in runtime. Yet how can the temporal material, as a metaphorical concept, be perceived? The perception of temporality, as Gilles Deleuze's cinematic philosophy below will show us, is not metaphorical but equivalent to the perception of constant changes involving different moments of varying saliency that draw our attention.

Deleuze theorizes a perspective of time in his two famous volumes on cinema. He points out that our natural perception introduces 'halts' or 'fixed points' in our everyday lives (Deleuze, 1986, pp. 22–23). We tend to intentionally 'immobilize' the continuous flow of life and slow down the intense 'flux' of data, in order to think (Colebrook, 2002, p. 149). Hence, we see time as the connection of those fixed viewpoints within some ordered whole. This model is best illustrated by the use of storyboards in filmmaking and interface design. To an interface designer, a storyboard helps her or him understand the connection between input and feedback. Apparently, time is just a sequence of alternating stimuli and responses. In other words, Deleuze points out that we had been used to creating a sequential concept of time, well before the advent of cinema. However, he also notes that 'cinematographic perception works continuously' (Deleuze, 1986, pp. 22–23). His major theses include the concepts of the 'movement image' and the 'time image'. The movement image refers to the early cinema enabled by the moving camera, indirectly informing the perception of time through movement. In such films, movement is not just a translation in space but also related to variation as a whole. On the other hand, the time image directly presents a continuous and simultaneous variation in time with irrational cuts that may jump in space and subject matter. Hence, time does not appear to be slices of sensory perception from a fixed viewpoint, but some constantly changing wholes involving divergent sections of varying saliency. He calls it the 'becoming' whole, which is supposed 'to change constantly, or to give rise of something new' (Deleuze, 1986, p. 9). I add that cinema makes this 'becoming' perceptible to humans, by scaling it appropriately to the human body and human perception. This idea of perception resonates with Merleau-Ponty's views that 'sight and movement are specific ways of entering relationship with objects' (Merleau-Ponty, 1962, p. 137). With this sense of time, the temporal material of computational objects in interactive environments should be able to present users with perceivable constant changes during different moments of use. In the same line of thought, users are readily familiar with these perceivable dynamic environments, and their attention is freed up for self-expression or evaluation.

Hence, for an interactive environment to be affectively engaging, the design should focus on the temporal 'pattern' of user engagement, including different moments of use, when and how users perceive and act upon the output, when and how the system processing continues in response to use. This goal can be achieved by integrating motion-based user input with constantly perceivable changes in the environment, the two defining qualities of enduring interaction. The perceivable changes have to reflect the continuing and diverging nature of Deleuze's 'becoming'. Some changes may arouse us and activate our bodily action, while others may slow us down and just sustain our attention. Here, I identify two states of changes in the temporal pattern, corresponding to how a computational object's dynamic surface, or interface, changes over time in two different moments of use. The first state relates to the common concept of use – user acting upon an object for a purpose. The second involves a holistic view of the word 'use' – sensing an object changing without achieving a predetermined goal.

STATE 1: DURING MOMENTS OF ACTIVE USE

In the first case, the interactive artifact's surface changes continuously in response to the user's bodily action.
An analogy: Use of the VTR jog dial
Consider the jog dial of a video tape recorder (VTR). When the user spins the dial, the finger motion, including speed and direction, conveys the intention of going forward or backward at variable speed (please refer to Figure 1.5). Meanwhile, the machine winds the videotape forward or backward accordingly and instantaneously displays the corresponding content. The output constantly changes with the motion-based input.

STATE 2: DURING MOMENTS OF INACTIVE USE

This state describes the exceptional case that the artifact's surface changes continuously in times of inactive use. That means the user is still using and engaging in the artifact, but taking no action.

An analogy: Use of a French press

An illustrative example is a French press for brewing coffee. After pouring hot water into the pot over ground coffee, the user covers the lid and waits. Taking no action does not mean nonuse. Instead, the user is sensing the gradual change of color in the liquid and the aroma in the air. Once the user feels the required strength is reached, he or she presses the filter down and pours the coffee (see Figure 3.1). During the idle time, the output keeps changing without any user action.

The above two states pertain to user emotions. They are in line with an energy-related dimension of core affect – arousal – in modern psychology, mainly advocated by James A. Russell (2003). Russell proposes a matrix of two dimensions, namely pleasantness and arousal, to describe the simplest raw feelings that exist within us, what he calls 'core affect'.

Figure 3.1   A French press in inactive use (the user sensing the changes in color and aroma) and then active use (the user pressing down the filter).

He believes all moods and emotions can be reduced to a blend of the two dimensions. Pleasantness is 'an assessment of one's current condition', which is similar to appraisal, and the result is between pleasure and displeasure. Arousal is 'one's sense of mobilization and energy', with which what I meant by the two states of use can be associated. Active use corresponds to one half of the matrix, where the user is mobilized to take action. English words positioned in this half include 'ebullient' (for pleasantly activated) and 'tense' (for unpleasantly activated). In the other half, the user is relatively inactive but still keeps perceiving or sensing. Adjectives include 'contented' (for pleasantly deactivated) and 'bored' (for unpleasantly deactivated).

J. J. Gibson coined the term 'affordance' to mean those environmental features that support what animals can do, and these features are usually directly perceivable. As Gibson puts it, 'affordances are properties taken with reference to the observer', and a property that is 'commensurate with the body of the observer' is 'more easily picked up' (Gibson, 1986, p. 143). Hence, affordances are relations between humans and environments in terms of their relative scales. The prior analyses about various moments of use show that affordances stem from the relative scales of the human body to an interactive environment not only in spatial, but also temporal terms. Combining Gibson's and aforementioned ideas, temporal affordance thus describes how an interactive dynamic property, or runtime presentation in the case of computational objects, is 'commensurate' with the human body and human perception in a 'becoming' world, in other words, how well it is able to match between a user's desire-driven action and the perception of resulting changes during different moments of use. This dynamic and continuous match of desire and appraisal in an interactive environment is said to have enduring agency. The two conditions of enduring interaction, requiring motion-based input and presenting perceivable constant changes, jointly enable the user to easily express felt needs and wants and continuously assess the current states, leading to an affectively engaging relation between the user and the environment. In general, they help develop closeness and intimacy between users and designs.

Illustrative (pre-) digital objects

Computational objects usually demonstrate temporal materiality through surfaces or interfaces with interactive dynamic properties. For the dynamic properties to be temporal affordances with which users easily become familiar, the temporal pattern of user engagement is crucial. The temporal pattern refers to when and how a user is engaged in motor action and sensory perception. The way of interweaving user input and system feedback over time constitutes the pattern (see Figure 3.2). The more continuous and simultaneous the temporal pattern is, the more easily the user becomes accustomed to and develops affection toward the digital environment. There are three kinds of temporal patterns ranging from the rigidly discrete to the highly continuous. Alternating engagement means that user input sections and system output sections are alternating, which is the turn-based conversational style of interaction. Coupling engagement refers to the pattern that input sections are coupled with output sections matching in time. This pattern corresponds to the moments of active use described earlier. If output sections sustain after input sections, the engagement is called sustaining. In other words, moments of inactive use render a sustaining pattern.

This array of engagement patterns provides a model for designing surfaces (i.e., interfaces) of computational objects aiming at a more engaging and affective user experience. Identifying the temporal pattern of user engagement with an artifact informs designers of promising ways to encourage users to develop familiarity, to exercise felt needs and wants more readily, and to open up possibilities for continuous appraisal in everyday life. As a result, users feel effectively engaged. To illustrate, we analyze the interaction mechanisms of some existing interactive artifacts, including both mechanical and digital ones.

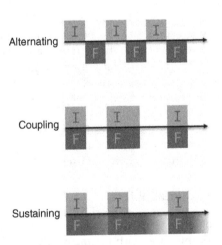

Figure 3.2   The three interweaving patterns of user engagement in terms of input and feedback.

Alternating engagement

Alternating engagement refers to the most rigid and discrete pattern of user engagement. The pattern is like the request-and-response style of verbal dialogue, involving discrete sections of motor input and sensory feedback taking turns alternately, forming alternating pattern on the temporal dimension. The sequential connection of these sections in a particular order in temporal terms is, in Deleuze's words, the 'immobilized' and 'fixed' nature of the interactive environment. Typical examples include the use of mechanical typewriters. The typewriter responds to each key tap with a corresponding character strike in sequential order. When a typist performs any one stroke without waiting for the completion of the preceding tap, a jam occurs. In other words, the input and feedback sections cannot overlap. This mechanical constraint leads to strictly alternate sections, resulting in the defining characteristic of alternating engagement.

The phenomenon of alternating engagement seems to be a result of the mechanics of the apparatus, yet this type of engagement is not limited to mechanical artifacts. As mentioned briefly in the beginning of this chapter, examples can be found in digital environments as well, including the command-line environment of MS-DOS or early text-based adventure games (a.k.a. interactive fiction, requiring players to input texts for the story to unfold), and the point-and-click mechanism in most graphical user interfaces. In these cases, a system always takes a user input, whether it is a tap of the 'return' key on the keyboard or a mouse click on an interface icon, and then responds accordingly. The system does not immediately process the next input until it completes the current output. If no input arrives after output, it waits indefinitely. Clearly the alternating pattern is a matter of design conventions, not physical constraints as in the typewriter example.

Alternating engagement can also be seen in some gesture-based interactions. Such systems have to recognize an iconographic gesture before taking corresponding action. Prevalent examples include the gesture unlock interface of some Android-based smartphones, as well as many handwriting input systems. Another distinct example is the video game *Ōkami* (2006) on both the PlayStation and Wii consoles. The action game allows players to pause a combat and draw a simple shape. Once the drawing is recognized, the system brings effects to the game world accordingly. Although the input is not a simple keystroke or point-and-click selection but of a graphical nature instead, the input–feedback pattern is still alternating.

Coupling engagement

Coupling engagement is a relatively continuous and simultaneous pattern. It differs from alternating in that user input sections seem to go hand in hand with system output sections over time. An artifact continuously accepts user input, which inevitably includes motion, and processes output instantaneously. This mechanism results in an illusion of synchronous response. A user is simultaneously engaged in performing motor action and perceiving sensory feedback without any practical time lag. When getting used to the interaction, one is able to develop more sophisticated abilities such as desire-driven action and continuous appraisal, resulting in affective engagement. The habituation makes one feel at home.

Examples of coupling engagement include, as mentioned, professional VTRs with jog dials that allow users to control video playback by rotating the knob. The motion components of the dial affect how the medium is presented. A clockwise spin results in fast-forward, whereas a counter-clockwise spin rewinds the tape. The faster it spins, the faster the tape plays. The case is similar to the mechanics of the zoetrope, the nineteenth-century optical device mentioned in Chapter 1. The viewer has to keep rotating the apparatus while simultaneously watching the animated images through the slits. The direction of rotation determines the direction of the animation, and the spinning speed matches the playback speed. These machines accept motion-based input and present instantaneous output, allowing users to manipulate outcomes quite variably. The power of manipulation gives users a sense of either satisfaction or loss.

Many so-called immersive computer interfaces entail similar interaction, continuously and simultaneously engaging users in action and perception. This kind of visual interface, whether two- or three-dimensional, is one in which users can navigate by moving a mouse, swiping on a touchscreen, or sliding a finger on a touchpad. The most classical examples include the interfaces of many first-person shooting games, like *Doom*, in which a player moves the mouse left or right to look around, forward to walk and backward to retreat, all the time being shown the matching animated contents accordingly. Multimedia websites enabled by technologies such as QuickTime VR (QuickTime Virtual Reality) or Flash often present interactive panoramic views or menus allowing visitors to pan across a space or a menu with the mouse (e.g., *Out My Window*, an interactive documentary by Katerina Cizek; see http://outmywindow.nfb.ca/#/outmywindow). Users of these interfaces, through practice, become competent in navigating through the virtual space and their attention is freed up to contemplate the conceptual meaning as intended by the designers. For example, the *Out My Window* website enables a visitor to readily 'navigate' around the globe by just rolling the pointer over a world map, a composite of apartments, or a strip of people's portraits. The instantaneous and continuous visual feedback in terms of color tone and scale gives the user a feeling of 'moving' among different places. One can concentrate on stories happening in those apartments that envelop the city life in different parts of the world, both those satisfied and concerned.

Similar forms of navigable interface can be seen in many handheld devices, tablet computers, or laptops. Users run fingers on the touch-screen or touchpad to scroll through screens or move the viewing window across a larger-than-screen canvas. Moreover, when a user of the Macintosh OS X system rolls the pointer (by sliding a finger on the touchpad) over the dock (a special container of user-selected application icons for easy access), the icons instantaneously vary in size to match the proximity to the pointer. The direction, speed, and even frequency of the motion-based input cause immediate and matching visual feedback on the screen. The user is engaged in motor action and sensory perception simultaneously. This coupling engagement again gives the user a sense of 'approaching' or closeness with the targeted application in a familiar environment. One can develop the habit of continuous appraisal and so become less vulnerable to clicking on wrong icons.

Sustaining engagement

Lastly, sustaining engagement describes those situations in which systems still show transformation for a period of time when users stop taking action. This kind of engagement is sustaining in that the changing environment continues to engage the user in the perception of changes during moments of inactive use. Meanwhile, the user is still using the artifact, and can resume action any time that is about to trigger a particular variation that will carry on. This 'becoming' whole is persistent and divergent. This holistic experience of use satisfies the user's desire to anticipate and to exercise control during different moments.

In the zoetrope case mentioned above, the viewer needs to spin the apparatus in order to see the animated effect. Unlike the VTR which immediately halts if the user stops spinning the jog dial, a zoetrope continues to show the animation for a while even after the user stops spinning, thanks to the inertia of the drum. Although for a short while the viewer is not taking any motor action, the apparatus is still in use and the engagement is sustaining, as one feels contented. The viewer's attention is caught by the animation, rather than by the motor habit to spin the drum.

Another good analogy is the tea-serving mechanical doll from Edo-period Japan (*karakuri*) mentioned in Chapter 1. After being wound up (which is a type of alternating engagement, though), the automaton paces slowly with a cup of tea to approach its user. When it bows, its gesture cues the user to pick up the teacup. If the user has paid attention to the cue and acts with pleasure accordingly, the doll waits for the return of the cup during this moment of active use. In case the user misses the cue and does nothing, which corresponds to the moment of inactive use, or when the cup is returned, the doll turns away, and comes back after a while. The user may look forward to its coming back. In short, the user engagement is sustaining from timely motor action to perception of the automaton's graceful retreat. The doll behaves differently at different moments of use.

Another exemplar of sustaining engagement in the early digital age is John Conway's classic computer program *Game of Life*. The 'game' is a two-dimensional cellular automaton in which the cells live, die, and reproduce according to pre-defined rules based on the neighboring cells. The game often looks like an animated work featuring vivid patterns that are constantly changing. Meanwhile, a user is always free to interfere with the growth of cells by putting extra cells in the two-dimensional grid neighborhood. This user input is motion-based, because to add cells the user has to move the mouse continuously, or a finger in case of the touchpad or touchscreens, across the grid (in some cases clicking is required, other implementations are initiated by mouse-over). During these moments of active use, the user is continuously and simultaneously engaged in bodily motion and perception of changes. One may feel excited in exercising intervention. When the user stops moving, the perceptual engagement still sustains for the moment of inactive use. The interaction between the user's motion-based motor action and the animated images of the whole cell habitat exemplify enduring interaction in a 'grid' of 'becoming'.

Video games that require players' time-management skill often demonstrate sustaining engagement in a comparable fashion to *Game of Life*. Such games often challenge players continuously and simultaneously, and show prominently visible changes in the game stage in order to give players a visual cue counting down to the end of a game. They feature what Espen Aarseth calls the transient property (Aarseth, 1997, p. 63) and can be seen in such game genres as casual games, mini simulation games, or mini real-time strategy games. Consider the classic casual game *Tetris*. In the game tetriminos, which are geometric obstacles requiring players to deal with them skillfully, keep falling down and piling up resulting in obvious constant changes. A player may be at one moment engrossed in the constant falling, and at another tensely busy with moving or orienting a tetrimino in mid-air to make it better fit the irregular stacked pile. What makes the engagement sustaining is the persistent game output even when the player temporarily suspends input. Meanwhile, the player can resume movement any time, which might lead to very diverging outcomes of the game (i.e., various ways of winning or losing). Similar patterns exist in other kinds of mini games that require micro time-management skills like *Diner Dash* (first released in 2003), *Cooking Mama* (2006), and the recent *KurukuruTakoyaki*.

Today, many handheld devices or tablet computers let users run their fingers along the touchscreen to scroll screens or move a window across some larger-than-screen canvas. Users of the Macintosh OS X system are able to scroll a Web page or a long document up or down by sliding two fingers simultaneously on the touchpad. Many of the above systems even implement an inertia effect making users feel as if they are physically panning a viewing camera or moving a canvas. The direction, speed, and even frequency of users' finger movements trigger immediate visual feedback on the screen. Users are engaged in motor action and sensory perception simultaneously. The motor–sensory feedback is comparable to that in the zoetrope. When a user stops swiping, the screen content keeps moving for a while due to the simulated inertia, and the user's eyes are still tracking what he or she looks for, resulting in hopefulness or disappointment. In other words, the user's engagement and attention are sustained.

Summary: Temporal pattern of engagement

In this chapter, I have argued that in contrast to the conventional turn-based view, interaction between humans and digital environments should be continuous and simultaneous in order to achieve a user engagement more affective in nature. It has been suggested that a digital environment has to accept user bodily motion as input and present perceivable constant changes. These two conditions underpin the notion of enduring interaction, which differentiates an array of temporal patterns of engagement that support the development of intimacy and affection to varying degrees with the temporal affordances and enduring agency. Alternating engagement refers to the discrete turn-based pattern with obvious time lag between input and output. Coupling engagement describes the continuous parallel pattern between motion-based user input and perceivable system change without practical time lag. Sustaining engagement means system feedback is extended beyond user input. From alternating to coupling and then sustaining engagement, a digital medium progressively achieves affective user experience.

The notion of enduring interaction can be summarized as a qualitative variable, *temporal pattern of engagement*, which can be alternating, coupling, and/or sustaining.

4
The Mind: We Interpret, We Imagine

As mentioned in Chapter 3, through repeated bodily engagement our bodies become habituated, automatically and fluently coping with mundane situations without employing high-level cognitive processing. Our attention is then freed up for more sophisticated mental activities like interpretation, remembering, and imagination. Some might have this experience: after traveling between home and a new workplace a few times, we do not need to pay too much attention to finding the way. It is because our body 'has absorbed' the path via continuous and simultaneous perception (e.g., recognizing that café around the corner) and bodily sensation (e.g., feeling that unpaved gravel road). We might instead divert our energy to mentally rehearse an upcoming presentation. Typing is another common experience showing the value of habituation. Putting the ten fingers on a keyboard and practicing the keys repeatedly, most of us can acquire the skill to type almost automatically. A typist does not have to explicitly locate the position of a certain key, but he or she can move his or her fingers accordingly while reading her handwritten notes. Hence, one can think about where to eat after work while typing. Similar habitual skills can be developed when using some 'easy-to-use' digital applications or interfaces. For instance, the gesture unlock interface of many Android-based smartphones now allows users to unlock the phone by running fingers to draw a pattern preset by the phone owner. Regular users of these phones will acquire the unlock habit quite easily, and so one's finger can move immediately whenever there is a felt need to access the phone. In short, habituation allows us to explore endless possibilities while our bodies take care of the routines.

In case of animated phenomena, people are concurrently and recurrently engaged in sensory perception and motor action. Habituation resulting from repeated engagements provides room for one to make further meaning of the sensorimotor experience. Since the perceived liveliness is reminiscent of everyday experience of life, one readily and even pre-reflectively compares a present animated phenomenon to a past experience, or familiar scenario, evoked by the phenomenon. For instance, when clicking an application icon in the dock of the Macintosh OS X system and seeing it responding with restless bouncing, a user might recall the experience, or imagine a common situation, of receiving an enthusiastic response from an attentive and motivated audience in a seminar. This comparison is a kind of metaphorical and embodied interpretation, which connects the source concept (e.g., the enthusiastic response) to the target phenomenon (e.g., the restless bouncing) in terms of the motor–sensory feedback loop (e.g., the point-and-click action and the bouncing animation perception) mobilized by the interactive system. Drawing upon cognitive science theories including material anchors and conceptual blends, this chapter argues that the interpretation of animated phenomena, which usually involve interactive dynamic presentation of images, can be so emergent that it triggers further interpretation and even imagination, resulting in what I and Harrell call 'material-based imagination' (Chow & Harrell, 2012), which hinges on our sensory and motor apparatuses, in contrast to the general notion of imagination as purely a mental activity.

Image interpretation: Across material and mental

Interpretation, which many regard as a highly conceptual task, can take place on the immediate, automatic, and pre-reflective level of cognitive processing. The most obvious examples include interpretation of one's mother tongue. Growing up speaking and listening to a language since early childhood, we do not have to identify every syllable we hear and consciously translate every meaning in day-to-day conversations. In fact, first language interpretation, as John Russon puts it, is not a 'two-stage act' of first receiving a recognizable unit of sound followed by translation (Russon, 2003, p. 15). Instead, we directly, and somehow inevitably, perceive the meaning of our everyday speech in first language without other options. It is because habituation is again at work. We have already developed the habitual skill to spontaneously 'process' the stream of familiar sounds we hear. To a certain extent we submit to this habit and have to pay extra attention and make an effort if we want to break away from habit and determine the meanings word-by-word in our conversation.

Image interpretation is another example in which understanding often works on an automatic, perceptual level. When perceiving an image, we are inclined to identify something in it. Once we recognize a person, an object, a logo, or a kind of bodily motion, it is hard for us to forget or unlearn it. Every time we are presented with the image again, we will automatically and immediately 'see' what we think it represents. The famous Dalmatian camouflage picture illustrates this phenomenon (Gregory, 1997, p. 12). Although there are always more reflective levels of interpretation, such as connotative meaning, in an image, the interpretation process is still grounded in sensory experience.

As mentioned in Chapter 1, in contrast to the classical semiotic approach that inclines to separate meaning from presentation in imagery, the latest thoughts explicating image interpretation as suggested by Wittgenstein, C. S. Peirce, Arnheim, and lately Stafford (2007), Hiraga (2005), tend to confirm the close relation between meaning and perception. Once we perceive an image in its material form, whether a digital image materially constituted by pixels on a computer screen or a shadow cast by a puppet in a shadow play, and recognize its referent or meaning, the perceived image becomes the mental image. This mental image may be missing some details of the original image, but it preserves the 'structural characteristics', in Arnheim's words, the 'shape' of the concept (Arnheim, 1969, p. 116). The distillation from the material to the mental makes the images generic enough for us to relate to. This connection between material images and mental images via perception is echoed by embodied cognition thought in cognitive science, which argues that human cognition, revealed from many intangible creations by humans including languages and culturally entrenched practices, is built upon bodily experience. In fact, quite a few cognitive science theories are grounded in the sensory experience of images. They all suggest we make sense of images in many of our cognitive processes through sensorimotor experience. Hence, they are particularly useful in articulating the interpretation of animated phenomena, in which people make meaning of interactive dynamic presentation of images through sensory perception and motor action.

Image schemas

Based on numerous examples in our everyday use of language, George Lakoff and Mark Johnson first uncover the fact that metaphor, instead of just being a rhetorical device, in fact plays a defining role in shaping our thoughts. What they call conceptual metaphors not only allow us to communicate abstract ideas by projection of similarities between concepts (e.g., computer virus) but actually largely structure our ways of thinking through entrenchment (Lakoff & Johnson, 2003, p. 6). Many of these conceptual metaphors are based on images resulting from our bodily and perceptual experiences in space. For instance, when we say 'see you in five minutes', we metaphorically picture that time as a container having a boundary separating 'inside' from 'outside'. Something inside the container is considered punctual while anything outside is late. A similar spatial relation exists in the metaphor of phrases like 'we have an exam ahead of us'. The particular event is 'seen' as a hurdle standing 'in front of' us. These kinds of metaphors are usually so conventional and entrenched that they have gone unnoticed by most people, and the corresponding mental images are so embedded in our minds that they exist as extremely skeletal and schematic images, what cognitive semantics calls 'image schemas' (Lakoff & Turner, 1989, p. 97). For the above two examples, they correspond to the container and front-back image schemas respectively. Both are built upon our perceptual and bodily experiences in a world of three-dimensional space.

Although the name includes 'image', Lakoff and Mark Turner have differentiated image schemas from common image metaphors mapping visual similarities (e.g., 'whose waist is an hourglass') in that the former is no longer images literally but instead very general spatial structures (Lakoff & Turner, 1989, p. 99). In other words, only structural patterns are preserved in the schemas for spatial reasoning. Some might agree that these highly distilled schemas are not images. I contend that they are images, but only highly abstract images that work as concepts, singling out some relevant properties (e.g., shape, angle, area, boundary, pattern, orientation, relative position, etc.) as structural characteristics while blurring others to allow possibilities of generalization. In Arnheim's sense, concentration on essential parts is a way of sharpening a concept, and the same applies to images. The distilling process sharpens the meaning of an image, even though it may result in loss of detail (Arnheim, 1969, p. 109). This is also a way that images span from the perceptual to the conceptual.

Hutchins's material anchors

While the theory of image schemas suggests that many of our concepts are built upon experiences with spatial structures of perceptual images, Edwin Hutchins's material anchors reciprocally show the distribution of concepts onto physical structures of images. Distributed cognition, an argument related to embodied cognition in cognitive science, posits that human knowledge and cognition are always distributed onto objects, instruments, environments, communities via social or cultural practices. One way information is distributed and retrieved is through images. Hutchins, being one of the initial major proponents of the idea, meticulously describes many of our everyday practices and instruments, such as queuing for tickets and analog timepieces, in which physical structures of the images perceived by participants or users represent elements for conceptual processes. For example, a participant queuing for theater tickets perceives himself or herself in a line of people. The service counter informs the head of the queue, and the number of people in front shows his or her position relative to the head. In case of an analog timepiece, the position of the minute arm and the target time mark on the clock face span a circular sector, the portion of which relative to a complete circle informs the user of roughly how many minutes to go. Based on similar analyses, Hutchins asserts that material structures and patterns, like marks, shapes, or diagrams, can provide us with stable images for even more complex mental operations, such as calculations done on paper or navigation with a compass. He calls these images material anchors, whose structures or patterns 'hold' information in place or incorporate constraints for mental manipulation (Hutchins, 2005). It follows that a material image in the physical world, for example, marks on paper or a compass rose, can carry information or constraints to act as direct input to the cognitive process. That is, the world's structural images are directly manipulated, and people do not need to hold representations in their heads. While Hutchins's analyses cover mostly goal-specific, instrument-oriented tasks, the material image of each artifact or instrument is equivalent to the mental image for manipulation. The major advantage of anchors to cognitive processes is that one can reduce memory and processing loads by building the constraints of the kind of task into the physical structure of the artifact.

Conceptual blends and material anchors

Fauconnier and Turner have built upon the insights of mental spaces (Fauconnier, 1985) and conceptual metaphors (Lakoff & Johnson, 2003) to result in conceptual blending theory (Fauconnier & Turner, 2002). The theory describes a basic mental operation that generates new meaning by integration of concepts. The operation constructs a partial match of elements between multiple input conceptual spaces and selectively projects from those input spaces into a novel 'blended' conceptual space. More importantly, blending is a dynamic process and successive blends give rise to an emergent conceptual integration network, which is pervasive in everyday life, as well as other creative feats such as rhetoric, reasoning, game play, and even interface design (Fauconnier, 2001, p. 279). The emergent and pervasive nature can be illustrated by the latest intriguing term 'The Great Firewall of China'. It combines some of the connotations of the Great Wall, including hugeness, boundary, and closeness, with the information technology concerning security, 'firewall', which itself is also a blend of the physical safety measure and the computing technology, to mean the tightly regulated Internet censorship. Interestingly, the censorship based on keyword scanning in turn generates many creative uses of analogies and homophones to 'climb over' (another new blend) the Great Firewall.

The blending theory also touches upon images. Fauconnier and Turner's analyses resonate with Hutchins's distributed cognition ideas as they examine everyday objects like watches and money to illustrate how our minds interact with the world in terms of images. Their discussion even extends to cover images of written and sign languages (Fauconnier & Turner, 2002, pp. 210–216). To this, Hutchins responds with doubts. He contends that the arbitrary relations between form and meaning in most linguistic signs make them a very weak type of material anchor, because not much analogical information is held in the material form of these signs. Each of them just provides a distinctive perceptual identity from one another (Hutchins, 2005). For example, the English words 'pan' and 'pen' share a certain extent of visual structure, but their referents belong to rather unrelated categories. Hence, to Fauconnier and Turner, a material anchor can just be a structural constant or perceptual identity for a concept, like the distinct images of different money notes or coins. In contrast, Hutchins claims that more information is loaded into the structures of material anchors. He argues that the compass rose, with all of its marks, has incorporated much more information and many more constraints, such as angular distance, than a distinctive coin did (Hutchins, 2005).

Glenberg's meshes

Although there are nuances between Fauconnier and Turner's interpretation and Hutchins's view, material anchors for conceptual blends mark an indispensable link by which part of human thoughts and memories can be projected onto world objects. In fact, Arthur M. Glenberg has also investigated the connection between human memory and the world in a way related to Lakoff and Johnson's observations regarding the embodied mind (Glenberg, 1997). Glenberg's article repositions memory as cognitive apparatus to combine, or in his words 'mesh', perceptual patterns projected from the environment with patterns of interaction from motor experience. The two patterns are compatible because they are both 'encoded' in one's body. One can recognize a walking path as the 'path home' using a match of patterns between the perceived environment and embodied motor knowledge in one's body memory. (This connection of visual perception and motor experience is in fact supported by neuroscience findings. Neuron activation patterns between acting upon something and just seeing it do overlap; see Johnson, 2008, p. 161). If material anchors suggest a 'download' of structural information from memory to artifacts via perception, Glenberg's notion of mesh recalls an 'upload' of spatial and functional meaning from the environment to memory through embodied interaction. The two ideas highlight different portions of a mind–matter continuum, but they definitely do not draw any boundary. Instead, they mobilize interplay between mind and matter through the body. And images with patterns resulting from bodily experience are the vehicles in this loop.

A short review of image interpretation

The survey of above major thoughts from a vantage point of image interpretation can be summarized as follows:

1. Perceptual images connect the material and the mental.
2. Perceptual images with structural features can be seen as concepts.
3. Perceptual images with structural features can be input to conceptual blends.
4. Perceptual images with structural features can be matched with patterns resulting from bodily experience.

Images with structural features cross the boundaries, if any, between mind and matter, mental and material, conception and perception. Structuring here does not imply static or stable images. In animated phenomena, images are mostly interactive and dynamic, possibly appearing variably on different occasions. As I shall show in the following sections, this peculiar type of 'animated' image constitutes a kind of understanding resulting from bodily experience, triggering imaginative construction and elaboration.

Embodied understanding of animated images

Hutchins's arguments for material anchors mainly focus on human-performed instrumental and operational tasks, so his material images have to be stable and faithful representations of the elements to be manipulated in the cognitive process. However, this faithfulness does not necessarily apply to cases in which the outcome is not a priori clear and task specific, such as process-driven, imagination-laden creative activities. For example in filmmaking, a storyboard is not strictly a faithful representation of the mental image inside the director's mind, but only a device for contingent reflection on a creative work-in-progress, projecting evocative sensation onto the work that goes beyond physical representation, and allowing subsequent imaginative images to be generated along the way.

Animated visual images cross the boundary between the original and the imaginative even more strongly, mobilizing viewers' motor–sensory connections and constituting embodied understanding of sensations. Consider that the storyboard of a film in progress projects the director's approximation of the intended outcome. At some point, the director will need an animated visual image, technically called a 'rehearsal', an 'animatic', or a 'rough cut', especially when one wants to elicit visceral sensations such as disgust, sorrow, and nervousness. There are many nuances to these 'gut feelings' that static images may not be able to convey. Instead, they have to be performed as actions in animated images. For example, a viewer is able to distinguish an animated character's giggling from trembling, because the viewer perceives and understands it as exhibiting lifelike qualities previously experienced in her or his everyday life. This is quite different than the use of culturally specific symbolic conventions (such as trembling lines) without which a still image could not convey these distinctions.

Recent neuroscience findings regarding activation of the peculiar brain structures known as mirror neurons are able to shed light on the visceral feeling induced by animated images. Studies of both monkeys and humans show that some neurons fire both when a subject performs an action and when the subject just sees another doing the same action (Rizzolatti & Craighero, 2004; Rizzolatti et al., 1996). While overlapping of neuron activation patterns in brain areas does not of course mean the equivalence of perception and action, it does inform the possibility of immediate understanding of action through perception by pattern recognition. These findings have been posited as suggesting that, when perceiving a performed action, for instance in moving images, the viewer's immediate interpretation relies upon evocation of the corresponding sensorimotor knowledge from a repertoire of his or her own bodily experience (Rizzolatti & Sinigaglia, 2008, pp. 94–98, 124–125). Furthermore, this coupling of perception and action may enable the viewer to 'recall' the associated sensation. Findings also show that certain neurons respond to both the perception of another receiving painful stimuli and direct experience of pain (Rizzolatti & Sinigaglia, 2008, p. 187). Certain neurons are activated both when a subject sees an expression of disgust on another's face and when he or she smells an unpleasant odor (Rizzolatti & Sinigaglia, 2008, p. 191). It suggests that when we see someone jumping restlessly, we readily understand the other's excitement, not by 'reading', but rather 'sensing' via our own comparable experiences. By the same token, a movie director can 'feel' whether an actor's performance is matching his or her mental image, or an animator can 'detect' if the animated object is moving right. In short, animated images constitute an embodied cognitive process. This kind of visceral understanding largely takes place on the immediate and pre-reflective level – requiring minimal cognitive effort.

As the philosopher Mark Johnson puts it, 'mirror-neuron phenomena suggest that understanding is a form of simulation' (Johnson, 2008, p. 161). Yet at present we do not have enough neuroscientific evidence for bodily understanding of every kind of sensation. Here, cognitive semantics research provides us with powerful accounts of understanding sensation through perception. When discussing animacy, Turner states that we cannot perceive others' sensations, so we can only infer their sensations by comparing their actions to our own reactions in similar situations (Turner, 1996, p. 21). He refers this analogical inference to a type of parabolic projection, or metaphor, in which partial structure of a source story of the perceiver, which primarily comes from one's own experience including action and emotion, is projected on to a target story of the perceived scenario. Hence, a viewer of an animated movie can infer the sensation by cognitively projecting her or his own experience to the perceived motion. A director or animator of the movie can even 'sense' the gap between the inferred sensation and what he or she actually looks for, and then make the necessary amendment. In the process, the act of 'inference' seems to be suggesting that the projection of a mini story takes place at a higher cognitive level, demanding conscious mental operation. In fact, some mental projections can be cognitively effortless. This point can be illustrated in terms of conceptual blending theory. The matches between two input mental spaces, what Fauconnier and Turner call 'vital relations' (Fauconnier & Turner,

2002, p. 92), of some blends can be so tightly compressed that they become automatic and unnoticed. Fauconnier has cited the computer interface phenomenon as an example of this kind of immediate blend (Fauconnier, 2001, pp. 264–265). For instance, when a user drags a window in order to move it, he or she slides the mouse on a desk. Meanwhile, the user's eyes track down the movement of the graphics on the screen that sits perpendicular to the desk plane. There is a set of mappings between the physical space and the screen space, including mousing over the graphical box, clicking to pick up, moving it away from the user to go up, moving it toward the user to go down, and so on. Most users, however, are unaware of the blend but just feel they are 'directly manipulating' the window.

In this regard, I add that, for directors or animators, there are possible blends of one's own experiences or familiar scenarios and the perceived actions yielding inferred sensations. A compression can be so tight that the animated image is immediately associated with the sensation. The image becomes an immediate and embodied input to the conceptual integration network.

The material-based reflective process

So far I have discussed the kind of understanding that is based on single-level blends. In fact, conceptual blending theory is powerful here for paving the way for further imagination, because it introduces the emergent structure of conceptual integration networks that allow imaginative elaboration. Together with material anchors, conceptual blends provide a good model for successive integrations of perceptual images and mental images, which I believe will give rise to articulation for the embodied kind of imagination emerging in animated phenomena. However, Hutchins's material anchors largely address stable images and seem to resist imagination. As mentioned, Hutchins coined the term 'material anchor' to mean those material objects or images with stable patterns and structures 'locking down' specific information or constraints for goal-specific, instrument-oriented mental operations. In contrast, I believe that animated visual images not only 'hold' information, but also 'embody' sensation or meaning, which will trigger imaginative elaboration in conceptual blending. Instead of focusing on goal-specific computation, I shall explore material-based, open-ended imagination through cases of fluid and flexible representations in the form of animated visual images.

These animated images are 'elastic' material anchors for conceptual blends, which hold sensation in place with flexibility and adaptability. They are elastic enough for one to match partial similarities (e.g., in motion or shape) with mental images to elaborate imaginative blends. I introduce the term 'elastic anchor' to describe these imagination-provoking artifacts. In the tradition of Hutchins's instrumentally oriented examples, material images and mental images are largely equivalent. The outputs of these blends, like the timepiece example, are fairly fixed as an entrenched cultural model (Fauconnier & Turner, 2002; Hutchins, 2005). For elastic anchors, the subtle difference and partial similarity between the bodily understood, immediately inferred sensation represented by the animated image and the mental image engenders nuanced imagination. A product designer has to sketch out his or her design concept (a mental image) on paper first and take a look at it (a material image) before further ideas can be developed. Someone practicing Chinese calligraphy has to write and look at the characters repeatedly, making continuous assessments and adjustments along the way. Practicing animators are also well aware of this kind of iterative processes. For example, an animatic sequence might suggest a visceral sensation, with which the animator can compare an intended mental image, immediately combining partial structures from the animated image and the mental image respectively to form a new imaginative image, and then triggering adjustment or modification to the material image, in this case the animation. This reflective process iterates and ultimately approaches the imaginative interplay of the material and the mental.

Such nuanced interplay goes even more unnoticed when the reflective process becomes instantaneous and continuous. It can be illustrated by a peculiar type of animated image: shadow play. Consider the difference between natural moving images (e.g., incidental shadows) and author-intended animated images (i.e., shadow play) (Figure 4.1). The two images can be materially the same. To Hutchins, neither representation is a powerful material anchor because their structural features do not seem to hold information; they are simply silhouettes. However, the latter can be an elastic anchor for conceptual blends in which the silhouette in motion embodying a visceral sensation is blended with the viewer's mental image of an entity (whether human, animal, or even an anthropomorphic object) moving in a similar fashion, thus forming an imaginative understanding that the shadow on screen is analogous to one cast by an actual character. On the audience side, this blended

Figure 4.1 Incidental shadow (left: the person did not intend to make it) vs. intended shadow (right: the person intentionally cast the shadow).

image is the meaning of the puppet show. On the puppeteer side, this might be an interim image which the puppeteer would fine-tune for upcoming animated shadows. In both cases, the material image blends with the mental image to give rise to the next imaginative image.

It follows that material images and mental images have a very intricate relationship. In goal-specific computational operations, they can be regarded as largely equivalent. In creative activities, to give an illustrative analogy, they may seem like dancing partners or boxing rivals irregularly approaching each other, whether collaboratively or oppositionally. Moving images such as hand shadows can be a vehicle for reconciling our understanding of this intricate relationship, because they constitute a specific type of embodied cognition process. Animated images, with their distilled visual forms, evocative movements, and the material-based reflective process, serve as an excellent elastic input to conceptual blends because the flexibility and adaptability facilitate partial structural projections between the material and the mental that give rise to new blends and imaginative images.

Coupling of animated feedback and motor input in digital media

If the animated images are instantaneously reactive, as in a shadow play, the elastic anchors include not only sensory perception, but also motor action. In digital interactive media, elastic anchors are even more adaptable and elaborative, because a user might interpret his or her motor input quite variably according to the perceived dynamic feedback. For an interactive system, dynamic feedback often defines, or redefines, the meaning of motor input action. For example, when a user of Macintosh OS X Tiger or Leopard version scrolls a window using two fingers on the touchpad, the scrolling effect defines the action as moving the viewpoint because the scrolling direction is the same as the finger motion. When a user runs a finger across an Apple iPhone screen, the contrasting scrolling effect (just in the opposite direction) redefines the action as moving the background instead. A few other examples follow. Turning a new page on the iPhone's screen by tilting the device defines the action as flipping. Leaving marks on a touchscreen defines the touch-and-move action as drawing. A swarm of particles following a pointer defines the action of moving the pointing device as choreographing. The magnification effect of the dock in Macintosh OS X defines the mouse-over action as searching. Giggling human figures in a viral interactive advertisement define the mouse-over as tickling.

As discussed in Chapter 3, Merleau-Ponty asserts that motility reveals our consciousness as ('not a matter of "I think that" but of "I can"') a move towards something. In other words, motion-based motor action embodies our consciousness tending toward something, representing intention and meaning. An illustrative example related to machine operation is the jog dial of a video tape recorder (please see Figure 1.5). When a user spins the dial, the motion, including speed and direction, conveys the user's various intentions of going forward or backward at variable speed. Likewise, in digital interactive media, motion-based motor input embodies users' consciousness 'moving' toward animated feedback. Since the animated feedback is dynamic, programmable, and variable, the embodied meaning of motor action becomes adaptable and emergent. It follows that a coupling of animated visual images and motor input may yield adaptive and evocative meaning through imaginative blends. Consider the magnification effect of the Macintosh OS X's dock; both animation (the magnification) and action (mouse-over) may seem non-representational, but the coupling is meaningful when it blends with some everyday experiences (e.g., an individual asserting 'pick me!' from a line of candidates, or an individual taking a closer look at every option on a list).

This coupling idea echoes with the motor–sensory feedback loop characterizing animated phenomena I mentioned earlier. Motor action triggers animation that in turn incites further bodily engagement. This loop sometimes is delayed, as in a hand-drawn animation pencil test, or computer animation preview that needs rendering. Occasionally, the loop is instantaneous and continuous, like that in shadow plays, or real-time interactive systems. This loop, which relies on the materiality of images that one perceives and acts upon, is the core of elastic anchors. And elastic anchors are elastic in the sense that the meaning is flexibly dependent on the dynamic nature of the animation and bodily interaction.

Illustrative digital objects

This chapter has argued that animation generated on the fly and presented in real time constitutes elastic material anchors for imaginative conceptual blends. What Harrell and I call material-based imagination is pervasive in today's digitally mediated environments. This section focuses on one particularly intriguing digital artifact in order to illustrate how this kind of imaginative conceptual blend takes place on different cognitive levels. The analysis is primarily based on the conceptual blending theory. For those readers without prior knowledge of the theory, the following is a brief summary of major terminology used in this book's analyses. These terms are just part of the specific vocabulary used by Fauconnier and Turner in their book *The Way We Think* (2002). I highlight them here because of their relevance in my analyses of material-based imagination. More rigorous definitions and a full glossary can be found in many other volumes of relevant literature in the field.

- *Mental spaces* are small conceptual packets constructed for local understanding and action (Fauconnier & Turner, 2002, p. 40), such as a particular scenario of transaction. They contain elements, such as who, when, where, and what, and are typically structured by *frames*, which are described as follows.
- *Input spaces* are input mental spaces for conceptual blends. Early examples in blending theory usually involved two input spaces.
- *Cross-space mapping* is the partial connection between counterparts in the two input spaces in a blend (Fauconnier & Turner, 2002, p. 41).
- *Selective projection*: Elements and relations from the inputs are only selectively projected to the blend.
- *Compression*: Cross-space mapping, also called 'outer-space' links between the inputs to the blend, will be compressed into relations inside the blend, or called 'inner-space' relations (Fauconnier & Turner, 2002, p. 92).
- *Vital relations* are important recurring relations in compression (Fauconnier & Turner, 2002, p. 92).
- *Frames* are long-term schematic knowledge (Fauconnier & Turner, 2002, p. 40), such as the sell-buy frame in modern society, which

includes roles for buyer and seller, merchandise, price, transaction period, terms of contracts, and so on.

The above terms will be mentioned in the following analyses or included in the related conceptual diagrams.

Now consider the 'water-level' battery meter interface of the Japanese mobile phone N702iS (Figure 4.2). The phone was manufactured by NEC Corporation in 2006. It comes with an intriguing gestural interface designed by Oki Sato and Takaya Fukumoto. The interface displays images visually resembling liquid water. The subtle movement of water in the interface invites the user to tilt the cell phone a bit, resulting in further reactive movement of the computer-generated water images. This motor–sensory feedback loop runs spontaneously and continuously, building a material-based mental space and holding the embodied meaning that this artifact affords tilt action and interactive animated visuals. The interactive image anchors this meaning as a direct input to the blend with the user's sensorimotor experience of tilting a bottle of water (similar to meshes of percepts with bodily experiences), yielding an imaginative construct of a water-filled cell phone, in which elements including animation (flowing), action (tilting), and artifacts (the cell phone and the water container) are selectively projected and compressed into the blend. These compressions rely on a match of motor and sensory patterns in the immediate situation and from memory, but the patterns encode not only spatial information (where to grip, which direction to tilt, etc.) but also temporal data (how fast to move, when to pause, etc.). These are motion-based input (as introduced in Chapter 3). Imagine how, if the water image did not flow to the tilted side, or it flowed with a delay of several seconds, the match and the blend

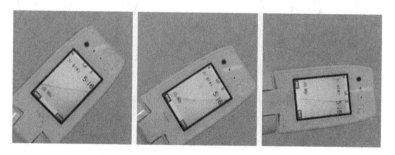

Figure 4.2   A mobile phone whose battery level is indicated via the illusion of water inside the phone.

would be rendered void. Hence, in blends involving elastic anchors, a spontaneous and continuous loop is the core.

The following diagrams illustrate two levels of blends emerging in the use of this artifact. Based on Fauconnier and Turner's traditions (Fauconnier & Turner, 2002), an integration diagram depicts the input spaces horizontally, with the output of the blend in the bottom. The lines between these spaces are mappings, selective projections, or compressions of vital relations. The top structure is the generic space, which encapsulates elements shared by all input spaces. In this structure, I add a circular loop to represent the aforementioned motor–sensory loop. Moreover, motor actions and perceptions are represented in terms of mathematical relations. For example, flow-inside (water, bottle) means that the liquid water flows inside the bottle, while tilt (phone) denotes the act of tilting the cell phone.

On the first level (Figure. 4.3), the generic space consists of a concept of the motor–sensory loop, together with a handheld artifact. For the

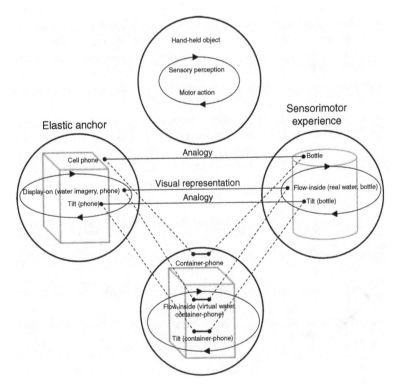

Figure 4.3 First level of conceptual blends taking place in the use of the water-level battery interface.

blend, there are compressions of outer-space representation links (vital relations between the representation of virtual water imagery displayed on the phone and actual liquid water flowing in a bottle), and compressions of outer-space analogies (e.g., tilting the cell phone cf. tilting the bottle), forming a new concept (the cell phone contains virtual water). The output is an imaginative blend of a water-filled container-phone.

What makes the artifact even more intriguing is that the computer-generated water level also tells us the battery level of the phone. The cell phone in use shows a descending water level over time reflecting the ongoing metaphorical water dissipation and actual energy consumption in the container-phone. This articulation further incites the secondary blend of water with energy in the battery (Figure. 4.4). The generic space now includes a concept of a level-type indicator, which reflects the amount of a particular resource left. In the blend, the outer-space analogy link between the water level and the battery level is compressed tightly into an inner-space category relation: the water level is a battery

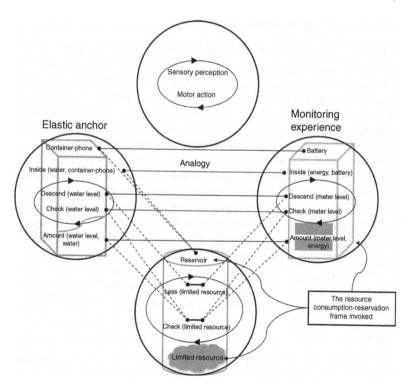

Figure 4.4 Second level of conceptual blends taking place in the use of the water-level battery interface.

meter. The blend might then be elaborated into an imaginative narrative about someone in some arid environment checking how much water is left or similar scenarios of water scarcity. The monitoring of water consumption invokes a common frame nowadays: conservation of energy or other scarce natural resources. The elaboration of such a blend leaves the user a strong and provocative message: 'Save the juice!'

It should be noted that if the water level does not spontaneously react to user action, or if it is not continuously descending according to power consumption, the message of the interface would be totally different. The first condition of having an immediate experience of spontaneous reactivity is necessary for the first level blend. I call this 'immediate level of understanding'. The second condition of coupling water level with energy consumption supports the imagination of a metaphorical narrative in the secondary blend (In Turner's sense, the narrative is a small spatial story; see Turner, 1996, pp. 13–19). I call this 'metaphorical level of understanding'.

Summary: Level of understanding

This chapter has posited that interactive animated images connect the material and the mental, matter and mind, in an embodied way, constituting a bodily understanding of sensation and meaning. When users act upon animated objects in a digital environment, the animated images act as elastic anchors for conceptual blends on the user side, enabling one's immediate interpretation and then imagination. Harrell and I call this kind of cognitive process material-based imagination, in contrast to the general views of imagination as purely mental activities. Extending the conceptual blending theory informs a way of analyzing how animated phenomena coupled with user input and animated images elaborate users' interpretation and hence, imagination on multiple levels of blends, including the immediate and the metaphorical. The former suggests an embodying environment, while the latter further implies its evocative and expressive potential.

The concept of material-based imagination can be represented by a qualitative variable *level of understanding*, which at the initial level will be the immediate and at subsequent levels will be the metaphorical.[1]

Notes

1. An extract of this chapter has been published as 'Understanding Material-Based Imagination: Cognitive Coupling of Animation and User Action in Interactive Digital Artworks', in *Leonardo Electronic Almanac*, *17*(2) (2012), pp. 50–64.

5
The Performer: We Improvise, We Create

Previous chapters articulated human experience of animated phenomena in terms of perception, action, interpretation, and imagination. Through bodily engagement in lively digital environments, people become aware of liveliness, build habits to interact with the medium transparently, feel at home in the environment, develop a sense of intimacy and pleasantness with it, make sense out of it, and are encouraged to imagine. They are also ready to explore further possibilities. With sophisticated habitual skills, they improvise with the environment, as all natural beings do in their habitat. Birds make use of found branches or leaves from surroundings to build their nests. A chameleon changes its skin colors to camouflage itself. A windsurfer knows how to make use of the wind and his or her weight to drive the board in a certain direction. As Daniel E. Koshland Jr writes in *Science*, improvisation with 'environmental challenges' is one of 'the seven pillars of life' (Koshland, 2002). Although Koshland's improvisation refers to the kind of 'slow', long-term, and fundamental adaptation of a being in response to its habitat, which differs from the sense in which I use the term, that is an adaptive, ongoing co-performance between a user and a digital environment, both ideas entail unplanned, unexpected, and unfinished changes, that is, the contingent nature of life. When it comes to animated phenomena, a user who improvises in a digital environment also perceives, maintains, interferes, manipulates, generates, or simply put, creates liveliness. A sophisticated gamer of *Super Mario Bros.*, in addition to just seeing the adversaries or treasures coming and going, can dexterously steers the hero to dodge or to seek adaptively, which may or may not lead to a favorable outcome. But it always catches the eye when the hero is on the razor's edge. The interactive installation *Shadow Monsters* (Philip Worthington, 2004) adds bizarre and 'nervous' graphics like horns and teeth to participants' shadows projected on a screen, and a smart participant can act out a crazy but entertaining shadow play in accordance with the gruesome appendages, attached by the system, which may come and go randomly. Even user interfaces not intended for entertainment sometimes can be a good interactive performing tool on stage. Well-known examples range from Douglas Engelbart's live demonstration of the computer mouse in 1968, to a series of seminars by the Apple co-founder, Steve Jobs, showing new and exciting features of his company's well-received gadgets. Although all these activities are not generally regarded as performance like drama or dance, and the related computing technology is not primarily intended for this purpose, the users or participants really establish a relationship not unlike performers and spectators in a live show. They all participate in creating the liveliness.

Among various forms of live performance, as discussed briefly in Chapter 1, shadow puppetry has the most in common with animated phenomena in terms of sensorimotor experience. This chapter therefore first delineates the phenomenological, as well as ontological, similarities between animated phenomena and the shadow puppet. It then introduces the idea of 'puppeteerly animation', which gives live performance a new meaning in the context of digital media. With examples from video games and other interactive multimedia artifacts, I argue that this new notion of liveness provides us with a theoretical device to investigate how an artifact manifests the contingent nature of life, providing audiences with possibilities of not only perceiving but also creating liveliness.

A word about animation and puppetry

Puppetry and animation differ in many ways. Puppetry has a long history in several cultures, such as China and Java, with deeply entrenched legends around the art. Animation is always said to be born out of nineteenth-century European optical toys like the zoetrope and the phenakistoscope. Apart from their contrasting origins, the two arts also have obvious differences in terms of technologies and practices. Animation is a sequence of drawings, cutouts, or objects manipulated by an animator frame by frame. Puppetry is a show of tangible objects or figurines directly manipulated by a puppeteer in real time. Yet there is ambiguity in certain niche areas. The noted silhouette filmmaker Lotte Reiniger has a book called *Shadow Theatres and Shadow Films*, that compares the two arts with a focus on her lifelong favorite medium: the shadow puppet (Reiniger, 1970). A glimpse at the illustrations in the book reveals a remarkable connection between puppetry and animation. The articulated figures used in the two media are basically the same. Since shadow figures are usually flat, an animator can take one from a shadow theater, lay it flat on a light box without the rod, and shoot it with an overhead camera, just like an ordinary filming setting for cel animation (Reiniger, 1970, p. 85). As Reiniger calls animation 'an entirely new kind of puppeteering' (Reiniger, 1970, p. 82), she believes the two arts have ontological similarities. Moreover, the projection of silhouette films, for example, Reiniger's classic *The Adventures of Prince Achmed* (1926), in the cinema looks very much like a shadow puppet show (although the latter is backlit while the former is a front projection). From the audience's viewpoint, the two media also have similar phenomenological characteristics, in the sense that both give life to some tangible inanimate objects. Hence, their ontological and phenomenological similarity gives rise to an ambiguous term, 'puppet animation', which can refer to films of tangible figures created with stop-motion filming techniques, or those directly recorded from live performance of tangible figures.

Interactive animation as digital puppetry

Today's real-time control and rendering technologies enable an interactive form of animation, closely resembling live puppet performance. This new breed emerges from what I call 'animated phenomena in digital media'. These allow computer users to 'puppeteer' visible digital objects, that is, to manipulate digital materials instantaneously and interactively. Meanwhile, users are presented with frame-based animated output in real time. The sensorimotor experience is particularly comparable to that of a puppeteer performing a shadow puppet show. As the following sections will show, interactive animation turns users, including computer animators and even general users, into puppeteers.

Computer animators as puppeteers

As mentioned in Chapter 1, shadow puppets are brought to life under the motor control of puppeteers via rods connected to puppets. Meanwhile, a puppeteer becomes simultaneously a performer as well as a spectator of the show, because the puppeteer also gazes at the 'animated' images and adjusts his or her motion behind the screen. The puppeteer's visual and motor apparatuses are wired with the movements of the animated puppet. The illusion of the puppet's self-movement is triggered and maintained by the puppeteer, and the illusion in turn engrosses the puppeteer and incites his or her continuing motor engagement with the puppet. To different degrees, this engaging motor–sensory feedback loop exists in other types of puppet theaters including marionette and hand-puppet theaters.

With recent advances in various real-time control and rendering technologies, animators who work on computer animation are engaged in a similar feedback loop. Computer-generated characters are comparable to physical puppets. For instance, by means of real-time motion capture, a computer animator is also a performer animating a human-like figure in virtual space, just like someone wearing a mascot costume performing live on stage (performers in costumes that cover all their body are theoretically regarded as puppeteers; see Kaplin, 2001). Data from motion capture are processed in real time and the virtual figure is rendered immediately (even though at a preview quality). The performing animator can thus act and see the figure moving at the same time. This correspondence between motion capture and full body puppetry has drawn the attention of performance studies scholar Steve Tillis. He makes use of a few similar comparisons in his attempt to reposition puppetry in the digital age. He also draws an analogy between real-time inverse kinematics in computer graphics and the act of moving strings or rods in puppetry (Tillis, 2001). With inverse kinematics, an animator can directly move a handle at the end of an articulated chain to a desired position, just like a puppeteer moving a string or rod. The virtual skeleton follows accordingly, as a physical puppet does. The difference is that the former's motion is determined by computational technology while the latter is moved physically. When the computer graphics character is rendered in real time, the animator can see the resultant movement of the work instantaneously, making the operation strikingly similar to that of a physical puppet. This synchronicity of operation and effect makes computer characters resemble their physical counterparts in ways that stop-motion puppets are unable to match. In this regard, real-time controlled and rendered characters are the 'digital puppets' of computer animators.

Computer users as puppeteers

The idea of 'digital puppets' can be extended from professional animation production to the use of many interactive multimedia applications and artifacts. These applications allow general computer users to control digital objects like animators manipulating their digital puppets. One intriguing example is the online entertainment application kit

Sodaconstructor (sodaplay.com), which allows Web users to build personal animated models: digital creatures composed of point masses and articulated by elastic skeletons. A user can drag a point mass and the creature's whole body will move along, like a puppeteer moving a rod attached to a shadow puppet. Another example is the open-source program *Animata* (animata.kibu.hu) designed to create on-the-fly animations in live performance. It supports the performance of a reverse shadow play, in which a participant, who is usually not a professional animator or puppeteer, moves his or her whole body in front of a white background. A camera detects his or her motion and a computer-generated Indonesian shadow puppet projected on a screen in front of the participant would move accordingly in real time. The puppet is like a full-sized avatar of the participant. Both cases demonstrate a kind of 'performance animation' enabled by real-time control and rendering technologies.

Tillis uses the term 'performance animation' to describe the kind of computer-generated figure that is anthropomorphic and puppet-like. I argue that the term should apply to any forms of animated objects, as long as there is synchronicity in both operation and reception, so fulfilling what he means by the double meaning of 'real time' (Tillis, 2001). On the operation side, real time exists in the synchronicity between control and resultant movement. On the reception side, it refers to synchronized generation and presentation. Real-time control and rendering technologies embody this double meaning in not only puppet-like characters but also general digital objects. For instance, the iPhone entertainment application *Spawn* generates real-time particles moving on the screen leaving trails behind them. A user can influence the movements by running a finger on the touchscreen, or trigger a firework explosion with a tap, among other actions. The result is like a live choreography of swarms orchestrated by the user. Although the digital 'puppet' here is non-representational and totally abstract in form, it does 'perform' according to the user's finger action and is received by the user's eyes simultaneously. The animated phenomena are generated on the fly and presented in real time, demonstrating the double meaning of real time.

We can regard GUIs, arcade games (e.g., *Tetris*), and platform games (e.g., *Super Mario Bros.*) as the site of everyday mini 'puppet' performance. Consider Jobs's demonstration of new gadgets in conferences, where the interface is projected overwhelmingly large on to the screen behind a stage. When Jobs demonstrated how to configure the home screen of the iPhone, he touched the screen and all the icons started to jiggle. He then moved an icon around and others shuffled to give way. The icons were choreographed like a puppet and the audience was amazed by this live 'interface' performance. Similar circumstances happen in the case of video arcades today. When a player struggles through a particular game level, there is sometimes a crowd of spectators around him or her. The action of the user-controlled character or 'puppet', whether it is abstract like a tetromino or figurative like Mario, appeals to the audience. This is because the interactive and divergent characteristics of the animated phenomena render the activities spontaneous and contingent. One can respond to user action, as shown by how a player controls Pac-Man with a joystick. One can also present divergent versions to viewers on different occasions (e.g., different tetrominoes fall into the field of *Tetris* in different rounds of the game). People are engaged in the contingency of the happenings.

Can computer users be performer-spectators?

In the above cases, computer systems invite and facilitate user participation by means of real-time control and rendering technologies. Users are responsible for some of the events, just like puppeteers, or performers at large. Yet some might argue that participatory users are still audience members and are by no means performers. In the context of a shadow puppet show, the audience views the front of the screen while the puppeteer watches behind it, and they see mirror images of the same thing. But although the performer and the audience see similar, though reversed, visual content, what they really perceive may be drastically different. This is because they have different selective attention.

Audiences often concentrate on intentional behaviors, those progressive actions usually leading to happenings that surprise them. For example, when a large desktop lamp in Pixar's animated short film *Luxo Jr.* (1986) suddenly 'wakes up' and 'flicks off' a rolling ball, one starts to wonder what the lamp is doing. This kind of behavior provokes audiences into taking what Daniel Dennett calls 'the intentional stance', speculating about the motives behind the actions (please see Chapter 2 for more details of the term, or see Dennett, 1987). In contrast, a performer does not need to make this speculation, focusing instead on the performance itself, or the pure motion. The nuances between intentional action and pure motion have been mentioned in performance studies. For instance, in his famous essay about the art of marionettes, 'On the Marionette Theatre', Heinrich von Kleist describes a fictive dancer who admires the unconscious and natural movement of puppets, which always follow gravity faithfully (Kleist & Neumiller, 1972). When one pulls the string attached to a puppet's torso, parts of its limbs resonate naturally. The resulting movement is a rhythmic balance of multiple forces. Kleist thinks that human self-consciousness upsets this 'natural grace' of movement. To the performer, the most elegant movement hinges on not just internal impulse but also this kind of natural resonance, that is, rhythmic body coordination. Animation theorist Paul Wells also makes a similar argument. For Wells, many works of hand-drawn animation featuring pure movement of abstract forms are very animistic because the pure movement depicted is a reflection of the automatic and preconscious coordination of the eye and the hand of the animator (Wells, 1998, p. 32). In fact, this preconscious motor–sensory loop is the ground of many animation productions. All in all, performers and animators inevitably favor pure motions, while audiences tend to detect intentional actions. Therefore, performers/animators and audiences take different perspectives on liveliness.[1]

However, today's real-time control and rendering technologies bring about a mutual sense of liveliness between performers and spectators, creating affinities between animators and audiences. For example, many multimedia-authoring environments provide animators with real-time animation previews, which turn an animator into a spectator of her or his own work in seconds. Conversely, instantaneous reactive features of many video games or applications allow players to feel the preconscious loop of motor action and sensory feedback in a way similar to what computer animators experience when 'tweaking' keyframes and reviewing the resulting movements. As soon as one is engaged in the transient and continuing interaction with the system, one has to make a timely response, and one's attention will be fully occupied by the motor–sensory coordination. The phenomenon is most obvious in such game subgenres as combat games, where the motion of a fighting avatar is like a martial arts performance 'coordinated' by the player. The players or users of an interactive media artifact become both the performer and the spectator. They experience the sense of liveliness from both perspectives through the real-time interactive system, which blends the two roles into a new form of live performance.

Puppeteerly versus viewerly animation

Animated phenomena enabled by real-time control and rendering technologies constitute a form of animation as live performance, a new notion blending the traditional concepts of puppetry and animation.

I call it 'puppeteerly animation', as opposed to the traditional film-based 'viewerly animation'. This neologism follows the rhetoric of Roland Barthes's 'writerly text', in which the reader produces, rather than consumes, the meaning of the text, like the writer (Barthes & Balzac, 1974). By the same token, in puppeteerly animation, the viewer creates, instead of receiving, animated phenomena, like the puppeteer in a live performance.

It may seem that this new form of animation, although comparable to puppet performance, should not be regarded as live, because the creators of the work (i.e., animators, designers, programmers, etc.) are not present at the show with the audience, or the user. It is the reason why a theatrical puppet show is live whereas a videotaped puppet show or a stop-motion puppet animation is not, as the puppeteer is absent during audience reception. Within this view, it follows that puppeteerly animation cannot be live since system designers, programmers, and animators are all absent during user interaction.

On the other hand, automaton demonstration is commonly regarded as live performance, even though the designers or inventors are usually absent, except insofar as they have preordained the possible actions of the automata. Automata, such as the mechanical duck or flute player invented in eighteenth-century Europe, or the tea-serving *karakuri* dolls created in Edo-period Japan, were designed to emulate a living creature and thus were 'programmed' through mechanical means to demonstrate self-movement, creating an illusion of autonomy. Some of them, like the *karakuri*, present an embodied and situated interaction with the audience. When someone takes the cup of tea from the *karakuri*'s hands, it stops pacing and waits patiently. Once the teacup is returned, it bows courteously and turns back. The action and reaction loop is embedded in the ritual of the Japanese tea ceremony. That is why automata can often perform live without the inventors. It follows that spatiotemporal co-presence of the creator is not a necessary condition of liveness, if the performing objects can act automatically.

Within today's technologized and mediatized contexts, Steve Dixon asserts that the essence of presence is no longer physical, but rather contingent upon audience interest and attention (Dixon, 2007, p. 132). This criterion applies to our televised culture, in which every marginally important event from any corner of the world is broadcast live on monitors in public places and private homes alike. Though viewers are not in the same physical space where the event happens, we still call it a 'live' broadcast. Similarly, 'telepresence' is commonplace in the context of entertainment and digital media, such as online chat-rooms and tele-videoconferences. Players of massive multiplayer online games – or performers in virtual worlds like SecondLife – are not particularly concerned about the respective physical and geographical locations of other participants. Ironically, they 'see' and 'feel' each other's presence merely by being on that particular platform at the same time.

Sometimes, the illusion of co-presence blurs the sense of concurrency. People get used to time fragmentation resulting from multitasking in digital media (social networking, instant messaging, video-on-demand, etc.). When users of social networking websites update their status, comment, or play mini-games, or when friends or colleagues communicate through instant messaging, they do not expect an immediate response, as they carry on with other tasks concurrently, expecting others to do the same. But they do think they are engaged in multiple ongoing activities simultaneously, which to them are all 'live'. As a result, they feel a sense of 'togetherness online'.

Hence, liveness in digital media does not require close proximity and immediacy. Interactive animation engaging its audiences, both their mind and body, in both operation and reception, should be seen as live, with the participatory spectators perceiving the illusion of 'being there'.

Defining liveness of animation

Interactive animation is a form of live performance in digital media, because the operation and reception are synchronized thanks to real-time control and rendering technologies made possible by modern computers. This technological phenomenon problematizes the traditional notion of liveness. It seems that physical presence, proximity, and immediacy are all outmoded requirements. Philip Auslander has made a provocative claim that there is no ontological difference between mediatized and live performance, so refuting the ontology of liveness altogether (Auslander, 1999, p. 50). He asserts that contemporary theatrical live performance is not only mass-consumed by a huge audience but also mass-produced and mass-reproduced from a recurrent text, just like other media content. Examples include Broadway plays that are adaptations of movies (e.g., *Billy Elliot*) and the pop singer Madonna's world tour concerts re-manifesting her own music videos. Following Walter Benjamin, live performance has lost its aura in the age of mediatization.

Meanwhile, real-time control and rendering technologies support interactive dynamic experiences in animated phenomena. Puppeteerly animation on computer systems can present divergent instances on every viewing and show responsive variations to audience feedback, which are phenomenologically similar to live performance. These experiences are scarce in the film or video form of animation (except for primitive operations like play, pause, reverse, or fast forward), and we need new vocabulary to describe this quality in a formal way. Here, Auslander's interpretation of liveness in today's mediatized culture may shed some light on the matter. He asserts that live performance exists only after recording technologies have engendered what we call mediatization. Before the advent of such technologies, all performances are intrinsically live. Inspired by Jean Baudrillard's dictum that the 'real' is something that can be reproduced, Auslander defines the 'live' as something 'that can be recorded' (Auslander, 1999, p. 51). Although some might see this kind of oppositional definition as paralipsis, it reminds me that real-time technologies have allowed the development of 'live' puppeteerly animation, in contrast to traditional 'playback' viewerly animation, just as recording technologies, in general, have redefined the notion of 'live' in the realm of mediatized experience.

So, to restate my position, I propose that real-time interactive animation should be regarded as 'live' in relation to playback of pre-rendered, stored animation. The latter is something already closed, complete, recorded, and materially stored in a certain medium, such as a film reel, videotape, disc, computer hard drive, or memory board. The former is still open, emergent, and subject to change through real-time generative processes, requiring a computer system to become live. Examples include machinima, video games, performance in virtual worlds, multimedia live performance, interactive installation, and even animated graphical interfaces. For this kind of 'live' puppeteerly animation, I define liveness to be inversely proportional to the quantity of stored or pre-rendered components. A high degree of liveness corresponds to less pre-rendered visual content for direct playback. A low degree of liveness means a high amount of stored content for playback. In this regard, a screening of a cutscene in *Final Fantasy VIII* or Oskar Fischinger's abstract films is not live while an instance of playing *Tetris* or running John Conway's *Game of Life* is highly live.

Improvisation and contingency of life

As mentioned, real-time control and rendering technologies have made possible a mutual sense of liveliness between the performer and the spectator, destabilizing their original perspectives. The designer, animator, or viewers of a multimedia artifact enabled by these technologies all participate in a co-performance. They all become 'performers' in the 'live' show of the artifact augmented with interactive animation. The multimedia artifact contributes to different versions of the performance, because the generative processes support pseudorandom variation, and interactivity facilitates human intervention. Hence, each presentation is like an improvised co-creation between the participants and the artifact. This kind of co-creation is more improvised than prepared because the designer can never exactly know how or when the participants would take action to interfere with the outcome.

In fact, the idea of improvisation is often positioned as an alternative to formal, well-prepared, and structured music performance. To explore the possibilities of music improvisation with computers, the trombone player, composer, and scholar George Lewis constructed the computer-driven interactive music system Voyager. Regarding the system's implications for the opposing 'composed' and 'improvised' traditions in music making, Lewis emphasizes the real-time intervention in improvisation lacking in composition. He believes an improvising machine should be 'open to input, open to contingency' (Lewis, 2000). His assertion also applies to animated phenomena, which entail improvisation between users and systems, bringing openness and contingency to an artifact.

Regarding contingency, Dixon also ties the concept closely to live performance. As he puts it, live performance is always somewhat contingent, carrying the possibility of the 'unexpected' happening (Dixon, 2007, p. 131). In other words, contingency is an integral part of liveness. The degree of liveness in puppeteerly animation mirrors the contingency of life carried by an animated artifact. The higher the degree of liveness, the less stored content, and the more variation can be generated by algorithms or driven by participants, the more uncertain the outcome will be. In short, liveness brings contingency of life to an animated artifact, providing audiences with a more embodied experience of the expanded illusion of life.

Contingency of animated phenomena

The aforementioned ideas of improvisation and contingency in animated artifacts labeled as liveness also inform a distinctive characteristic of interactive animation and digital media at large. Regarding the nature and properties of digital media, a number of media theorists have already conducted sound and relevant discussions, including Janet Murray's four essential properties of digital environments (Murray,

1997), Lev Manovich's principles of new media (Manovich, 2001), Peter Lunenfeld's aesthetic of 'unfinish' in digital media (Lunenfeld, 1999), and others. This section, rather than arguing for a particular point of view, attempts to augment the lively discussion by marking the role of contingency in today's digitally mediated context. Animated phenomena in digital media, with its contingent nature, destabilizes the respective roles of performers and spectators, animators and audiences, throwing new light on the broader theoretical context of post-structuralism.

Barthes's dictum 'Death of the Author', which marks the birth of post-structuralism for many, provokes the subversion of an author's hegemonic authority, turning the reader from a consumer into a producer of meaning (Barthes, 1977a). At the end of his essay, he writes:

> A text is made of multiple writings, drawn from many cultures and entering into mutual relations of dialogue, parody, contestation, but there is one place where this multiplicity is focused and that place is the reader... we know that to give writing its future, it is necessary to overthrow the myth: the birth of the reader must be at the cost of death of the Author.

In another essay 'From Work to Text', he further talks about the consumption of a text, suggesting that we 'abolish (or at the very least to diminish) the distance between writing and reading' (Barthes, 1977b). He draws an analogy from the art of contemporary music, in which the performer or interpreter is regarded as the co-author of the score, to advocate reader collaboration and improvisation in writing. The idea is comparable to Umberto Eco's notion of the open work or its sub-genre work-in-movement, which refers to the kind of works that are always open for interpretation and intervention, or to be completed (Eco, 1989). He gives a wide array of examples, including James Joyce's *Finnegans Wake*, Alexander Calder's mobile sculptures, abstract expressionist paintings, and even live television broadcasts in which each director is free to choose from a set of cameras in order to complete his or her narrative. However, Eco's view is less radical than Barthes's concept of writerly text, because Eco presumes that the direction of 'movement' in a work is still intended, proposed, and so steered by the author (Eco, 1989, p. 19). In fact, Eco's work-in-movement is similar to Nelson Goodman's notational system of art, like a musical score or a woodblock print, of which the constitutive component is usually prescribed by the author while the contingent component is open to the performer or the printer (Goodman, 1976, pp. 116–118). All in all, these (relatively) contemporary thoughts mark the contingent nature of the world of creativity.

Actually, what Eco and Goodman describe are author-intended rule-based systems with contingent instances reactive to user actions, which also lie at the heart of interactive animation. Instead of completely subverting the role of the author as did the writerly text, puppeteerly animation still assumes that the author plans, designs, or programs the expanded illusion of life, while the user and the computational artifact co-create various versions of the live performance. The degree of liveness is inversely proportional to the amount of pre-rendered or stored material content. Hence, a higher degree of liveness indicates less certain output, resulting in more divergent possible outcomes. The notion of liveness I have been arguing for incorporates the idea of improvised co-performance, better describing and capturing the contingent nature of digital media, in which users' experience is different in each system instantiation and outcomes vary with every user intervention at all times.

Illustrative digital objects

Liveness of interactive animation imbues digital media artifacts with the contingent nature of life, contributing to an expanded illusion of life. A higher degree of liveness in an artifact implies a more embodied experience of life. To illustrate the idea, I list several examples of artifacts in ascending order of their respective degrees of liveness.

Slightly live

As mentioned, the traditional film forms of animation, including stop-motion, hand-drawn, and CGI animation, are not live, as long as the presented content is a direct playback of pre-recorded or pre-rendered materials stored in a certain medium. On the other hand, playback of stored visual content with very minimal user interaction (just a little more than hitting the 'play' button) in a digital environment can be slightly live. This degree of liveness enables users to select stored media materials (e.g., animated images, sound clips, etc.) to arrange in varied orders of presentation or nuanced ways of composition. However, all possible outcomes are predetermined by the designers. The upshot includes some contingency in the process, but the endings are planned. The structure is like the so-called branching plot. Users are provided with a couple of options at certain decision points during the presentation. What one selects would lead to destined endings preordained by the author. This degree of liveness is commonly demonstrated by those fairly prevalent interactive Web movies, for example, *La Linea interactive* by Patrick Boivin on YouTube (an interactive remake of the noted Italian animated series of the same title), enabled by the latest interactive multimedia technologies. This kind of interactive Web movie allows audiences to select the next clip to play (through a mouse click), resulting in divergent but preordained sequences.

While interactive Web movies can present divergent orders of movie clips, some visual-based adventure games may show even more varied ways of composition. Good examples can be seen in visual novel-type adventure games. This special subgenre of video games, which is quite prevalent in Japan and other East Asian markets, resembles a combination of interactive fiction and anime (Japanese animation). Interactive fiction (a.k.a. the text-based adventure game) is the precursor to a major genre of computer games: adventure games. It relies on alternating textual user input and system feedback for a narrative to unfold. The visual novel allows users to make choices in a graphical interface and presents visual feedback in anime style, commonly featuring 'limited animation'-type loops. *Phoenix Wright: Ace Attorney* (first released in 2001), available on many handheld gadgets, is a typical example of this kind. The game is about the court cases Phoenix Wright, a defense attorney, faces. Players take on the role of Wright in court, deciding on different actions like 'cross-examine', 'object', and 'present evidence'. The game interface is divided vertically. The upper screen displays limited animation loops in the courtroom, while the lower screen is like a control panel, providing users with options. Not only can players control playback of and pause these animation clips, they also can obtain varied responses from the characters by taking different actions on separate occasions. For example, when a player selects 'object', Wright will point confidently to the court. Conversely, if the player retreats, Wright will sweat submissively (see Figure 5.1). This means the same character on the same background can show different actions according to user selection. Although most character actions are animation frames pre-rendered by animators and stored, other visual elements like backgrounds and dialogue boxes are stored separately and composed with the characters on the fly. In this sense, the animation in this game is slightly live.

Moderately live

This degree of liveness allows users to compose stored media materials at more granular and modular levels (down to individual stenciled

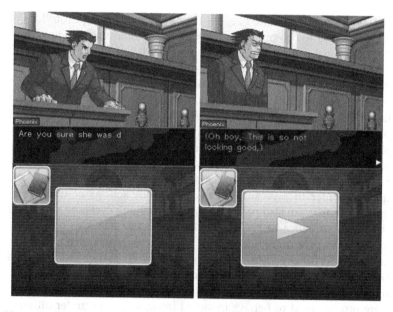

Figure 5.1 Two screenshots of *Phoenix Wright: Ace Attorney* showing two different performances of the main character resulting from two different actions taken by a player. *Phoenix Wright: Ace Attorney* © 2005 Capcom Co., Ltd.

graphics) than the case of slightly live, resulting in more divergent outcomes. But the possible ways of composition are still fixed in number and mostly programmed by the designers. The act of composition can be implicit and even unconscious to the users.

A few interactive animated comics on the Web or other digital platforms can be moderately 'live'. Examples include Han Hoogerbrugge's works, such as *Modern Living* / Neurotica series, published in Hoogerbrugge.com and Erik Loyer's 'opertoon' (a cartoon story one can play like a musical instrument) *Ruben & Lullaby*. These animated comics are usually composed on the fly from hand-drawn animated graphics with simple variations in composition or timing according to user intervention. For instance, a mouse rollover in *Modern Living* / Neurotica series might trigger the main character to vomit electrical appliances at random. In *Ruben & Lullaby*, a user's gestural input (shake the handheld device or stroke the touchscreen) would gradually change the character's facial expression to anger or sadness. They sometimes involve very limited real-time manipulation of stored materials, such as color manipulation, image processing filter effects, timing or speed control, and the like. Yet they all demonstrate possibilities of making the stored components fairly live by combining them in various dynamic ways and allowing real-time manipulation by the user.

Many video games in the maze or platform subgenres exhibit this degree of 'moderately live' animation. These games usually display a maze in a top or side view. Sometimes the maze just fits the screen (as in *Pac-Man* or *Mario Bros.*) or the player can pan to see different parts of the maze by moving the avatar (as in some versions of *Super Mario Bros.*). These mazes or platforms are usually composed of static visuals pre-rendered and stored (many mazes are composed of modular graphics and only these modules are stored instead of the whole maze in order to save storage space). Various actions of the avatars and adversaries are also pre-rendered (e.g., walking cycles of Mario and the death sequence of Pac-Man). Players are free to move the avatars to any part of a maze (depending on individual dexterity) and take any allowed actions. Meanwhile, non-player characters (NPC) would perform various stochastic and situated actions based on artificial intelligence algorithms. For example, the four ghostly enemies of Pac-Man were programmed to behave in varied intriguing ways under different conditions. Therefore, playing these games often results in contingent happenings with characters, items, adversaries, and backgrounds all put together in many ways in real time. For example, Pac-Man could get caught by the ghosts from behind, in the front, or on both sides in a passageway or at a corner, and then the pre-rendered death sequence would be played there.

Highly live

This degree of liveness relies even less on pre-rendered materials and grants more control to users, meaning that outcomes are nearly non-deterministic.

Most highly 'live' animated phenomena can be found in the GUI of many computer systems. Exemplars are those commonly seen generic-styled screensavers, which can be traced back to John Whitney's renowned abstract computer animation. There can be very limited or even no stored materials in the running of those screensavers. They are purely live. Meanwhile, animated GUI mechanisms in Macintosh OS X, such as the magnification effect in the dock, the genie effect of windows, bouncing of icons in response to user click, and others, can also be called 'live' animation because the stored materials are limited to still graphic imagery, like icons or fonts, and the changes are generated on the fly.

Other alternative, but equally salient, examples of highly live animation can be seen in many works of interactive art. Prominent examples include Camille Utterback and Romy Achituv's *Text Rain* and Philip Worthington's *Shadow Monsters*. *Text Rain* shows a projection of animated letters falling like raindrops. A participant standing in front of a camera sees his or her image projected with letters raining upon him or her. When one moves his or her body, the projected mirror image also moves accordingly to catch, lift, and then let fall the letters. During this embodied interaction, the only stored content is those falling alphabets. The motion and reaction of letters, together with the participant's image, are all produced and composed on the fly. As mentioned in the beginning of this chapter, *Shadow Monsters* adds bizarre and variable appendages to participants' projected silhouettes on the screen. The bizarre graphics are stored in prototypical form, and then manipulated in size and composed in the presence of the participants' shadows. These creative works demonstrate intriguing ways of presenting highly live animated performance out of simple stored data.

With recent advances in real-time rendering technologies, many digital games today employ highly live animation, especially those rendered in three-dimensional graphics, such as first-person shooters, vehicle simulation games, sports games, combat games, and the like. Most of the visual content in these games, including characters, settings, and backgrounds, is rendered and composed in real time. The only stored materials may be textures to be mapped on the three-dimensional models during rendering. This category includes a wide array of sophisticated games, such as the latest hit *Wii Sports*, in which every play scene is a live performance of avatars particularly instantiated with user-defined faces and user-controlled movements. The stored materials, besides some rudimentary models, include a modular graphics database that generates all the avatars' faces.

The highly live category also includes a 'classic' arcade game regarded as almost antique, with very simple graphics. *Pong* (1972) was arguably the first arcade video game in the sports category. The game simulates a table tennis game with a rudimentary two-dimensional graphical representation of two paddles on opposite sides and a ball. The ball bounces back and forth between the two opposing paddles, which are controlled by two competing players, or one player versus the computer, but both constrained to move in only one direction (horizontally or vertically, depending on how the monitor is placed) to hit the ball. As with traditional sports games, *Pong* can be seen as a form of performance. The animated phenomena shown in this performance is highly live because the amount of stored visual content is kept to a minimum. The paddles and the ball are represented only by a bar and a dot, which need not be pre-rendered and stored, just generated on the fly. The motion of the computer paddle and the ball is simple enough that it can be computed in real time. The high degree of liveness in *Pong* implies that the game is very contingent, and it can be regarded as an improvised performance between the system and the player. The player can enjoy being both the performer (when hitting the ball) and the spectator (when seeing the opponent running for it) of the game. As these examples show, it is the ratio of stored information to user intervention that results in relatively less or more 'liveness', not the overall sophistication of the storytelling, imagery, or any other factor related to design or technical development.

Summary: Degree of liveness

This chapter has uncovered a subtle connection between interactive animation in animated phenomena and live puppet performance in terms of sensory perception and motor action. Computer users in digital environments can also act like shadow puppeteers, as both the performer and the spectator in the pursuit of illusion of life. I call this peculiar phenomenon puppeteerly animation, as opposed to viewerly animation that means the direct playback of film form of animation. Puppeteerly animation entails improvisation as in live performance, bringing the contingent nature of life to a digital environment and resulting in an expanded illusion of life. The less pre-rendered and stored media material a computational artifact carries, the higher degree of liveness it displays, which means granting more user intervention and opening up more possibilities in the process of creating liveness and pursuing the illusion of life.

The idea of puppeteerly animation is closely related to a qualitative variable, *degree of liveness*, which, depending on the design, can be highly live, moderately live, or just slightly live.[2]

Notes

1. Readers may find the two perspectives on liveliness here comparable to the two types of liveliness introduced in Chapter 2. The nuance is that the latter is considered from the view of the spectator only, while the former takes into account the performer's viewpoint. To certain extent, one may say secondary liveliness (mentioned in Chapter 2), which has been less dominant on the spectator side, usually gains more attention from the performer side.
2. A short version of this chapter has been published as 'Puppeteerly Animation: Animation Becoming Live on Digital Platforms', *Animation Journal*, *19*(Special Issue: Animation on the Fly) (2011) pp. 4–19.

Part III
Analyses of Designs

Human experience of the latest new media technologies includes both bodily and mental engagement: sensory perception, motor action, immediate interpretation, elaborate imagination, and creative improvisation. Part II sequentially investigates these aspects and delineates four theoretical principles, namely holistic animacy, enduring interaction, material-based imagination, and puppeteerly animation. In order to better encapsulate the notions of the four principles in the context of digital design, I propose a set of qualitative variables describing the characteristics of a digital media artifact.

The observer: Variety of liveliness

A digital media artifact can exhibit various types of liveliness. Primary liveliness concentrates the observer's attention on action that shows obvious linear tendency toward a result (i.e., a goal). Secondary liveliness distracts a user with a complex transformative whole that lacks clear, linear end. The balance and spread of the two types of liveliness resonate with East Asian holistic views of life, spanning a spectrum that includes humans, animals, and other dynamic phenomena in natural or even digital environments. Hence, the variety of liveliness of an artifact shows how immersive a medium is with respect to holistic animacy.

The body: Temporal pattern of engagement

When a user acts upon digital objects in a digital environment, he or she also perceives its changes. The two conditions, continuous motion-based user input and simultaneous perceivable constant changes, jointly describe the notion of enduring interaction, which suggests an approach toward, not just a bodily, but also an affective engagement. The two conditions intertwine to result in three possible patterns of engagement in terms of temporality. Alternating engagement is the discrete turn-based pattern of input and output with obvious time lag between them. Coupling engagement refers to the continuous parallel pattern between input and output without practical time lag. Sustaining engagement means the extended pattern of perceivable changes without user input. The order reflects the temporal affordances of a digital product that allow varied degrees of intimacy and affection among human users in terms of sensorimotor experience.

The mind: Level of understanding

Interactive animated images enable viewers to understand the meaning or sensation carried via conceptual blending. On an immediate level of understanding, the images act as elastic anchors, holding a viewer's sensory perception and motor action, and blend with the viewer's past sensorimotor experiences, to yield a largely automatic and unnoticed concept bridging the virtual environment and the physical reality. On a metaphorical level, the images further evoke an imaginative story with a simple structure at the viewer's end, usually within a well-recognized frame (or schema), resulting in more evocative messages. An animated artifact or system can be labeled as embodied if it incorporates tight immediate compression of cross-space mapping. Meanwhile, tight metaphorical mapping implies an evocative and expressive artifact.

The performer: Degree of liveness

Interactive animation is open to user intervention, like an improvised live performance. The degree of liveness measures this openness, and also the contingent nature of an animated artifact or how far a user can explore the possible contingencies in animated phenomena. A high degree of liveness corresponds to what I call puppeteerly animation, which usually comprises a very minimum amount of stored material content in playback. In contrast, low-degree liveness describes media artifacts inclined toward viewerly animation, with a high content of pre-rendered or pre-recorded playback. Those in the middle of the continuum can be called moderately live.

The above four qualitative variables and their possible values are summarized in the following Tables 6.1:

Table 6.1 The four variables and their possible values

Variables	Values
Variety of liveliness	Primary liveliness Secondary liveliness
Temporal pattern of engagement	Alternating Coupling Sustaining
Level of understanding	Immediate level Metaphorical level
Degree of liveness	Slightly live Moderately live Highly live

With different possible values, these four variables form a multidimensional continuum for describing the features of any particular animated phenomena with respect to those four threads of human experience. For instance, a video game, such as *Pong* (1972), might show primary liveliness, enable only immediate level of understanding, implement largely coupling engagement, and present highly live co-performance. Meanwhile, a work of interactive art, like *Text Rain* (1999), might show secondary liveliness, evoke a metaphorical level of understanding, entail much sustaining engagement, and also demonstrate highly live improvisation. These four qualitative variables, each of which is devised from one of the four principles of technological liveliness, constitute a descriptive framework for analyses of design artifacts exhibiting animated phenomena.

A multi-threaded taxonomy

Toward analyses of animated phenomena emerging in digital media, I propose an unconventional taxonomy in which a thoughtfully composed corpus of digital media artifacts will be categorized according to the four variables mentioned above. All these variables together span a multidimensional space in which each dimension refers to one variable and the corresponding possible values distribute along the axis. In this abstract space, each artifact in the corpus articulated by this taxonomy will be threaded by the four variables to one specific point. In other words, each artifact will have a profile of these variables in particular values (for example, variety of liveliness: primary; level of understanding: immediate; pattern of engagement: coupling; degree of liveness: highly live, or variety of liveliness: primary, secondary; level of understanding: metaphorical; pattern of engagement: sustaining; degree of liveness: moderately live). These articulations render the proposed taxonomy radically different from a conventional classification with simple distinctive boundaries between its classes.

While the word 'taxonomy' is usually concerned with classification of organisms, the use of the term here is relatively metaphorical. It identifies different species of artifacts, especially those mediated with machines or computers, which have been evolving with our technologies, cultures, communities, and economies. Today, they have developed into many different sorts of everyday objects. We are used to regarding them separately as video games, user interfaces, interactive installations, websites, multimedia applications, and the like. This folk classification can also be seen as the basic-level categories in digital media.

Based on studies in cognitive psychology and other fields, basic-level categories refer to the level of categorization on which children first learn about categories and objects (Lakoff, 1987, p. 14). It is the 'level of distinctive actions' (Lakoff, 1987, p. 32). For example, people 'play' video games, 'browse' or 'navigate' multimedia websites, and 'read' or 'appreciate' digital artworks. It is also the level at which things are first named and used most frequently (Lakoff, 1987, p. 32), such as 'video game', 'website', and 'user interface'. Further down the hierarchy subordinate categories, such as 'action game', 'role-playing game', 'simulation game', and others come under 'video game'. Conversely, working up results in certain superordinate categories, such as 'digital media artifact'. However, to categorize digital media artifacts according to the basic-level categories, such as 'video game', 'user interface', or 'interactive installation', is to oversimplify the nuances and to erase the differences within each category, which may not be helpful in revealing their intricate qualities in the long-standing human pursuit of the illusion of life.

For such reasons, Ludwig Wittgenstein raised the classification problem of games (Lakoff, 1987, p. 16). The classical theory of classification implies clear separation among categories. Each category has a set of common properties shared by all its members. This classical model does not apply to games because there is not any common property shared by all games. Yet games are like families. One game might have something in common with another game, which might in turn share other properties with a third one. These connections spread and form an intricate network among all games. Wittgenstein calls it 'family resemblance'. By the same token, the digital media paradigm is like games and families. We might not be able to single out a set of properties shared by all the digital media artifacts that present animated phenomena. The variables I suggest here do not mean the rules all these artifacts must follow, but instead sketch out the directions and possibilities that members of this emergent kind are inclined to. Hence, the taxonomy based on these variables does not aim to subdivide the corpus of artifacts into some mutually exclusive and pre-defined subcategories, but to disentangle and uncover subtle qualitative links in the corpus constituting the illusion of life.

Unlike a classical 'box' classification (Bowker & Star, 1999, p. 10), the taxonomy I propose does not precede the corpus itself. Instead, it is a 'vehicle' toward convergence of qualitative analysis and humanistic interpretation of the corpus. The upshot is three-fold:

First, the variables establish for us a novel but accessible vocabulary. Based on the theoretical underpinning described in previous chapters, the variables provide us with a shared analytical tool for describing and discussing the features of any artifacts in relation to animated phenomena. Each of the variables marks a particular inclination of an artifact. On one hand, this qualitative data coding allows us to focus on the disposition of one particular attribute among a group of works. For instance, one can compare the secondary liveliness of a John Whitney analog computer animation with that of an ordinary screensaver on a desktop computer. On the other hand, and more importantly, the coding helps differentiate the nuances between intertwined attributes of an intriguing work, which may be overshadowed by the tight integration of form, content, function, and context of today's multimedia artifacts. Consider the water-level cell phone interface mentioned in Chapter 4. It is primarily a utility application: a battery meter. Yet, its function is manifested in the form of computer animation and implemented in the context of everyday use of consumer electronics, altogether bringing out a provocative message. It seems that the function, form, and context are all tied together with the content. The variables help us resolve and understand the complex nature of an artifact by rethinking from four different perspectives one by one: how we perceive the lively movement, how we act upon the device, how we interpret the interactive animated images, and what possibilities there are. Through determining the value for each variable, we iteratively look into the connection between human perception, bodily action, and cognition in relation to the artifact.

Second, the taxonomy and the corpus are persistently evolving to reflect the emergent nature of digital media. After identifying each artifact by assigning a value to each variable, we can build a corpus of artifacts that distributes in the multidimensional space and sketch out an abstract terrain. By examining possible links between attributes and works, we look for patterns, norms, and peculiarities. Any unbalance in distribution would suggest a review of the corpus selection and composition. For instance, if the majority of the samples incline to the secondary type of liveliness over the primary one, a researcher may consider whether it is a recent tendency in digital media, or only due to sample bias as some typical or salient candidates are overlooked. That means the collection of samples is a dynamic and explorative process, aiming at a comprehensive and illustrative distribution of the properties of artifacts best demonstrating animated phenomena. Overall, the corpus represents a paradigm of and also a design perspective on digital media artifacts. I admit that the corpus presented in this book to a certain extent also reflects the vantage point and cultural baggage of the writer. I am open to any suggestions of adding certain artifacts to the corpus with a primary objective of upholding the pervasiveness of animated phenomena in the basic-level categories of digital media (more discussion on the corpus is included in the next section).

Third, the taxonomy and the corpus constitute an interpretation of animated phenomena in the digital age. In the taxonomy, the variable values determine the profile of an artifact in the multidimensional space. The variables describe the interactional properties of the samples rather than the inherent ones. Interactional properties are based on our interactions with artifacts provided with our bodies and cognitive apparatus, that is, how we 'perceive them, image them, organize information about them, and behave toward them' with our bodies (Lakoff, 1987, p. 51). Inherent properties are common ones defining the boundaries in the classical theory of classification. As a result, a comparison between the distribution of the samples in the multidimensional space and their cognitively established basic-level categories reveals useful information for researchers and animation scholars. Basic-level categories of digital media such as 'video game', 'user interface', and 'digital artwork' are the most commonly used labels. Each of them has its own image in our minds. However, they also largely overlap in the multidimensional space with only minor discrepancies, implying that they enable comparable perceptions and interactions. Hence, it is sensible to speculate that they might belong to a greater superordinate category. I believe the results would shed new light on basic-level effects (Lakoff, 1987, pp. 46–47) in the study of digital media and suggest an embodied cognition approach to the understanding of animated phenomena in digital media. It is like understanding the concept of furniture, which exists at the superordinate level of categorization, and requires mental images of basic-level objects, such as chair, table, bed, and the like (Lakoff, 1987, p. 52). Each type of furniture differs from others in terms of form, function, and motor requirement, but their interactional properties form 'clusters' inclining to furnishing a living or working environment. Likewise, to understand digital animated phenomena, we require a corpus of subordinate basic-level digital media objects orienting toward an expanded illusion of life.

The corpus

The corpus consists of diverse kinds of artifacts. The collection apparently has no specific focus on a particular media form, yet there are reasons for its broad scope and particular selection. This intentional diversity serves the following purposes:

First, the corpus consists of works from a range of media categories, including video games, user interfaces, and digital art objects. A variety of media types is intentionally included in the corpus to reflect the ubiquity of animated phenomena in today's digitally mediated environment. Most people are, to some extent, exposed to them.

Second, the corpus includes works from creators with very different motivations or ambitions. Some works might have practical purposes, such as user interfaces. Some of them are intended for entertainment, for instance video games. Some others aim to express poetic messages or to provoke critical thinking, such as digital art. Furthermore, a few of them were created for demonstration or experimentation of novel ideas. The vast differences in intents and genres show that animated phenomena are independent of the genre, context, purpose, or meaning of a work. Works of completely contrasting intents might be congruent in projecting an illusion of life.

Third, there are both canonical and unorthodox works in the selection. Some of these works are classical examples of their kinds (e.g., the GUI of Macintosh OS X and the arcade game *Pong*) whereas some others are more eccentric, but still salient, examples (e.g., the water-level mobile interface, and the art-game *Passage*). I include each of them in order to illustrate that animated phenomena are not limited to either typical or extraordinary artifacts – they are a pervasive paradigm in the digital age.

Most important, the diversity in the corpus does not mean that the selection of samples is arbitrary. In fact, the samples exemplify the principles of technological liveliness in terms of the properties captured by the variables. All in all, artifacts from these basic-level media categories constitute the superordinate notion of technological liveliness. The following three chapters walk through the three major categories, namely user interface, video game, and digital art. They largely correspond to the three major human activities with digital media, including control and communication, entertainment, and creative expression.

6
User Interfaces

The corpus of digital media artifacts demonstrating animated phenomena includes works from an array of media types. One of these is the user interface. This kind of artifact, which can be a device or a program, is created to mediate between users and machines, mostly computer-based in today's context, for effective communication and control. Since the demonstrations of Ivan Sutherland's Sketchpad (1963) and Douglas Engelbart's early computer mouse, user interfaces have become one of the indispensable constituents of computer-based systems, giving rise to a new area of study in the computing discipline: human–computer interaction (HCI). The initial objective is to enable users to complete certain tasks such as data processing, information access, content creation, or telecommunication. One of the design criteria is to make interfaces more 'user-friendly' or 'usable'. Following the views of Donald Norman (Norman, 1988), Jakob Nielsen (Nielsen, 1993), and others, these terms generally describe a tool that is easy and rapid to learn, to understand, or to operate. Their ideas have led to the prevalent user-centered approach to interface design. The paradigm emphasizes usability, effectiveness, and efficiency.

On the other hand, the idea of direct manipulation usually accredited to Ben Shneiderman (Shneiderman, 2003 [1983]), together with the innovative designs from Xerox PARC and Apple, have steered user interfaces toward a graphical presentation, resulting in the so-called graphical user interface or GUI. In recent years, the advances in technologies such as computer graphics and interactive multimedia have even 'animated' most GUIs, not only on personal computers but also on many handheld devices and electronic gadgets. For instance, icons in the GUI of Macintosh OS X, menu items on many recent websites, or even digital buttons on smartphones will show certain animated visual effects when highlighted or rolled over. These animated effects might seem to some people just decorative, or even opposed to Shneiderman's original concept of direct manipulation. In fact, Shneiderman dismisses the idea of adding animation to user interfaces. He thinks that 'anthropomorphic representations destroy the users' sense of accomplishment', giving a feeling of loss of control over the systems (Shneiderman & Maes, 1997). Yet, as I have explicated in Chapter 1, animated phenomena refer to not strictly anthropomorphism or human-like behavior but rather 'human-familiar' everyday experience. Instead of feeling the loss of control, users develop a sense of familiarity with an interface environment imbued with liveliness.

As other parts of this book have shown, animated phenomena have already started to pervade the user-interface environment. For example, the common kind of electronic book interface on tablet computers features animated page-flip effects in response to user tap or flick, as introduced in Chapter 1. Another animated scene, the genie effect of Macintosh OS X, is even more salient. When discussing enduring interaction in Chapter 3, the textual command-line interface of MS-DOS is said to show alternating engagement, although the turn-based request-and-response pattern features a very minimal degree of liveliness compared with GUIs. The Web of today demonstrates many animated interfaces. One salient design that has been touched upon also in Chapter 1 is the event website *Ecotonoha*, whose main page features a graphical tree that automatically extends its branches when users click on a leaf. All these are noticeable examples of animated phenomena in interface environments. However, they are not illustrative enough to demonstrate the four principles of technological liveliness. The corpus suggested in this chapter starts with a typical and also prevalent lineage of GUIs, the Macintosh OS X and iOS environments. What follows is the distinctive interface of a Japanese cell phone. Finally, the corpus includes the interface of a very distinctive messaging website. All in all, these works show how user interfaces span a wide terrain in terms of the four variables in technological liveliness.

The GUIs of OS X and iOS

In the early 1980s, Xerox, Apple, and others started to offer GUIs for their own computer systems. Just a couple of years after this, Apple released the first version of its most successful series ever, Macintosh OS 1.0. The GUI of this initial version already incorporated most basic concepts of today's user-interface design, including the desktop, folders, files, and trash, as well as the typical windows and icons. A similar framework was adopted in many later variants and clones, with major front-end advances in number of colors and graphical details only until the release of Mac OS X (latter renamed as simply OS X) around the turn of the century. The brand new operating system imbued its interface environment with many animated visual effects, including the bouncing effect of icons, the 'genie' effect of windows, and the magnification effect of the dock (alias icons grouped at the periphery of the screen). As briefly mentioned in Chapter 1, these effects started to emerge as animated phenomena in digital interface environments. In 2007, Apple started to release its handheld products and developed the operating system iOS based on the OS X framework. The two systems have much in common on the interface level, including the dock and some gestures such as pinch, except that iOS has more adaptations to the touchscreen interface. All in all, they share the same interface design philosophy upheld by the company and so are worth putting together for analysis.

Variety of liveliness

Interface objects including icons, windows, and the dock in the GUI of OS X exhibit both primary and secondary liveliness. The obvious and seemingly intentional effect is mainly achieved by two lively widgets, namely the bouncing icon and the stretching window at the dock. When a user clicks on an icon at the dock to launch the corresponding application, the icon often responds with restless bouncing for a while. Sometimes, a launched application icon not in user focus will pop up and down on the dock, because it has a message or request that needs the user's attention. This unanticipated but arresting action looks as if the icon is jumping up and down in order to arouse others' attention, inciting the user to take Daniel Dennett's intentional stance (as described in Chapter 2) and to think about what the application wants to communicate. Moreover, a desktop window, in response to a 'minimize' command click, would stretch and twist into the dock. Conversely, it would 'twirl' back into place when being clicked again. It amazingly resembles a playful genie coming up from its oil lamp. On seeing this 'body gesture' for the first time, a user likely wonders about the motive behind this act. The window seems to 'show off' its magical power that previous versions of operating system do not have. These erratic behaviors from the extraordinary widgets project primary liveliness.

Besides this, the OS X interface environment also shows secondary liveliness via the magnification effect of the dock. The dock contains a list of user-selected alias icons made easily accessible to the user. When one runs the mouse pointer across the dock (either by rolling the mouse or by running a finger across the touchpad), the icons scale up and down successively and continuously, just like an audience performing a wave at a sporting event. Yet this wave is always reversible in direction. When the pointer runs back and forth, some icons will go up while the others will descend. Icons move simultaneously in various ways. It is not easy for the user to focus on just one particular icon movement because the others always distract him or her. Instead, the whole dock of icons transforms itself into a waving, swaying ribbon going back and forth without a wave being sent down in one clear direction.

Following the OS X design trajectory, the iOS interface entails a certain degree of liveliness too. Instead of the usual windows and desktop arrangement in the OS X environment, the iOS interface, like a variant of the OS X specially adapted for handheld devices, presents application icons in a more structured, gridded layout. Yet users are free to re-arrange the tiled icons by directly 'touching' and 'moving' them. When a user touches any one icon for a while, all the icons start to jiggle restlessly. The user can then drag an icon to any part of the screen, or move an icon into or out of the dock. When the icon is moved along, other icons just automatically and adaptively shuffle to make way for it. In this animated scene, the user is presented with both primary and secondary liveliness. All the jiggling icons are competing for the user's attention, in other words distracting the user, but they do not seem to have very clear and directed goals. It is secondary liveliness. On the other hand, when an icon is moved into the dock and the neighboring icon makes way, the action-and-reaction link is relatively obvious. The intents of such motion are rather clear – a new icon is introduced and others have to give way. It is primary liveliness. But in case the icon cuts across the gridded crowd and there are too many neighbors moving around simultaneously, what the user observes would be something between primary and secondary liveliness. With the spread and balance of the two kinds of liveliness, the OS X and iOS environments immerse their users in holistic animacy.

Pattern of engagement

Since Sutherland's Sketchpad and Engelbart's computer mouse demonstrated the spatial manipulation feature of pointing devices, the mouse, the stylus and tablet, and lately the touchpad, have broadened the horizon of user input other than the command-line interface's turn-based mechanism. The GUI paradigm draws user attention to the dimension of space and, to a lesser extent, some motion parameters, such as direction and distance. For instance, the arrangement of desktop items always depends on where and how far the mouse pointer moves. The main menu and the dock in the OS X environment are usually set on the periphery of the screen, because the user can easily reach them by running the pointer far enough in a particular direction. However, the conventional point-and-click mechanism does not pertain to other motion qualities such as moving speed or motion path. The bouncing of clicked icons or the genie effect is not affected by the speed of a click, or a tap in the case of a touchscreen. Instead, these effects are restricted to the turn-based click-and-show pattern. Hence, the pattern of engagement in the GUI is largely alternating.

One exception is the magnification effect of the dock. When moving the pointer across the dock, a user can perceive the docked icons scaling up and down continuously and simultaneously. The engagements between action and perception are coupled in a temporal sense. A comparable situation takes place in the iOS environment during rearrangement of tiled icons. The user is engaged in dragging an icon to the desired position, as well as simultaneously perceiving how the others make way for it, which enables the user to evaluate along the way, thus feeling a sense of control. These salient features demonstrate coupling engagement.

Lastly, both the OS X and iOS environments seldom show perceivable changes without user input (except with the start of screensaver programs). They involve no sustaining engagement (although some screensavers do show visual effects playfully altering the appearance of the desktop during moments of inactive use, these effects do not actually change the desktop arrangement because everything would revert once the user activates the machine again.) Yet the coupling pattern of continuous user input and simultaneous system feedback still provides ground for users to develop a sense of familiarity in sensorimotor experience via the temporal affordances of the systems.

Level of understanding

As Pixar's animated short film *Luxo Jr.* (1986) and some other character animations did with still objects, the GUIs of OS X and iOS anthropomorphize the widgets. When the mouse pointer moves across the dock in OS X, the docked icons scale up and down successively. If the user clicks on one of them, the icon will respond with restless bouncing. The user understands that the application icon is taking responsive action by conceptual blending at the immediate level. The user spontaneously and effortlessly blends the motor action and sensory perception with the sequence of motor action and sensory perception including moving across icons, clicking, and seeing bouncing feedback, with socially recognized forms of the body language of keen enthusiasm. Imagine a teacher trying to pick a monitor from a class. The teacher points his or her finger along each row of seats as he or she makes a choice. Then students respond by sitting up straight when the teacher points at them. The student chosen to be the monitor jumps up and down with joy. The blend includes, among others, a compression of moving the mouse pointer across icons and moving a pointing finger across candidates into selecting from a list of 'competing' icons, as well as a compression of bouncing icons and jumping candidates into 'excited' successful icons. The output of the blend is an anthropomorphizing concept of selecting from a list of 'attentive' and 'enthusiastic' candidate icons.

More blends take place after an application has been launched. If the user clicks to minimize the application window, it will 'enact' a playful genie, stretching and twisting into the dock; when clicked again, the minimized window icon will reveal itself with another twist. The user acquires the connotative meaning when blending the click and the perceived twist, analogous to what a genie does in movies or TV shows. In the blend, the motor–sensory feedback loop of user click and window twist has a counterpart in our sensory experience of seeing a cartoon film (e.g., Disney's *Aladdin*), in which someone rubs an oil lamp and then the genie comes out. The outer-space link between the user click and the rub is compressed into an analogy relation: an imaginative act of summoning in the GUI environment. The links between the window twist and the genie twist, as well as the desktop and the film background, are also compressed into a virtual and magical spectacle. The new concept yielded in the blend is a genie kind of window in the GUI environment. Figure 6.1 illustrates this blend in a conceptual integration diagram.

There are similar blends in the iOS environment. When the handheld device user tries to reconfigure the home screen layout, he or she starts by moving one of the jiggling icons across a grid of others, and the others automatically move around to make way. The user can blend the jiggles and shuffles with one's common experience of rearranging seats in a classroom or hall. The mapping between jiggling icons and slightly nervous tenants preparing for relocation is compressed into nervous but prepared icons waiting for user reconfiguration. The mapping between quick shuffle and smooth relocation is compressed into well-prepared action. The blend results in a concept of 'cooperative' and 'well-prepared' icons in response to rearrangement.

The above blends mostly take place on the immediate level. Users usually acquire the corresponding meaning quite spontaneously and effortlessly. In addition, users can elaborate these blends to a metaphorical level. It is well known that the icons at the dock, the windows, and the tiled icons are all visible interfaces of applications. They can be regarded as various 'incarnations' of the same set of applications in the digital environment. In the metaphorical blend, the incarnation frame is evoked. Attentive docked icons, magically helpful genie windows, and cooperative, prepared tiled icons are all mapped to incarnations of applications, which are compressed into 'personified', and even 'spiritualized', representations of the applications always at your service in a 'spectacular' multitasking environment (see Figure 6.1).

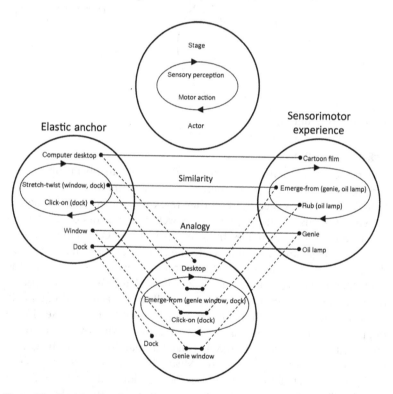

Figure 6.1 Two levels of conceptual blends taking place in the OS X environment. The immediate blend (above) results in a concept of a genie-window, and then the metaphorical blend (below) yields an imagination of personified and spiritualized applications.

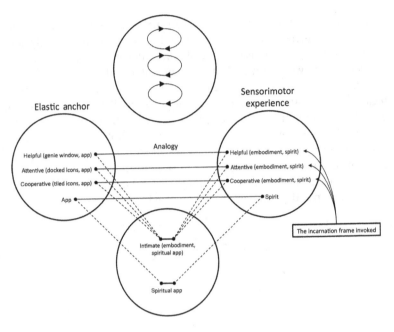

Figure 6.1 (Continued)

Degree of liveness

It is quite an alternative view to see the use of an operating system through the GUI as a performance. As I have argued in Chapter 5, today's operating systems, like other real-time control and rendering systems, turn users into puppeteers as well as spectators of the performance animation enacted by those widgets. In the OS X environment, users can trigger and then appreciate the genie-like performance of windows, or orchestrate and gaze at the harmonic wave sliding across the dock like a choreographer directing a line of dancers. On the other hand, heldheld device users can drag a jiggling icon across other equally nervous ones and see how others move around in response, like a puppeteer pulling his or her puppet in concert with others. In these animated visual effects, the stored visual materials include all the graphical icons and the window motif. Meanwhile, the resizing of docked icons, the stretch and twist of desktop windows, the restless jiggles and shuffles of tiled icons are all rendered in real time. The amount of pre-rendered, stored contents is limited, and the degree of liveness is highly live, indicating that the GUI environments are quite contingent and open to user intervention at all times. Users are free to create liveliness in a myriad possible ways. For instance, users of OS X can keep very different application icons at the dock, adjust the magnification factor, and of course control the speed and rhythm of pointer motion in order to give different waving performance. In a similar way, iOS users choreograph jiggling icons moving around the gridded stage.

The mobile interface of NEC FOMA N702iS

While the term 'user interface' primarily refers to a point of interaction on computer platforms, today many electronic devices and gadgets also have user interfaces. Compared with homogeneities like the desktop and window metaphors in the GUI of personal computers, the designs of device interfaces are much more diverse because the uses of these devices differ substantially from one another. For instance, touchscreen-based interfaces may be convenient for digital camera users to select a focus point, but may not be safe for a motorist trying to make a call on the road, who may prefer the tactile sense of physical numeric pads. Meanwhile, the varied contexts of use also open up possibilities of novel designs. An example is the water-level interface of the NEC mobile phone FOMA N702iS described in Chapter 4. The distinctive and intriguing gestural interface displays computer-generated imagery of liquid water that looks as if it is 'contained' inside the mobile phone. When a user tilts the phone, the rendered water surface also shakes and tilts in response (please see Figure 4.2). As an informative interface, the water level represents the battery level. That is, the interface is also a real-time battery meter.

Variety of liveliness

The perceptually realistic water effect displayed in the distinct mobile interface constitutes a kind of secondary liveliness. When a user shakes the phone, the virtual water surface shakes restlessly. Although the water movement is reactive to the user's hand action, the dynamic tension is not very obvious in the animated images because the direction of movement is not consistent. The water surface moves up and down out of phase at different positions. It is not easy for one to detect a unanimous result or a direction of movement. Instead, a user's attention is diffused over the whole water imagery.

In fact, the water surface is overall descending due to continuing consumption of energy. Yet the rate of change is so subtle and slow that it has gone nearly unnoticed by the user. It hardly keeps the user's focused attention for a duration long enough to detect the directional 'movement'. As a result, the mobile interface is inclined toward secondary liveliness, thus lacking the primary liveliness necessary to be immersive with holistic animacy.

Pattern of engagement

The dynamic water surface shown in the mobile interface seems to invite a user to tilt or even shake the phone. The user action will be accurately tracked by the built-in accelerometer, and the responding water waves will be simulated on the fly and displayed in real time. That is, the moment-to-moment changes in speed and orientation of the user's motor action determine how the virtual water surface reacts. The interface is sensitive to continuous motion input, as well as being spontaneous in giving animated feedback. The user's action and perception are coupled during these moments of active use. This results in a coupling pattern of engagement.

Meanwhile, the interface is able to sustain the user engagement in two scales of temporal dimension. In the short term, the water surface will stay rough for a while after a tilt or shake. The user might hold the phone and gaze at the animated pattern, as the water moves quite differently on different levels. The divergent movements keep engaging the user in terms of perception. In the longer term, the water level is steadily descending with or without user input. Although the rate of change is slow, a user would be aware of it when checking out the phone intermittently. This subtle but persistent transformation, like the minute arm of an analog clock, cues or reminds the user of a piece of important information – how much energy is left. The user is engaged (relaxingly or anxiously, dependent on the water level) in this perception of change from time to time. To sum up, the interface couples users' action with perception during moments of active use and sustains the engagement in perception of changes during moments of inactive use. This extensive engagement ties the interface to the human body by achieving an appropriate scale between bodily action and sensory perception.

Level of understanding

The basic water flow simulation in the mobile interface surprisingly invokes multiple levels of understanding in the user's mind. As described in Chapter 4, the first blend takes place immediately and effortlessly. The subtle water movement first incites the user to slightly tilt the mobile phone, which in turn detects the user-driven motion by means of the built-in accelerometer and computes and displays the reaction of the water surface. This motor–sensory feedback loop constitutes an elastic anchor, blending with the user's remembered experience of holding a bottle of water, yielding an imaginative conceptualization of a water-filled mobile phone. The representation relation between the water imagery and actual liquid water is tightly compressed into a virtual form of water (which differs from real water at least in mass), and the analogy relation between the phone and the bottle is compressed into a new concept of container-phone. Readers can refer to Figure 4.3 for the integration diagram of this imaginative blend.

The secondary blend emerges on a metaphorical level, when the user notices the gradually descending water level that informs the ongoing energy consumption in the container-phone. This articulation gives a concept of a level-type indicator, which is shared by the water-level interface and the ordinary battery meter. The analogy relation between the acts of checking the water level and reading the battery meter is compressed into monitoring the availability of a resource. The frame of conservation is invoked with elements such as limited resource, reservoir, indicator, and others. The blend elaborates an imaginative narrative about someone in a harsh environment monitoring the use of a limited resource, getting across a provocative message: 'Save the juice!' Readers can refer to the discussion in Chapter 4 and Figure 4.4 for more details on this blending process.

Degree of liveness

Like the GUI of personal computers, mobile device interfaces are generally not related to any sense of performance. First, they are designed for individuals, which makes them very personal artifacts. Second, the design criteria are inclined to functionality and efficiency, rather than entertainment or recreation. However, after a series of engaging and engrossing seminars by Steve Jobs with his popular and prevalent 'companion', the iPhone, on stage, it is completely sensible to say that interaction with a user interface of today can be a form of live performance. The water-level interface invites the user to take action at any moment, and engages him or her with highly responsive moving water images, which are totally rendered on the fly. There is nearly no stored visual content in the interface. The user can explore almost unlimited possibilities of action and reaction, such as shaking vigorously, turning the phone upside down, or laying it flat on a table. What is more, the animated effects look substantially different when water levels differ, resulting in very divergent spectacles. Hence, the mobile interface is very live, echoing the contingency of life.

The Web interface of SnowDays

Messaging is a major activity on the Internet, and quite a number of websites have incorporated a messaging feature. For example, one can easily find on Amazon.com a hyperlink labeled 'Share with Friends', which allows one to send friends an electronic recommendation of an item. While many of these websites make messaging an explicit option, SnowDays (snowdays.me) incorporates this feature more seamlessly and elegantly in its virtual world. The popular website depicts a scene of a snowy day in which every falling snowflake was previously 'handcrafted' by an earlier website visitor. The visitor may leave a message 'inside' the flake and the receiver will be notified by the website. The receiver, or in fact any other visitor, may go to the page, look at the system-generated snow, appreciate the magnificent details of the user-submitted flake, and respond to any of them. In other words, the website gives visitors an illusion of messaging through snowflakes in the virtual world (please see Figure 6.2). Launched in 2002, the website had accumulated over 11 million user-generated snowflakes by the end of 2012.

Variety of liveliness

The SnowDays webpage displays a graphical representation of an outdoor open space, with a few trees covered in snow. Snowflakes of

Figure 6.2   SnowDays features cutout snowflakes tailor-made by individual users. SnowDays © Always Snowing LLC.

different sizes, some of which are large enough for the feathers to be seen, descend steadily all over the graphical scene. Simulating the so-called motion parallax effect (i.e., closer objects seem to move faster than far objects), larger snowflakes fall slightly faster than smaller ones. As it falls, each flake also rotates variably and sways differently to reflect the air buoyancy. With these nuances in individual movement, each flake seems to have its own destined path and pace. It is hard for viewers to detect or focus on one particular impulse driving the flakes. In addition, the flakes look distinct from each other because each is tailor-made. They show off their own beauty simultaneously to compete for viewers' attention, constituting secondary liveliness.

On the other hand, the flakes also show a limited extent of primary liveliness in terms of their reaction. When a viewer rolls the mouse pointer over any one flake, the flake immediately scales up and shows its full details together with the user's name, date of creation, and the attached message. When the pointer rolls out, it retreats and returns to the snow scene. During this close-up process, the snow pauses. The zooming transition draws the viewer's attention toward the selected flake. In other words, the flake has a clear, immediate goal that is to present its meticulous details and wholehearted message to the viewer. This results in some primary liveliness. Hence, the snowing interface immerses viewers in the secondary liveliness of emergent falling flakes, together with the primary liveliness in the direct interaction between mouse input and animated feedback.

Pattern of engagement

The sensorimotor experience of using the SnowDays website relies not only on the animated graphics it presents, but also the bodily engagement it affords. When starting to present the snowy scene, the website invites the viewer to catch a falling snowflake. One can move the mouse pointer freely to pick up a flake, but timing and motion path have to be spot on. Since all flakes descend continuously, the visitor has to employ hand–eye coordination to move the pointer to roll over a targeted moving flake. If the visitor does not act swiftly enough, the flake might fall out of frame and not come back in the near future. If the visitor moves the pointer too hastily, the pointer might hit and zoom in at the wrong flake along the way. This mouse interaction mechanism hence requires the continuous pointer movement and simultaneous tracking of the moving flake, exhibiting a coupling pattern of user engagement. Although the zoom-in interaction, which is triggered by mouse-over and pauses all flake movements, entails a form of alternating engagement, the flake-catching process still engages users continuously.

In addition, SnowDays also demonstrates sustaining engagement. When a visitor stops any mouse action, the website still continues to snow. Although the virtual snow on the ground will not become any thicker as time goes by, the scene does show other constant transformations to reflect the change in time, or in Deleuze's term, 'becoming'. With Internet connection, SnowDays is able to vary the background color and atmosphere according to the actual time of day and weather. For instance, the site shows an orange sky during the sunset. Sometimes there is a mist in the scene. The interface environment is always changing. Furthermore, with unlimited numbers of Web visitors at all times, there are always new snowflakes falling into the scene. Even if a user just gazes at the scene without taking any action, the snow scene constantly shows perceivable changes in terms of flake patterns, composition, and background color, sustaining user engagement in perception of the changes. During these moments of inactive use, the user can resume mouse action when noticing any particular appealing flake. Therefore, the virtual snowy space enduringly affects the user, and the pattern of engagement is sustaining. This shows that the website matches human users' scales of bodily action and perception, allowing its users to act out desires and evaluate continuously, giving them a sense of intimacy.

Level of understanding

The recurrent snowing images in the website constitute multiple levels of understanding. When a visitor gazes at the graphical scene and moves the mouse pointer over any particular falling snowflake, a close-up view of it pops up and an immediate conceptual blend comes about. The link between the falling sprite (a computer graphic cutout) and an actual falling flake is compressed into a representation relation in the blended space: a piece of virtual flake in delicate sixfold symmetry. The motor action of moving the mouse, or running a finger across the touchpad, forms an elastic anchor with the act of catching a real snowflake in real life. Our past sensorimotor experience informs this analogy. Similarly, the perception of the zooming effect connects to the act of looking closely at something. These links are compressed into an imaginative act of moving a pointer to examine a virtual flake when looking through a window 'teleporting' a snow scene. This immediate imaginative blend is illustrated in the following diagram (Figure 6.3).

Apart from exhibiting the beauty of ice crystals, the virtual flakes in SnowDays have other even more intriguing features. First, each flake carries a message from its creator to a particular receiver. This messaging function makes the flake comparable to airmail, a long-distance call, or even a note brought by a pigeon. The website shortens the distance between the sender and the receiver. Second, with the provided tiny Web tool, the sender creates a snowflake tailor-made for the receiver. The tool simulates the little trick that many of us learned in elementary school to construct our own symmetrical paper cutouts. Such experiences can be integrated with the sensorimotor experience of using the website, and then compressed into an imaginative act of constructing a tailor-made handcrafted snowflake, sending it together with sincere written greetings and then letting the sky send it to someone special (see Figure 6.3). In this blend, the 'season's greetings' frame is invoked with

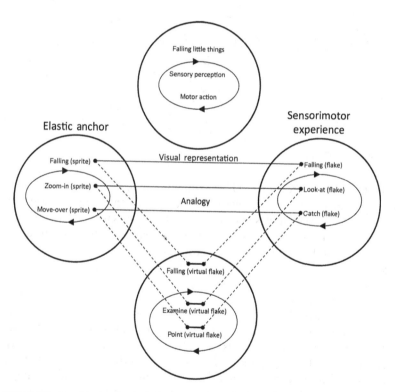

Figure 6.3 Two levels of conceptual blends taking place in SnowDays. The immediate blend (above) results in an embodied concept of catching flakes in virtual space, and then the metaphorical blend (below) yields an imagined thought of mailing handcrafted flakes through the sky.

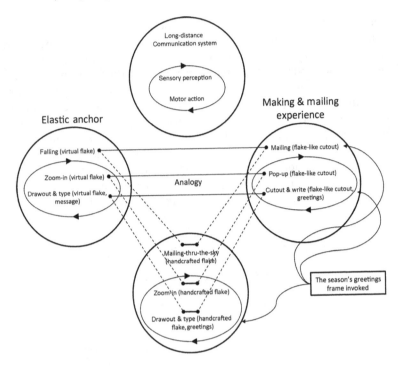

Figure 6.3   (Continued)

the tailor-made greeting card, greeting messages, mailing, and possibly replies. This metaphorical blend elaborates an imaginative narrative of exchanging heartfelt blessings and handcrafted gifts with someone from a distance on a lonely winter day. With such visceral and nostalgic associations, the hidden meaning is evocative and affective: 'You are not alone!'

Degree of liveness

The SnowDays website enables its visitors to create their own snowflakes, tag on messages, and then let the flakes fall in the virtual world. Visitors act like wizards in this imaginative world, consecutively and collectively participating in the virtual snowing show. Meanwhile, they are also individual spectators of the beautifully simulated scenery. In short, what SnowDays presents is an improvised live performance between the website and its visitors. In this emergent performance, the major visual components include all the graphic sprites. With millions of flakes, the number of sprites should also be huge. Fortunately, all

Table 6.2 The four variable values of selected user interfaces

Interface environments	Variety of liveliness	Pattern of engagement	Level of understanding	Degree of liveness
The genie effect on windows in OS X	Primary (twisting into place)	Alternating (click and then twist)	Immediate (magically helpful windows) Metaphorical (the incarnation frame)	Highly live
The magnification effect on the dock in OS X	Primary (bouncing) Secondary (magnification)	Alternating (click and then bounce) Coupling (roll over and magnify)	Immediate (attentive icons) Metaphorical (the incarnation frame)	Highly live (icons)
Home screen configuration in iOS	Secondary (jiggling) Primary (shuffling)	Coupling (drag and shuffle) Sustaining (jiggling)	Immediate (cooperatively prepared icons) Metaphorical (the incarnation frame)	Highly live (icons)
The water-level interface of N702iS	Secondary (waving)	Coupling (tilt and wave) Sustaining (waving and descending)	Immediate (water-filled cell phone) Metaphorical (the conservation frame)	Highly live
The Web interface of SnowDays	Secondary (snowing) Primary (zooming)	Alternating (roll over and then zoom) Sustaining (falling, changes of background color and atmosphere)	Immediate (teleporting snowing scene) Metaphorical (the season's greetings frame)	Highly live (stored snowflake graphics)

flakes are sixfold symmetrical. For each flake, the system only needs to store the user-defined cutout path, and a complete sprite can be generated by simple procedures. In other words, less than one-sixth of graphic content is really stored, together with other static background elements. Since all the snowing and changing sky color effects are also generated on the fly, the resulting performance is highly live. The website opens up diverse contingencies for Web surfers to generate ongoing liveliness in the virtual world.

Summary

This chapter examines a set of user interfaces epitomizing the phenomenon of technological liveliness. They include one prevalent stream of GUIs, one distinctive mobile interface, and one notable and well-received website's interface. These interfaces are initially intended for different purposes, respectively control and management, information delivery, and social communication. Yet, they all have their attributes elaborated from primary functionality and usability to affectivity and expressiveness through animated phenomena. The analyses of the four variables have shown that regardless of the differences in the design intents, these user interfaces jointly span a wide terrain in the dimensions of the four principles. Table 6.2 summarizes the variable values describing these interfaces.

7
Digital Entertainment

People consume digital media in many ways, for various purposes. Some use it to organize resources, access information, or communicate with each other, as discussed in Chapter 6. Apart from these productivity-oriented objectives, others use digital media for enjoyment, amusement, or entertainment. They play video games or have fun with entertainment apps (a new breed of application category that has flourished on smartphones and tablet computers aiming at an engaging and enjoyable experience rather than competitive, goal-specific gaming pleasure). No matter how a piece of digital entertainment engages its players, whether in relaxing or exciting mode, animated phenomena are prominent and pervasive in their corresponding digital environments. This chapter looks at these emerging phenomena of liveliness.

Video games provide quite some good examples of technological liveliness, because they often show motion graphics that are seemingly autonomous, reactive, and transformative in real time. The phenomenon is relatively obvious in such game subgenres as action, sports, simulation, time-management strategy, and casual. The discussions in Part I and II touch upon various video games from arcade game classics such as *Pong* (1972), *Pac-Man* (1980), and *Phoenix* (1980), to the computer platform/maze game *Lode Runner* (1983), the casual (but addictive) game *Tetris* (1984), the first-person shooting game *Doom* (1993), the visual novel-type adventure game *Phoenix Wright: Ace Attorney* (2001), the 'sandbox' game *Electroplankton* (2005), and other console games such as *Ōkami* (2006) and *Wii Sports* (2006). They demonstrate different qualities in terms of the four principles of technological liveliness. Some of them, including the action-adventure game *Ōkami*, entail a certain amount of alternating engagement, while others, like the classical casual game *Tetris*, feature perceivable sustaining engagement nearly all the time. Regarding the degree of liveness, the category spans the slightly live, as in the adventure game *Phoenix Wright*, and the highly live, such as the sports games *Pong* and *Wii Sports*. The qualities of the animated phenomena of a video game seem to be independent of its genre.

Since there are innumerable examples in each genre, the corpus of digital entertainment artifacts exemplifying technological liveliness for the discussion in this chapter is limited to just one example from each of these genres – arcade, casual, and 'sandbox'. This is because the qualitative variable values of these games already cover a reasonably wide terrain. *Pong* is definitely an arcade game classic that is regarded as almost antique, but is still influential in terms of game mechanics. *Angry Birds* is a recent casual game that is highly popular and addictive (like its early counterpart *Tetris*). It has many variants and sequels, not to mention that all-pervasive merchandise. Lastly, *flOw* started as an indie flash-based game, and later became available in the console. It does not provide any obvious goals for its players and can be regarded as a kind of sandbox game. This chapter examines these examples in great detail. Readers should note that the analyses in this book are not intended to focus on common parameters of game studies such as rules, narrative, or gaming cultures, nor do they attempt to revitalize the confrontation between the ludologist and narratologist camps (Aarseth, 2004; Eskelinen, 2004; Jenkins, 2004; Murray, 2004). Instead, this chapter concentrates on how these games demonstrate the emerging animated phenomena in digital media.

The classic arcade game *Pong*

Pong was arguably the first arcade video game in the sports category, released by Atari Inc. in 1972. The game simulates a table tennis game with a rudimentary two-dimensional graphical representation of a ball and two vertical paddles on horizontally opposite sides separated by a dashed line. The ball bounces back and forth between the two opposing paddles, which are controlled by two competing human players, or a human player and the computer in some later versions supported with artificial intelligence (AI) techniques. A player has to move the paddle to hit the ball on his or her side, but the movement of the paddle is constrained in only one dimension. To me, the game is more like a tabletop air hockey game in that all movements take place in a two-dimensional plane rather than three-dimensionally as in the case of table tennis. Although *Pong* is an early video game, its mechanics is very influential on many of its variants and descendants. Today we could still find some mini-games that have implemented similar gameplay, such as *Break 'Em All* (2005), released on the Nintendo DS platform, which is one of the contemporary descendants of another arcade classic, *Breakout* (1976), seen as a 'lonely-hearts' version[1] of *Pong*. Some recent *Pong*-like sports games include the popular iOS app *Touch Hockey* (2009), available for free download. I choose *Pong* not just owing to its legacy in the history of video games, but also because it predictively epitomizes many of its descendants in terms of the four principles of technological liveliness. Moreover, readers should be able to access many of its demonstration videos or those free remakes on the Internet for a first-hand experience of its liveliness.

Variety of liveliness

Pong features three prominently active characters, the two paddles and the ball. Just having a look at some demonstration videos or play a few games from the remakes, one notices the primary liveliness in each of these simple objects. First, the paddles (including the AI-driven player's paddle) in the game definitely demonstrate very clear and goal-directed movements. To an observer or a human player, they move as if racing toward the 'slippery' ball. The AI paddle is also programmed to move and match the ball's vertical position as much as possible. While the ball just keeps bouncing and seems relatively passive, it always directs players' as well as observers' attention from side to side. These motions make the dynamic tension between these running characters clearly visible, and this is the primary liveliness.

Second, the interaction between a paddle and the ball, even though it might be computer-controlled, sometimes will surprise and provoke an observer or a player into taking the intentional stance and speculating on its tactics. The AI paddle does not align the ball's position all the time; otherwise it would be unbeatable. In fact, it is programmed to make mistakes occasionally. It sometimes loses track of the ball and seems to miss. Yet at times, for instance when the ball bounces at a wall, it readjusts and picks up again (for a more detailed explication of the AI implementation, please see (Montfort & Bogost, 2009, pp. 38–39)). This misalignment and realignment mechanism simulates human error in game play making the computer paddle's behavior less expected and more likely to catch one's attention. This adds to the primary liveliness. Furthermore, even in the original arcade version without AI player, the ball still shows non-trivial trajectories. It will automatically accelerate after a few hits. This is a trick the inventor, engineer Al Alcorn, added to make the game more challenging and exciting. Alcorn even programmed the ball to bounce at different angles when hit with different segments of a paddle (Kent, 2001, p. 41). All the above intriguing features jointly render the computer paddle and even the ball seemingly autonomous. All in all, the interactive and dynamic visible objects in this game present a large extent of primary liveliness.

In fact, the dynamic tension in *Pong* is so clear and directed that there is no trace of secondary liveliness. The player's attention always follows the ball flying from side to side, and meanwhile other distraction in the game environment is minimal. Hence, the game is not holistically immersive. With the advances in real-time computer graphics, descendants of *Pong* have added more animated elements to the game field with a view to increasing the liveliness. For instance, the tennis game in *Wii Sports* features not only the two tennis players and the ball, but also an excited and animated audience around the tennis court. These animated characters give the game a lively ambience and distract players to a certain extent, resulting in a better balance of two kinds of liveliness and immersing users (both players and observers) in holistic animacy.

Pattern of engagement

As a sports game, although highly abstract in its presentation, *Pong* is able to engage its players in both sensory perception and bodily interaction. The game presents on-screen animated images that are interactive in real time. The player's hand connects to the on-screen paddle through a rotary knob, a special control device preceding the joystick and other game controllers. The knob enables the player to move the paddle intuitively, with the rotation of the knob linearly and immediately mapped to the translation of the paddle. How fast one turns the knob determines how fast the paddle runs. Rotating too slowly, a player would of course miss the ball, but turning too fast might result in passing the hit point and also failing to bounce the ball back. In other words, *Pong* accepts continuous motion-based input from the player and simultaneously generates perceivable changes, allowing the player to perform continuous appraisal. This coupling engagement of motor input and change perception in real time is essential to the dexterity challenge of this kind of two-sided ball game.

In addition, *Pong* also features some degree of sustaining engagement. When a player stops turning the knob, the corresponding paddle halts at the same time. Yet the ball in this case will still continue to go its way, and the opposite paddle, if controlled by the computer, will run and bounce back the ball. Even if both paddles stand still, the ball will still fly and reach the bottom line of either side, followed by a score update;

then the game resumes by sending off a new ball again. In short, a game of *Pong* shows frequent perceivable changes until it is over. This sustaining pattern has become more obvious in *Breakout*. This 'lonely-hearts' variant of *Pong* simulates a squash game, with a rainbow-colored thick wall facing and also 'opposing' the 'lonely' player. The player has to hit the ball to bounce on a brick and knock it off the wall. Once the wall is broken through, the ball gets to the other side of the wall and keeps bouncing for a while. In the meantime, the player can pause the action and just watch the ball knock off the bricks with a sense of achievement. This perceivable change in the game environment sustains for a while without user input, until the ball gets back to the player side again.

With the coupling and sustaining patterns emerging in game play, *Pong* and its variants feature temporal affordances that tightly connect to their players through sensorimotor experience.

Level of understanding

As with many other sports games succeeding it, immediate conceptual blends take place in *Pong*'s game mechanics, entailing the motor–sensory connection between player action and animated visual feedback. In the original arcade and home versions of *Pong*, a player is provided with the rotary knob through which one is able to move the corresponding paddle along the bottom line to hit the ball back to the opponent. When the player turns the knob, he or she can see his or her paddle moving accordingly to hit the ball. How fast and far the paddle goes instantaneously and continuously reflects how the player turns the knob. This motor–sensory feedback loop makes the virtual paddle an extension of the player's body, constituting an elastic anchor for an immediate blend with the player's sensorimotor experience of playing tabletop air hockey, table tennis, or even tennis. In the blend, the mapping between the movable short solid line and a player with a racket is compressed into an imaginative identity relation of paddle as avatar in the game environment (this is the reason why some players move their bodies along with paddle motion when playing the game); the mapping between the white dot and the puck or ball is compressed into a visual representation relation with the virtual ball; the mapping between the screen and the table for the sport is compressed into an analogy relation of a background as a slippery black table. Meanwhile, player action (e.g., turning the knob) and sensory perception (e.g., seeing the ball bouncing) are selectively projected. The output of the blend is a concept of hitting a ball with a paddle in virtual space. The integration diagram illustrates the structure of this blend (see Figure 7.1).

With the immediate blended concept, a player or an observer can elaborate metaphorical blends. As the game is called *Pong*, the pronunciation easily reminds us of table tennis (a.k.a. ping-pong, transliterated from Chinese), invoking the associated frame. One major property in this frame is a quite unique skill in this sport: adding spin to the ball. A player can readily imagine the possibility of moving the paddle quickly sideways when hitting the ball with a hope of adding spin to it. As mentioned when discussing the variety of liveliness, the engineer Alcorn intriguingly programmed the ball to bounce at different angles when hitting different parts of a paddle. This trick unintentionally but wittingly creates an illusion of spin effects. When a player sees the ball being hit by the paddle at an awkward angle, he or she

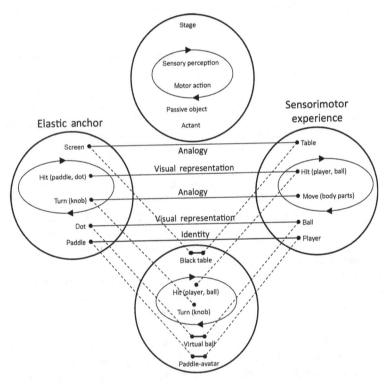

Figure 7.1 Two levels of conceptual blends taking place in a game of *Pong*. The immediate blend (above) results in an extension of the player's body to virtual space through the virtual paddle, and then the metaphorical blend (below) yields an imagined idea of adding spin to the virtual ball.

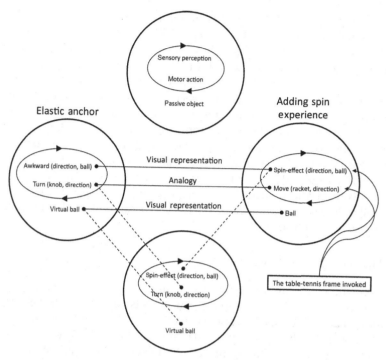

Figure 7.1   (Continued)

may imagine a spin on the bounced ball. Although the spin feature is not actually included in the game mechanics (at least for the original arcade and home versions), the coincident blend of the visual effect and the non-existent spin effect yields an imaginative concept of adding spin to the virtual ball, resulting in higher excitement. The integration diagram is shown in Figure 7.1. This integration could actually give rise to emergent ideas, like different paddles for different types and power of spins, for the possibilities of more sophisticated variants of the game.

Degree of liveness

Pong as a sports video game, like the actual sports, can be seen as a form of performance. The animated phenomena shown in this performance are also highly live, because the amount of stored media content is kept to a minimum. The paddles and the ball are represented only by solid lines and a dot, which need not be pre-rendered and stored, but can just be generated on the fly. Their motion is also simple enough to be computed in real time. The high degree of liveness in *Pong* implies that the system is full of contingencies for players to explore, and the game can be regarded as an improvised performance between the system and a player. The player can enjoy being both the performer (when moving the paddle to hit the ball) and the spectator (when seeing the opponent running for the ball). One manipulates the paddle (directly) and the ball (indirectly) to orchestrate the performance. The manipulation is even more obvious in the case of experienced players, who might explore various ways to 'send' the ball to the opposite bottom line. Though not as vividly animated as other newer sports games boasting advanced real-time control and rendering technologies, *Pong* lets its player enjoy a similar degree of contingency nonetheless, because of the high degree of liveness involved.

The casual game *Angry Birds*

From the classic arcade games, let us move to a recent casual game garnering a phenomenal reception. Since its first launch on the iOS plat-form in 2009, followed by versions on other touchscreen-based systems, *Angry Birds* has been hugely popular around the globe. The game is a simple physics-based mini-game, combining gravity and slingshot with meticulously stacked structures and charged with black humor derived from the absurd story background. A player has to use the virtual sling-shot in the game to shoot birds at pigs within stacked structures to destroy all pigs (because the pigs have stolen the birds' eggs!). The game works best on touchscreen-based systems, as the player can touch and drag a bird directly on the slingshot and release to shoot. Eliminating all pigs in the game field keeps advancing the player to the next level, and different types of birds with different capabilities will become available. Like most mini-games, *Angry Birds* initially targets casual gamers but then they become addicted to it, largely due to its simplicity, con-tingency, and comical style. Such addiction is further reinforced by the numerous updates with additional levels and variations for special sea-sons, such as the Halloween-themed and the Valentine's Day-themed ones. The phenomenon has also pervaded the social media when mes-sages and images of the game posted by players go viral. The craze is not confined to the virtual world either. With the prevalent physical mer-chandise, licensed peripherals and outdoor marketing campaigns, such as a campaign for T-Mobile in Barcelona with a real-life version of the game,[2] *Angry Birds* has inevitably become a fad in social reality.

Variety of liveliness

The major dynamic visible objects in the casual game include various types of birds, the pigs (shown only with their heads), and components such as stones and wooden blocks constituting the stacked structures. Their movements are mainly governed by the simulated physics of the system. When a player launches a bird from the slingshot, it flies in a parabola and lands on the target. The motion directs the player's attention to the hit point, which shows that the flying bird seems to have a clear and determined goal. This is obviously the primary liveliness of the game.

Once the flying bird hits the stacked structure, another kind of liveliness emerges. If the bird hits a pivotal point, the whole structure collapses according to the computer-simulated physics. Stones, wooden blocks, and other fragments subsequently fall down here and there. The player will be anxious to see if the collapse can destroy all the pigs. Yet the collapse is like a chain reaction in which the dynamic action and reaction are so complex that one may not easily accomplish the mission in one particular blow. Moreover, since the pigs hide in different compartments of the structure, one's attention will inevitably be distracted by simultaneous pig destructions scattered over the game field. The whole structure is transforming, but without an obvious goal. In other words, secondary liveliness dominates in this part. Sometimes, one last pig might still survive by the end of the serial collapses. The player's attention will be drawn to what happens in the end, and primary liveliness takes over again.

In short, with the two types of liveliness distributed in different parts of the game play, *Angry Birds* is able to immerse its players in a lively digital environment.

Pattern of engagement

While the arcade classic *Pong* makes use of the proprietary knob, *Angry Birds* builds its game play on the touchscreen. When a player puts his or her fingers on the bird and drags it across the touchscreen, the bird is pulled backward to provide the power of the projectile. The player can always fine-tune the projectile angle and strength by subtly dragging it to different spots with his or her finger. Before releasing the finger to launch the bird, the player is engaged in moving the finger and watching the bird position change continuously and simultaneously in order to estimate the projectile path. During these moments of active use, the game features coupling engagement. This coupling of motor action and sensory perception along the temporal dimension resonates with Ben Shneiderman's original thoughts on direct manipulation, which include physical action and continuous representation (Shneiderman, 2003 [1983]). It is this coupling that provides players with a sense of direct manipulation and control, which is one of the major features that make the game addictive and also affective.

On the other hand, once the player lets go of the bird, the game enters the moments of inactive use. The player has his or her fingers off the touchscreen and just watches how the bird flies and hits the stacked structure. Although the player does not take any action during these moments, he or she is still playing the game in terms of appraisal and desire. First, he or she is still captivated by the perceivable constant change in the game state, as it tells how the score will be. Second, he or she is paying attention to the bird's projectile because certain bird types allow the player to change the projectile with a tap. For example, the big white bird will drop explosive eggs like a bomber in midair when a player taps the touchscreen. The blue one will split into three separate smaller birds in midair to cover a larger area when the player taps the screen. With these various types of birds, a player always has a felt want to trigger the special attack at any time. Hence the player is still engaging with the game during the moments of inactive use, because he or she knows that the next action he or she takes will lead to major changes in the game outcome. This thought sustains the player's engagement.

Both the coupling and sustaining patterns of engagement persist during a shot cycle, resulting in an embodied and affective relation between the game and its players in terms of sensorimotor experience.

Level of understanding

When playing *Angry Birds* on a touchscreen device, a player touches and drags the bird on the slingshot backward with a finger first, and then fine-tune its position subtly before releasing his or her finger. The bird is then shot into the sky in a parabola. This sensorimotor experience, together with the illustrative representation of the slingshot, readily evokes a familiar scenario of using a physical slingshot in the player's mind. One immediately compares the interactive animated images anchoring the experience to the actual use of a slingshot, forming a conceptual blend. In the blend, only the motor action and sensory perception in the two input spaces are mapped, while the force feedback is ignored (because the touchscreen device and the system do not support this feature yet). The mapping between moving the bird and pulling the slingshot is compressed into an analogical concept of pulling the animated bird on a virtual slingshot. The mapping between seeing the bird flying and seeing a physical projectile flight are compressed into a similarity relation. Although there is a lack of sensation of force feedback, the coupling of dragging the bird backward and seeing it launched still gives the player an embodied meaning of pulling an elastic band on a slingshot. The blend yields a new possibility of launching a bird, like shooting a projectile at a target (see Figure 7.2).

More secondary blends emerge from what follows the launch. When seeing the propelled bird heading for the target, exploding, and hitting the structure, the player instantly recognizes and interprets the bird as a stone or even a missile. The military attack frame is invoked, including weapons, bombers, and the like. This frame gives rise to a series of

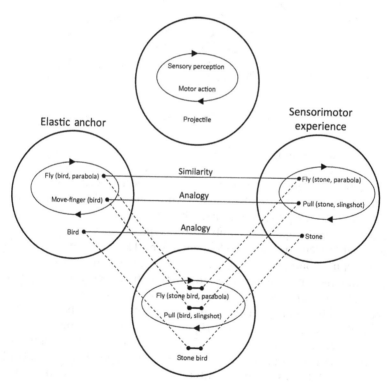

Figure 7.2 Two levels of conceptual blends taking place in a game of *Angry Birds*. The immediate blend (above) results in an embodied concept of propelling virtual birds, and then the metaphorical blend (below) yields an imaginative concept of a bomber-bird.

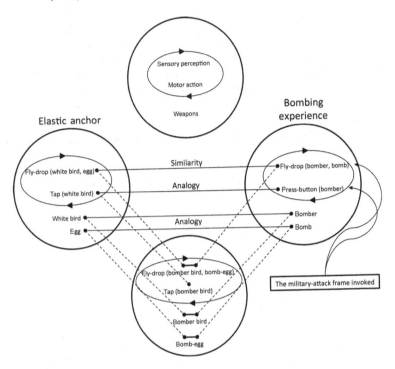

Figure 7.2   (Continued)

metaphorical blends, as demonstrated in the special attacks displayed by various birds. As mentioned, the big white bird can drop an explosive egg midair at the player's command (by tapping the screen), very much like a bomber dropping a bomb. In this type of attack, the player can elaborate a blend between the flying white bird and a common scenario of dropping bombs from an aircraft. The mapping between user tap and pressing the control stick button in the aircraft, as well as the mapping between dropping eggs and dropping bombs are compressed into the blend, yielding an imaginative concept of a propelled bomber-bird. This particular blend is illustrated in Figure 7.2. Another example of special birds generating blends is the aforementioned blue bird that splits into three separate ones upon user tap. This special capability echoes a kind of ninja dart. In this blend, the output consists of a concept of propelled ninja-bird. It follows that each type of bird generates its own blend. With an array of special birds and the associated blends (not only in the original version but also in other special editions), the interactive casual game materializes an imaginative conceptual integration network.

Degree of liveness

Just like most casual mini-games, *Angry Birds* presents animated images in two-dimensional graphics only. The stored visual content is limited to graphics of each type of bird, pig, wooden block, stone, and some pre-rendered debris. Various movements including parabolic propelling, bouncing, falling, and the like are all generated on the fly based on the simulated physics of the game engine. This high-degree liveness results in myriad diverging ways a game can unfold, because a bird can fly on countless possible projectile paths with special attack triggered at countless points in midair, leading to almost unlimited forms of structural damage or collapse. Meanwhile, the game provides players with an infinite number of trials, and so one can explore the various possible contingencies of a particular level. The exploration can then be regarded as a kind of live performance directed and enacted by the player and supported by the system. The player might want to have more of an audience. This is the reason why some fans have uploaded walkthrough videos of successful attempts to the Web, while others have conversely shared screenshots of tricky and curious happenings at some levels. They just want to share what they have performed and created on this highly live platform.

The indie game *flOw*

While most action games have clear goals for players, such as defeating the opponents in both *Pong* and *Angry Birds*, some games do not make the goal explicit but just provide a game milieu for players to explore, develop, and create. This kind of game is sometimes called 'sandbox game', giving players digital 'spades', 'rakes', and 'tubs' for building digital 'sandcastles'. One of the best known and once most prevalent examples is the *SimCity* series, which allows players to build their own self-evolving virtual cities. The interactive music game *Electroplankton* (described in Chapter 2) in which users 'fiddle' with animated plankton to generate music is also one of this kind. Without an explicit goal, a sandbox game can be addictive too. This section introduces another example that demonstrates technological liveliness to the full extent. The game *flOw* originated independently from its creator Jenova Chen's Master of Fine Art thesis, and started in a Flash-based version on the Web in 2006 (http://interactive.usc.edu/projects/cloud/flowing/). The online version features a peculiar 'aquatic organism' (as described in the official website) in primitive two-dimensional graphical form, swimming autonomously in a virtual 'blue' environment. A user can move the mouse pointer to lead the microorganism to explore the milieu. On its way it can eat other organisms and assimilate its prey into its own body (but some prey might be harmful!). There are special organisms that can bring one to a deeper, darker level or back to the shallower, lighter one. Therefore, a player can ambitiously dive into the deep sea or aimlessly navigate between levels with the central organism constantly evolving in form. The goal of the game is not singular but plural and contingent upon user intentions. The rising fame of the independent online version takes the game to the console PlayStation 3 with a more vivid and sophisticated three-dimensional graphics presentation.

Variety of liveliness

Although the game *flOw* does not give players an explicit and particular long-term goal, it presents the user-driven central organism with some immediate targets. There are various other organisms on different levels surrounding the central one, ranging from single-celled to more complex ones. A player can always roll the mouse pointer over any one nearby organism, and then the central organism would gradually swim toward the user-identified target. This clear, goal-directed motion sustains the player's undivided attention, because the target is always moving subtly as if 'floating' in the sea and the player has to make nuanced adjustments in order to make the central organism's mouth (represented by an arc) reach the target. Once having eaten the prey, the central organism immediately changes its form. This clear action-and-reaction phenomenon also engrosses the player at that moment. In short, the game environment entails primary liveliness to draw players' attention.

Meanwhile, the digital, fluid environment is imbued with secondary liveliness too. The various organisms inhabiting the environment always 'flow' and 'wander' without an obvious direction. They do not seem to attract or repel each other. In other words, the dynamic tension between them is not instantly noticeable. Yet they all move, spin, or show changes in pattern quite autonomously. These subtle and diverse events compete for player attention simultaneously. On one particular level, the central organism will be surrounded by a few of these ceaselessly moving little things, and the player is distracted by what happens over the screen in different places. Sometimes, a couple of rippling circles appear near the edge of the screen, giving players a visual cue that more organisms exist at that end. Players have to look here and there from time to time. In addition to being distracted by what happens on the same level in a two-dimensional sense, a player sometimes (usually on deeper levels) comes across blurred shadows of organisms from an underlying level. This further diverts player attention to another dimension of depth, which requires players to look for certain organisms to eat for inter-level travels. All these distractions show that the secondary liveliness in the game is pervasive and persistent. With prominent primary liveliness and pervasive secondary liveliness, *flOw* is able to immerse its players in a holistically dynamic virtual environment.

Pattern of engagement

Chen named the game *flOw*, and he seems to want it to achieve fluidity in all aspects, including input and feedback. Although the initial Web version solicits player inputs via the mouse or touchpad, it accepts and actually requires continuous, motion-based input. Once a player moves the pointer over a target organism (either by rolling the mouse or by running a finger across the touchpad), a central organism starts to swim toward the target. Yet this control has to be continuously updated. On one hand, the target organism is always flowing, and the player has to track the target continuously. On the other hand, the central organism is programmed to have some degree of autonomy. If the mouse pointer holds still for a while, it seems to have lost interest in the signal and starts to wander. In order to keep the central organism's attention, the player has to keep moving the pointer, albeit subtly, around the target. This nuanced but acute interaction mechanism forces players to give input continuously, or to keep the input flowing at all times. Meanwhile, both the target and the chaser are moving simultaneously. The player has to monitor whether the chaser's mouth can pick up the target and then make the necessary input adjustment. Hence, one is engaged in the coupling of continuous motor action and simultaneous sensory perception for the desire to eat and appraisal of success rate.

In addition to the coupling engagement, players of *flOw* also experience a sustaining pattern of engagement. When a player stops moving the pointer, as mentioned, the central organism will keep swimming toward the pointer just for a while and then it will wander. At these moments of inactive use, the player is not engaged in taking any action but is still able to perceive possible changes in the milieu. Since other organisms are always moving around, one can patiently wait for more organisms to flow nearby and resume pointer movement to pick them up. Sometimes, this pause-and-resume tactic may be better than proactive hunting because it renders the predator less aggressive to its preys and so the latter becomes less cautious. Hence, an experienced player would only take action rhythmically, and at other times one might let the organism wander gracefully, embodying the spirit of 'flow' between coupling and sustaining engagements during the time of play. With the temporal affordances of the game environment that enable motion-based input and perceivable constant changes, the enduring interaction gradually becomes familiar and even second nature to its players.

Level of understanding

As mentioned, the central organism in *flOw* is programmed to follow the mouse pointer. The organism, however, will lose track of the pointer and wander if the pointer holds still for more than a few seconds. This protocol requires players to keep the pointer moving by, for example, circling or sliding their fingers subtly in the target direction on the touchpad. In response, the central organism will gracefully swing its body and crawl along in that direction. Sliding a finger continuingly while seeing the organism 'swimming' simultaneously, a player quite readily compares this motor–sensory feedback loop enabled by the interactive animated images to his or her sensorimotor experience of swimming in which one has to keep working various parts of the body in order to advance. In both cases (of mobilizing the organism and actual swimming) a subject stops advancing and just floats if he or she stops moving his or her body parts. The interactive animated images anchor the act and feel of mobilizing the organism in this immediate conceptual blend. The mapping between seeing the organism crawling and watching oneself's swimming is compressed into a visual similarity relation. The mapping between rubbing a finger on the touchpad and doing a swimming stroke is compressed into an analogy relation, together with the finger and the body forming a part–whole relation in the blend. The output is an imaginative concept of dragging a finger or a mouse to swim in the virtual sea of the game (see Figure 7.3).

When a player yields an immediate blend resulting in 'swimming' in the virtual sea, he or she can practice navigating and hunting in this peculiar environment. One has to develop the motor habit of doing a stroke to propel and steer. Since every other organism in the game has the adaptive ability to avoid collision or direct attack, one has to learn how to approach one's prey via a roundabout path. After acquiring the skills of being a predator, the player will notice that in most cases the central organism assimilates what it eats into its body. Some prey organisms add length to the tail of the predator, while others may change the nuanced circular patterns on its segments. There are also some apparently hazardous organisms, for example jellyfish-like complex structures, which degenerate or literally shorten the protagonist's organism when approached. In short, eating or approaching different neighbors results in diverging outcomes in the body form of the playable character. These animated phenomena invoke the diet frame from our everyday lives, and trigger the elaboration of metaphorical blends. The kinds and the mix of food we eat not only nourish our body but also determine our health and form. Deficiency in protein undermines the development, while over-consumption of refined carbohydrates or fat may lead to diabetes or obesity. In other words, as the saying goes, 'we are what we eat'. In the blend, the analogy mappings from eating and transforming in the game environment to nutrient intake and body matter development in one's diet experience are compressed.

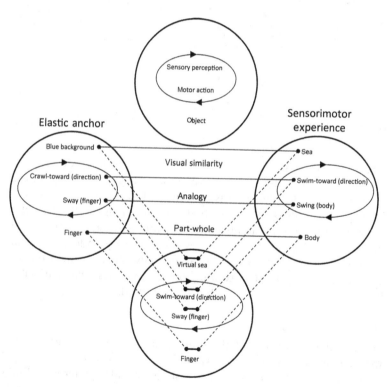

Figure 7.3 Two levels of conceptual blends taking place in a game of *flOw*. The immediate blend (above) results in an embodied concept of swimming in virtual space by swaying finger, and then the metaphorical blend (below) yields the message: 'We are what we eat'.

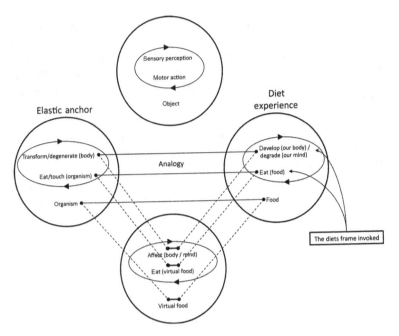

Figure 7.3 (Continued)

The output is an imaginative possibility of virtual body development via one's virtual eating habit. Furthermore, the saying metaphorically applies to 'food for thought' as the kind of information or knowledge we acquire may also affect our mental wellbeing. This association further elaborates the conceptual integration network (see Figure 7.3). The central organism degenerates or even reverts to its early undeveloped stage when subject to contact with the harmful jellyfish. This might provoke a player into thinking that exposing oneself to undesirable materials or information is hazardous to both body and mind.

Degree of liveness

The initial Web version of the indie game presents the virtual environment with very primitive two-dimensional graphics. The central organism is composed of a string of simple circular patterns and dots with a thin arc as the mouth. Other single-celled organisms are mostly presented in ellipses with thin and short strands as their limbs. Even complex structures like jellyfish are also formed by squares, triangles, dots, and the like. In short, the game system can have only a few rudimentary stored graphics, and all the composed organisms and their movements are generated on the fly and presented in real time. With this high degree of liveness, the game provides its players with nearly unlimited possibilities for exploration, development, and performance. A player can develop its organism into very divergent forms by navigating to different terrains and eating different food in different orders. One can even just 'swim' elegantly in a neighborhood of system-animated autonomous organisms, like choreographing a dance performance with the game system. The corresponding screenshots can be seen as a beautifully improvised ballet dance. In other words, *flOw* is not a mainstream competitive game that has set explicit goals requiring players to run for them, but rather an unorthodox sandbox game that has provided tiny actors (i.e., autonomous organisms) allowing players to improvise emerging and contingent happenings.

Summary

There is a myriad video games and lately entertainment apps in the domain of digital entertainment. In this study, it is impractical to closely examine each and every one of them. The corpus introduced in this chapter comprehensively focuses on representatives from three contrasting categories, namely the action/sports genre in arcade games, the casual mini-games, and the 'sandbox' games. They are distinctive from each other in terms of the rules of play, context of play, game mechanics, styles of presentation, and target audiences. But they all rely on animated phenomena enhancing the experience of play. The analyses of the four principles of technological liveness have shown that animated phenomena are vital to the reception of these video games. The corresponding values are summarized in Table 7.1 as follows.

Table 7.1   The four variable values of selected video games

Video games	Variety of liveliness	Pattern of engagement	Level of understanding	Degree of liveness
Pong (with the variant *Breakout*)	Primary (sliding, hitting, missing, bouncing)	Coupling (turn the knob and move) Sustaining (ball and opponent continue to move, keep bouncing in *Breakout*)	Immediate (movable paddle, hittable ball in virtual space) Metaphorical (the table tennis frame: adding spin)	Highly live

Table 7.1   (Continued)

Video games	Variety of liveliness	Pattern of engagement	Level of understanding	Degree of liveness
Angry Birds	Primary (parabolic flying) Secondary (collapsing)	Coupling (drag and pull backward) Sustaining (continue to fly, bombard, and collapse)	Immediate (sling-shoot a bird) Metaphorical (the military attack frame)	Highly live (simple animated graphics)
flOw	Primary (swimming, eating, transforming) Secondary (wandering, silhouettes from other layers)	Coupling (move pointer and crawl toward it) Sustaining (continue to wander, others may approach)	Immediate (slide finger to swim) Metaphorical ('we are what we eat')	Highly live (primitive graphics)

Notes

1. Please see a brief description from *Time* magazine: http://techland.time.com/2012/11/15/all-time-100-video-games/slide/breakout-1976/
2. For a journalist report and video documentary of the campaign, please refer to: http://www.creativeguerrillamarketing.com/guerrilla-marketing/real-life-angry-birds/

8
Creative Expression

After examining animated phenomena that are pervasive in such domains as user interfaces and digital entertainment, this chapter looks at the phenomenon of liveliness in the realm of art, which has long been a platform for humans to express, to interrogate, and to experiment. Contrasting with the previous types of digital artifacts in terms of creators' intentions or consumers' motivations, fine art practice still shares some features with them in animated phenomenal terms. Many works of art, such as mobile sculptures by Alexander Calder, mechanical automata by Jacques de Vaucanson, and others, revolve around the illusion of life, not to mention numerous arthouse animated movies. For an expanded illusion of life, works of digital art are particularly illustrative. By 'digital art' I mean the field of work whose discourse processes rely on the use of digital technology. This kind of work usually incorporates computer programs to produce variable and dynamic instances that show autonomous, reactive, transformative, and contingent behaviors. Hence, John Conway's *Game of Life* (1970) as mentioned in Chapter 3 belongs to the category by definition. The tiny but distinctive program, as the name tells, simulates the mechanics of evolution on the cellular level and projects an image of life on a two-dimensional plane. The pixels in the grid turn on and off continuously and responsively in a seemingly autonomous fashion, resulting in a diverging pattern similar to the evolution of cells. The analogy discourse on the respective rules of game and life could not be manifested without the incorporation of computational technology. On the other hand, interactive installations, including the Camille Utterback and Romy Achituv's previously mentioned *Text Rain* (1999), Wolfgang Muench's *Bubbles* (2000), Philip Worthington's *Shadow Monsters* (2004), Alvaro Cassinelli's *The Khronos Projector* (2005), and many Scott Sona Snibbe's works, are definitely major examples of digital art. These works usually make use of real-time computer graphics, full-body motion detection and image processing technologies to create human-sized, immersive experience. The topics in discourse are undoubtedly diverse, but they are all embodied with the support of digital technology. Sometimes, even a website, a mobile application, or a video game can be intended or regarded as a piece of art. Examples include Han Hoogerbrugge's series of interactive Web comics *Modern Living / Neurotica series* (1998–2001) and Erik Loyer's interactive storytelling app *Ruben & Lullaby* (2009), both mentioned in Chapter 5. Another equally atypical work is Jason Rohrer's *Passage* (2007), which is presented in the form of a classical and pixelated platform game, but aims to deliver a poetic, poignant message about life.

Among the numerous works of digital art that have emerged in recent decades, the corpus to be analyzed in this chapter highlights only those featuring animated phenomena and exemplifying the four principles of technological liveliness in terms of the four variables. They include the interactive installation *Text Rain*, the interactive Web comics *Modern Living / Neurotica series*, and the expressive art-game *Passage*. Although these different works run on very divergent computer-based platforms, animated phenomena are indispensable to their creative discourse processes. This chapter looks into each of these phenomena closely.

Camille Utterback and Romy Achituv's *Text Rain*

Interactive installation is one of the major formats emerging in digital art. It usually involves the use of various sensors to detect users' full-body motion and real-time rendering engines to generate dynamically composed, human-sized images. The coupling of motion input with sensory feedback not only makes the installed or projected images highly responsive but also lets the audience participate in making the work's meaning. The responsive and participatory nature of interactive installation has caught the attention of many artists. Key precursors such as Myron Krueger have inspired countless successors: Wolfgang Muench and Scott Snibbe among others. Ever since Krueger's early work *VIDEOPLACE* was shown in 1969, various interactive installations have been included in canonical international art festivals such as Ars Electronica and SIGGRAPH Art Gallery. Quite a few of them were acquired for the permanent collections of prestigious art museums and galleries. Among the array of highly regarded salient works in the Hall of Fame, *Text Rain* is chosen to be included in the corpus here. It has been widely discussed and closely examined by digital art theorists and critics, such as Jay David Bolter and Diane Gromala in their seminal work, *Windows and Mirrors: Interaction Design, Digital Art, and the Myth of Transparency* (Bolter & Gromala, 2003). I do not intend to re-celebrate its influence here with respect to art theories and practices. Instead, this section focuses on how this exceptional work manifests technological liveliness in terms of the four variables.

The work shows a human-sized projection of animated English letters falling like rain or snow. A participant standing in front of the screen sees his or her immediate mirror image projected on the screen, and the falling letters shower on his or her image (see Figure 8.2). Any body movement will cause the projected image to interact with the falling letters – catch them or let them go. A stretched arm may catch a string of letters, which may form a verse from a poem by Evan Zimroth (Utterback, 2004, p. 221). Hence, the audience is invited to actually take part in uncovering meanings made by the text rain.

Variety of liveliness

Text Rain presents participants with their own monochromatic mirror image on the projected screen. The image is in fact produced by flipping horizontally the moving images captured in real time by a live camera on the screen. When a participant raises his or her left hand, the projected image will lift his or her right hand. In other words, the installation works as if the participant is looking at himself/herself in a mirror. Hence, the participant can 'move' his or her body so as to move the projected image to catch, lift, and then let fall any letters. The overall moving images on the screen, including the falling letters and one's mirror image, demonstrate both primary and secondary liveliness.

When the projected image moves in the rain, letters might bounce off and fall from the projected body as if due to gravity. An observer of the installation would spontaneously take Daniel Dennett's physical stance to perceive this seemingly natural physical interaction. The action and reaction between, for instance, one's hand, and raindrops are clear and direct. Meanwhile, each raindrop is actually a letter from a poem, and sometimes a participant might want to look for, catch and hold on to a word or a phrase. Such action results in abrupt movement or bizarre posture so that an observer is tempted to take the intentional stance to read which word or phrase the participant is targeting. Here, the participant's action and the caught phrase draw the audience's undivided attention. This is the primary liveliness in *Text Rain*.

On the other hand, participants and falling letters also contribute to the secondary liveliness of the work. Since different letters fall ceaselessly and randomly all over the screen at seemingly varying speed due to motion parallax (a visual effect that things in the front are moving faster than those in the back), they actually compete for the audience's eyeballs. An audience might be distracted by the falling letters over the whole screen, just like gazing into the rain in real life. Sometimes, participants become excited enough to dance and strike different poses in the virtual rain. They move rhythmically and gracefully. Some even bring their own little props such as umbrellas or cloths in order to generate wavelike patterns from the falling letters.[1] These moving patterns are not related to any obvious goals but just engross the audience in a transforming whole. These visuals correspond to the secondary liveliness of the work. With both the primary and secondary liveliness, the installation immerses its audience in the holistically lively virtual rain.

Pattern of engagement

Making use of real-time live video capturing and processing technologies, *Text Rain* is able to detect and respond to users' full-body motion input without an intermediary. Whilst a participant stands in front of the screen and moves his or her body, the projected image immediately mirrors those movements, together with the reaction of animated letters in real time. During this apparently direct interaction, nearly all motion qualities of motor input are continuously tracked by the system. For instance, a participant can tilt his or her hand slowly until the caught letters finally start to slip and fall. Meanwhile, looking at the projected image, he or she is always free to lift his or her hand again to stop the letters from falling off his or her hand. With continuous motion-based input and simultaneous animated feedback, participants' motor and sensory experiences are coupled all the time. The coupling engagement allows one to move the body with impulsive desire and continuously evaluate the posture. A participant will become accustomed to 'catching' or 'fiddling' with the virtual rain very soon.

The interactive environment in *Text Rain* is also able to sustain user engagement. In the moments of inactive use (say, when there is no participant, or when the participant just stands still) letters keep falling all the same. Since the words from the poem are randomly selected and let fall, the resulting raining pattern on the screen is constantly changing. If the participant misses a particular falling verse of the poem, one can wistfully wait for it to reappear somewhere some other time. The participant's engagement is temporarily inclined to perception of constant changes. Once the verse shows up again, the participant will have a felt want to resume action to hold it and become engaged in the coupling of action and perception again. Hence, the ever-changing environment features both coupling and sustaining patterns of engagement. Users facing the *Text Rain* environment will feel that the virtual rain's autonomous and reactive behavior is compatible with their bodily action and perception, resulting in an intimate relationship.

Level of understanding

As a poetic work of art, *Text Rain* is expressive. It entails both immediate and metaphorical levels of understanding. When a participant moves and then sees his or her mirror image doing the same in the showering letters, one immediately blends the sensorimotor experience, which is anchored by the interactive animated visuals on the screen, with one's remembered sensorimotor experience in actual rain (see Figure 8.1 for

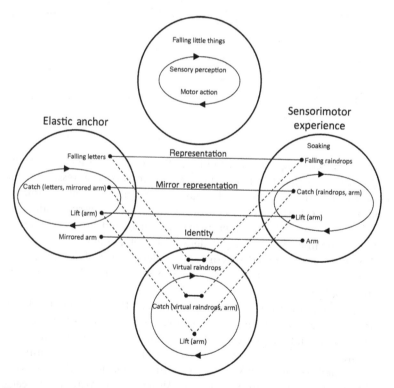

Figure 8.1 Two levels of conceptual blends taking place in *Text Rain*. The immediate blend (above) results in an embodied concept of dancing in the virtual rain, and then the metaphorical blend (below) yields a particular imaginative thought of receiving poetic messages via the body.

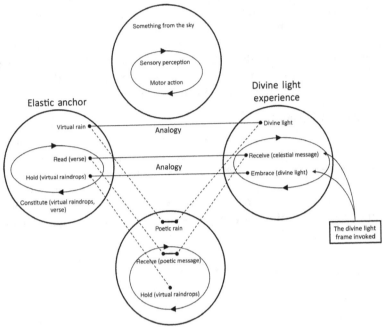

Figure 8.1   (Continued)

the integration diagram). In the blend, the outer-space representation link between falling letters and falling raindrops is compressed into a concept of virtual raindrops. The outer-space link between the mirror image and the participant is compressed into an inner-space identity relation. As a result of the blend, seeing a projected image of oneself catching the imaged rain is equivalent to oneself being in the rain. The elaboration of this immediate conceptual blend results in an imaginary space in which the participant can dance in the virtual rain without getting soaked.

The metaphorical understanding emerges as the participant notices that letters caught on his or her silhouette seem to form meaningful words or phrases. The text, in the original version of the work, is excerpted from Evan Zimroth's poem *Talk, You* (1993), which implies an imagined narrator 'conversing' with the reader in accordance with bodily actions such as 'turning around'. Whenever the participant reads the line of letters held by the body silhouette and makes sense out of it, he or she feels as if he or she is hearing someone whisper through the body gesture. The experience may be interpreted as analogical to receiving via the body gesture a celestial message from the sky. The 'divine light' frame is invoked, including a scene involving a visible beam of light carrying an immaterial and even spiritual sign from above, and triggering metaphorical blends (see Figure 8.1). The analogical relation between the virtual rain and the divine light is compressed into a new concept of poetic rain, which carries conversational messages. The action of outstretching arms and holding virtual raindrops may be analogical to the action of embracing 'divine light' from the sky. This particular blend is not predetermined, and there are other possible elaborations as well. However, a documentary photo of the work at the Boston CyberArts Festival showing a lady receiving the falling letters with her face up (Figure 8.2) does accord with the interpretation that the work evokes a metaphorical narrative of someone receiving celestial and spiritual messages via the body and the environment. The animation of falling letters, and the viewer's interaction with them, generate an imaginative integration between the physical and the spiritual.

Figure 8.2 In *Text Rain* (1999), a lady receives falling letters with her face up. Image courtesy of the artists (Utterback and Achituv).

Degree of liveness

As an interactive video installation that projects the participant's real-time moving images on the screen, *Text Rain* is intended to be a platform for live improvisation between the system and the participant. As some documentary videos on one of the creators' official websites have shown (please visit http://camilleutterback.com/projects/text-rain/), many participants enjoyed taking part in the performance, with their own creative inputs. For example, someone brought in a real umbrella to perform 'dancing in the rain'. Several others stood hand in hand and made wave to bounce off the rain. They all actively participated in creating animated phenomena in the performance facilitated by the system. When it comes to liveness, the only stored visual components are the typographic characters of the poem. The participant image captured and projected in real time interferes with the motion of the falling letters on the fly. In other words, the installation demonstrates a very high degree of liveness, which means that the work opens up nearly endless contingencies for participants to intervene.

Han Hoogerbrugge's *Modern Living / Neurotica series*

Like many works of art, *Text Rain* is exhibited publicly in an art gallery or similar setting. In contrast, another work to be discussed here emerged on a strikingly different platform. It was originally intended to be shown on the Web. Since 1997, the Dutch comic artist Han Hoogerbrugge has used the Internet to publish interactive animated comics on his website Hoogerbrugge.com. The first work of the project, *Modern Living / Neurotica series* (1998–2001), featuring nearly 100 short animated films, addresses small observations from the artist's personal life, which also resonates with some users' lives, including workaholism, social impositions, and the like (please visit http://ml.hoogerbrugge.com/). Apart from a few simply looped animated sequences, most of the animated comics are interactive. The collection can be seen as a documentation of the artist's experiments with mouse-mediated interaction. They are inspirationally successful in remapping conventional mouse action like point-and-click to different intentions. For instance, in #43, 'Itch', a mouse click makes the character (a self-portrait of the artist) 'itch' wherever the mouse pointer is located. Through various couplings of motor action and animated feedback, the peculiar work mobilizes motor–sensory connection and projects an expanded illusion of life.

Variety of liveliness

Within the archive of animated comics in *Modern Living / Neurotica series*, both primary and secondary liveliness are pervasive. The former can be seen in many pieces in which the character tends to 'get away' from the mouse pointer. For example, in #61, 'Drowning', a user can move the pointer to play hide-and-seek with the character. The character just sinks into the water on mouse-over and rises elsewhere. In #54, 'Jumpy', a mouse-over action seems to drive the character to jump around. In #68, 'Obedience', keeping the pointer over the character's head can 'bring' him to his knees, and after a kowtow he immediately stands up again. All these action-and-reaction animated phenomena demonstrate clear dynamic tension between the mouse pointer and the character. Whenever it jumps away or kneels down, the character's motion directs the user's attention to a clear result. This interactive phenomenon shows primary liveliness.

On the other hand, some other pieces show secondary liveliness by displaying multiple reactive characters that distract a viewer with many animated objects all over the frame. In #60, 'New Religion', dozens of characters line up to form four rows. When the pointer moves across the characters, they stand up and then bend down continuously forming a wave like those spectators make in sporting events, also in a way similar to the magnification effect in the dock of OS X. In #85, 'Material Guy', when a user runs the pointer across the faces of the characters, they swell up and vomit home appliances – washing machines, dryers, toasters, and the like – in random order. There are often simultaneous happenings and movements in the frame, which is distracting. Moreover, the action-and-reaction relationships in these pieces are unstable. That is to say, one can reverse the pointer movement any time and the animation would more or less rewind with the character resuming its starting appearance. Hence, the overall transformation does not show any clear direction of progression but purely changes. This emergent nature echoes secondary liveliness. The archive of the animated pieces presents not only the multifaceted modernity of today but also the holistic animacy of life.

Pattern of engagement

In *Modern Living / Neurotica series*, most animated pieces are interactive. The system usually considers the position of the pointer and the timing of a click in user input. For example, in #70, 'Eternal Love', the position of the pointer determines whether the character in the foreground or the picture in the background is in focus. In #87, 'Vaudeville', many 'dummy' versions of the character travel across the frame at various speeds. A user can point and click on any dummy head to pop it open, like in a classic carnival game. Whether a head pops open certainly hinges on where and when the user clicks. In these interactive pieces, a mouse-over or click action usually sets off a corresponding animated feedback. Strictly speaking, the input and output sections are alternating. Yet there are pieces involving more continuous input and simultaneous feedback. For instance, in #97, 'Rash', when the mouse rolls over the character's head, spines grow out of its head around the pointer. When the pointer moves away from its head, the spines recede. A user on one hand has to continue to move the pointer and on the other inevitably gazes in awe at the spines that go in and out of the face. One's motor action and sensory perception are coupled continuously throughout the game.

In case of no user action, most pieces just come to a halt. Even though a few pieces do show some changes, like #63, 'Perfect Day', in which the character keeps swinging along the background music, the audio and the visuals are just in very simple loops. The environment does not exhibit really perceivable changes until the user resumes action and moves the pointer. Hence, the enduring interaction of *Modern Living / Neurotica series* largely hinges on coupling engagement, which forces users to take action in order to experience the pieces but loses their attention during the moments of inactive use.

Level of understanding

As mentioned, many pieces in *Modern Living / Neurotica series* remap conventional mouse actions to novel meanings. These new mappings are formed with the help of immediate conceptual blending. Furthermore, some pieces even provoke metaphorical understandings. To illustrate, I focus on an example. In #83, 'Possessed', the character sits behind a task table facing the user. It seems as if he is using a computer mouse. When the user rolls the mouse pointer over the task table, the character will move his mouse to follow. This interactive animated figure acts as an elastic anchor, capturing the sensation emerging from the sensorimotor experience. It follows that the immediate blend lets the user understand how to control the character in an intuitive way, just by sliding his or her mouse to a desired spot. The mechanism is like controlling a shadow puppet with moving rods. The analogy mapping between the elastic anchor of moving the character and the sensorimotor experience of controlling a rod puppet is compressed, together with the analogy link between the character and a rod puppet from two input spaces. The output of the blend is a concept of virtual puppet in the animated piece (see Figure 8.3). Hence, when one moves the pointer, the virtual puppet moves his hand.

What makes 'Possessed' eccentric is the strange apparitions that appear on the character's face and the curious noise he makes while the user moves the pointer around. This effect may invoke the 'Web surfing' frame in the user's mind, suggesting a metaphorical blend of the piece with an imaginative but familiar scenario – net surfers often being distracted by the many unexpected pop-ups and hyperlinks. In the blend, the mapping between the character and the user, both using a computer mouse, is compressed into an inner-space identity relation. An analogy

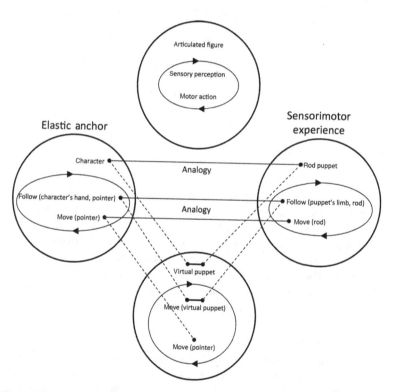

Figure 8.3 Two levels of conceptual blends taking place in *Modern Living / Neurotica series*. The immediate blend (above) results in an embodied concept of moving a virtual puppet, and then the metaphorical blend (below) yields an imagined reflection of how hyperlinks distract our minds.

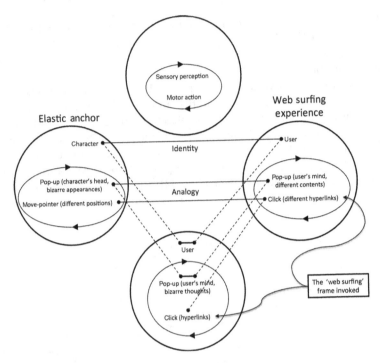

Figure 8.3   (Continued)

link is compressed between the elastic anchor of bizarre apparitions on the character's face and the sensorimotor experience of unexpected pop-ups when browsing the Web. In this case, the character's head is also analogical to the user's mind. The output of the metaphorical blend is a novel concept of how the Web materials affect our thoughts (see Figure 8.3). The interactive comic acts like a mirror reflecting the mental status of the user. This example shows a typical way in which *Modern Living / Neurotica series* resonates with our personal experiences.

Degree of liveness

Although *Modern Living / Neurotica series* is intended and regarded as a series of interactive Web comics, it also opens up possibilities of improvisation between the user and the artist, with the support of interactive multimedia technologies. An example best demonstrating this idea is #71, 'El Mariachi'. The piece features five identical characters on stage, each of which is holding a guitar in a different pose. A user can roll the mouse to cast a spotlight on any particular character, and that character will start to play. Although all characters and guitars look alike, each of them makes a different sound. Hence, by moving the pointer the user is like playing a real-time sound synthesizer with five different instrumental tracks. The result is a live performance orchestrated by the user on the fly. In this performance, the stored components include short audio clips and a few animated drawings prepared by the artist. Meanwhile, the spotlight effect is added to the comic during runtime. Hence, this particular interactive piece from *Modern Living / Neurotica series* can be called highly live. It allows users to arrange the audio clips coupled with the animated visuals in any order for any duration, opening up almost unlimited possibilities for composing an ongoing audiovisual performance with the five simple tracks and the animated characters.

Jason Rohrer's *Passage*

Art takes many forms; so does digital art. Interactive installations and interactive Web graphics, as exemplified by *Text Rain* and *Modern Living / Neurotica series*, are two common approaches to digital art, although they occupy very different spaces in art practice. Besides, innovative art practitioners are also interested in other digital media forms such as video games. Like their physical counterparts, video games generally pit players against each other within the 'magic circle' of certain logics, rules, and conditions. Although as mentioned in Chapter 7, alternatives such as sandbox games, which do not impose explicit competition framework, do exist in practice, they still motivate players' exploration in order to entertain. On the contrary, artists make video games for self-expression. They may not be very keen on making the games addictive, but more interested in the meanings the audience makes out of them. This is the reason why the following discussion is included in this chapter. A very distinctive example is Jason Rohrer's mini computer game *Passage*.

Rohrer is an independent game designer, who has made several mini-games that have been very well received on the Internet and among both the indie game and academic game studies communities. One of his notable works is *Passage*, an expressive art-game written as a reminder of mortality for gamers to meditate on the subject (please visit http://hcsoftware.sourceforge.net/passage/). As Rohrer puts it in his creator's statement, '*Passage* is a game in which you die only once, at the very end, and you are powerless to stave off this inevitable loss' (Rohrer,

2007). In other words, no player can win the game. The concept of 'winning' violates the basic premise of the game, making it more a work of art than a game. He believes that computer codes could 'make us cry and feel and love' and intends to turn video games into artistic vehicles for exploring the meaning of life (Fagone, 2008). Hence, *Passage* is imbued with evocative metaphors of 'life is a journey', which is presented literally, visually as a long horizontal screen of a maze. A player starts the game with a character walking alone in a maze with many obstacles. The character's position on the screen gradually shifts from the left edge to the right within the five-minute game time. Simultaneously, the character becomes increasingly older in appearance (going bald and grey-haired, hunching its back, etc). Along the way, the player accumulates points. One may also collect treasure chests for additional points, or walk with a companion for double points. However, once the character bumps into his spouse, the couple walk hand in hand and become less agile in collecting treasures. Players have to make a trade-off. Lastly, the most poignant part is that no matter how many points one has got, the character has to die after reaching the right end in five minutes.

Variety of liveliness

Unlike most other maze games, *Passage* does not involve any computer-controlled adversaries who disturbingly challenge the player character. The only character other than the player character is his potential spouse, who contributes only to a minimum extent of primary liveliness to the game. In the beginning, the lady just stands still in the maze. Once the player character walks close enough to her, she snaps to the player character and they start walking side by side. The couple shows a magnetic type of action and reaction in the game. The dynamic tension is clear and directional. Besides, when the player character, with or without his spouse, is exploring the maze, an observer may take the intentional stance, speculating whether the character is looking for treasures nearby. In other words, the game characters always direct viewers' attention toward some objects or certain parts of the maze, giving the game its primary liveliness.

On the other hand, secondary liveliness is not prominent in *Passage*. As mentioned, there is no non-player character (NPC) wandering in the game environment, which is a main difference from other ordinary maze games. In fact, the only active element in *Passage* is the player character (the spouse only snaps and attaches to him). Players' or viewers' attention is always focused on the protagonist, without much distraction from other objects. Although the maze itself moves steadily and unnoticeably to the left like a camera panning slowly to the right, the transformation is too subtle and also too directional to be called secondary liveliness. In this sense, the game can only draw players' focused attention whilst overlooking their peripheral attention.

Pattern of engagement

As a mini maze game like *Pac-Man* (1980), *Passage* allows its players to control the motion of the main character in only four directions, namely up, down, left, and right. In the computer version, players press arrow keys to move the character. This kind of motor input is not very closely related to motion, because a control finger pressing buttons only is not moving with the character's motion in any way. That is, qualities of finger motion like direction and force do not have significant effect on the resulting character movement, except maybe when the character changes direction. In the mobile version, however, the arrow keys are turned into four touchscreen buttons arranged in the four directions accordingly. This button arrangement allows the control finger to just 'slide' across the screen, thus to 'steer' the direction in a more 'continuous' way, and the character keeps walking and turning simultaneously. The player feels as if he or she is directing the character in motion by moving a finger around. This fairly motion-based input can also be achieved in the computer version if the touchpad (a basic input device in laptop computers nowadays) is taken into consideration. The player's motor action can be coupled with perception of animated feedback. Hence, *Passage* is able to manifest a coupling pattern of engagement.

Since there are not many active elements in *Passage*, it may seem that the game cannot sustain a player's engagement if one stops the input. This is actually not the case. If the player stops taking action and the character stands still in the maze, the character position relative to the game view would incrementally shift toward the right at regular time intervals. That means even though the character's absolute position in the maze does not change, the screen position changes due to the game camera's panning movement. In the meantime, the rendering on the right side of the screen gets clearer and clearer, whilst those on the left side become hazy. In short, the game environment still shows endless transformations without any user action. Apart from the constantly changing game environment, the character also gradually turns from a young guy to an older man no matter he moves or not. If the player resumes control, the camera continues to track the character again. Therefore, *Passage* engages its players during various moments of use, active or inactive. With both coupling and sustaining patterns of engagement, the game environment contains temporal affordances that closely match players' scales of bodily action and perception, as well as enduring agency in which one can perform continuous appraisal with respect to his or her felt wants, easily resulting in a sense of intimacy.

Level of understanding

Although *Passage* only involves two characters and a passage, there is a wealth of metaphors provoking multiple levels of understanding. At first glance the work looks like a primitive maze game with the player character wandering and searching around. Yet the presentation of *Passage* differs from an ordinary maze game in at least two ways. First, the screen is intentionally made to be exceedingly wide such that only a horizontal slice of the maze can be seen. Second, in the early stage of the game, the far right end of the frame seems to shrink and blur. Those visions will become clearer and clearer only when the character moves forward. These nuances render an immediate conceptual blend in *Passage* more compressed than those in other maze games or platform games. In *Passage*, when a player presses an arrow key on the keyboard, the screen scrolls and reveals more walkway ahead of the character, and also in front of the player. Compared with a fixed overview of the maze in such maze games as *Pac-Man*, this incremental unfolding is more reminiscent of our sensorimotor experience of exploring an unfamiliar walkway in which the further you move, the more you see. This action–perception coupling in the game environment acts as an elastic anchor to the immediate blend. The identity link between the player and the character is compressed into an avatar relation in the blend, an embodied extension of the player in the virtual space. The representation link between pixel graphics of the maze and an unfamiliar walkway is compressed into a virtual passage. The output of the blend is a new concept of exploring an imaginative maze, as illustrated in Figure 8.4.

As mentioned, *Passage* is imbued with metaphors related to the conventional saying 'life is a journey'. First, the game presents the view in a long horizontal slice, and the character gets older and older as the game time goes by. When the character walks from left to right in the maze (and also on the screen), it becomes obvious that space is a metaphor for time. It then follows that the journey on the wide screen is a metaphor for the character's lifespan. In the end, the character approaches the right edge and then leaves only a gravestone, a conventional symbol of death. The five-minute journey represents the character's short life. Second, in the course of his journey/life, he may meet a lady. One could approach her to establish a life-long companionship, or just leave her alone. The two options correspond to two fundamentally contrasting lifestyles. In a relationship, the character is unable to explore the narrow passageways aggressively and collect treasures along the way. Together, the couple can only go through the mainstream passage. This limitation echoes with the common frame of marriage, likely bringing out the author's intended imaginative perspective on how having a family and commitments limits possibilities. These rules and constraints form the secondary blend of the game with a story of life and death. As shown in Figure 8.4, the analogy link between the screen journey and a life with marriage, and another between a narrow pathway and a niche career or business opportunity, are compressed into inner-space relations in the new blend, together with the representation of death by gravestone.

Figure 8.4 Two levels of conceptual blends taking place in *Passage*. The immediate blend (above) results in an embodied concept of walking through the virtual passage, and then the metaphorical blend (below) yields a particular message of how marriage and family commitment limits possibilities.

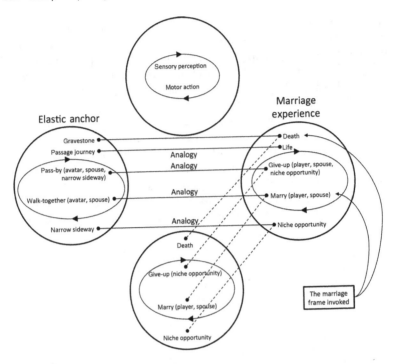

Figure 8.4 (Continued)

In the blend, the message: 'Till death do us part!' is invoked. Whilst the integration diagram here only depicts one possible imaginative blend, the work also provokes other metaphorical understandings such as the adventurous and treasure-hunting lifestyle of the celibate. The analysis here only emphasizes one possible interpretation of the game.

Degree of liveness

Compared with rudimentary action games like *Pong* or *Pac-Man*, *Passage* has relatively more stored visual assets (e.g., character graphics, maze terrains, audio, etc.). The pixel graphics of the characters and those few treasure chests were pre-rendered and stored. The structure of the maze together with its modular components were defined in advance, whilst the full rendering, especially the shrunk and hazy effect, is likely to be generated on each instantiation, because the final view depends on how a player navigates in the maze. Furthermore, the compositing of characters, items, and the maze onto the screen display is definitely executed on the fly during game play. In other words, the only stored visual materials are still images of some modular pixel graphics. It means a moderately high degree of liveness. Although unlike ordinary games that usually have myriad divergent outcomes between winning and losing, there are still a few contingencies in the game. For example, the character may die anywhere in the maze. One may collect many treasures and score high, but be alone till death. Others may join a partner and walk straight back to the start point to wait till the game is over. Every game in *Passage* is a moderately live improvisation between the player and the system. When the character is wandering around, the player is a performer. When the player observes the steadily changing environment and the aging character, he or she becomes a member of the audience too.

Summary

Not all works of digital art rely on animated phenomena in their creative discourse, but quite a number of them entail various forms of dynamic elements in their presentations, which can be visuals, sounds, or even physical materials. This chapter introduces for discussion three distinctive works that foreground the phenomena of technological liveliness. Their initial stages of presentation are diverse, ranging from an installation in physical space, through a Web publication on the Internet, to a mini computer game. Both their forms and meanings vary greatly. Nevertheless, they unanimously span a wide terrain in the variables of technological liveliness. The corresponding values are summarized in Table 8.1 as follows.

Table 8.1 The four variable values of selected works of digital art

Artworks	Variety of liveliness	Pattern of engagement	Level of understanding	Degree of liveness
Text Rain	Primary (catching, holding) Secondary (raining, waving, dancing)	Coupling (body movement and mirrored image motion) Sustaining (continuously raining)	Immediate (dancing in the virtual rain) Metaphorical (the divine light frame)	Highly live (only stored letters)

Table 8.1   (Continued)

Artworks	Variety of liveliness	Pattern of engagement	Level of understanding	Degree of liveness
Modern Living / Neurotica series	Primary (jumping, hide-and-seek, etc.) Secondary (simultaneous up and down, swell up and vomit, etc.)	Alternating (click and then pop up) Coupling (roll over and spines come out)	Immediate (puppeteer the character) Metaphorical (the Web surfing frame)	Highly live (animated drawings and audio clips)
Passage	Primary (striding)	Coupling (sliding finger over touchpad to steer) Sustaining (maze view continues to pan; avatar continues to age)	Immediate (navigable virtual maze) Metaphorical (the marriage frame)	Moderately live (animated sprites, some contingencies but convergent outcome)

Notes

1. For a look at how participants 'creatively' play with the 'letters' rain, please see the video documentation on one of the creator's website: http://camilleutterback.com/projects/text-rain/

9
Implications

In the previous three chapters, we have conducted a close reading of an array of digital media artifacts which belong to the basic-level categories including user interface, video game, and digital art. These three commonly separate groups of artifacts generally contrast with each other in terms of both the creator's motivation and the consumer's expectation, but the works included in the corpus resonate in the pursuit of liveliness. As the analyses in previous chapters have shown, the properties of these artifacts with respect to the four qualitative variables exemplify the principles of technological liveliness. They are able to immerse their users in a virtual environment with both primary and secondary liveliness; they entail coupling and/or sustaining patterns of engagement that match users' bodily motion and perception, resulting in a sense of intimacy; they anchor sensation for immediate conceptual blends yielding embodied concepts of virtual space, followed by elaboration of metaphorical blends; they generate output on the fly and in real time, supporting users to explore diverse possibilities in outcomes. In short, they all rely on animated phenomena to give human users immersive, familiar, embodied, evocative, and divergent kinds of experience. This study is not intended to be an exhaustive survey of all digital media artifacts, and inevitably there are many other salient examples that demonstrate comparable values in those four variables. For the sake of controlling the corpus size, they are not included in this book. Only the best representatives of their kinds are covered. The upshot shows that technological liveliness is pervasive in such domains as control and communication, entertainment, and creative expression. And the corpus in this book epitomizes its pervasiveness.

On the other hand, there are many other digital media artifacts that do not exemplify every qualitative variable. One may exhibit holistic animacy in terms of both types of liveliness, without providing users with exploratory contingencies. For instance, the animated installation of *Along the River During the Qingming Festival* analyzed in Chapter 2 is immersive with the integration of primary and secondary liveliness, but it is not live because of the largely pre-rendered visual content in presentation. The salient website Ecotonoha briefly mentioned in Chapter 1 featuring dynamic user-submitted messages in animated graphics is highly live, as it allows visitors to expand different branches of the virtual tree by leaving new messages. Yet it does not entail much coupling or sustaining engagement, unlike the website SnowDays. In addition, certain computer games, particularly in the action, simulation, and time management subgenres, usually engage players in coupling patterns during moments of active use, and even sustain their engagement in perception during inactive use, but not many of them trigger material-based imagination on metaphorical levels, as *Angry Birds* and *flOw* do. In short, those works not included in the current corpus may not be relevant to the discussion of certain qualitative variables, meaning they have room for further development toward achieving an all-round technological liveliness. Hence, the four qualitative variables indicate how far an artifact is from the notion of fully fledged technological liveliness. An ideal representative would include both primary and secondary liveliness, entail coupling patterns or even sustaining patterns of user engagement during various moments of use, provoke not only immediate understanding but also metaphorical imagination, and be highly live. A representative far from technological liveliness would only present one type of liveliness (or even none), limit user engagement to an alternating pattern of input and output, engender only immediate levels of conceptual blends, and be slightly live or even of a passive viewerly nature. Expanding the corpus by including those less exemplifying artifacts in one or two variables can be a way to reflect the media landscape more comprehensively, informing designers or researchers of further design strategies for pursuing technological liveliness.

As mentioned in the beginning of Part III, the corpus can be persistently evolving, as long as each artifact in it is articulated by the four variables. The current corpus I include in this book represents a paradigm of digital media artifacts across user interfaces, video games, and digital art objects that exemplify technological liveliness. In fact, the corpus can be reformed to represent another paradigm. For instance, it can be those latest artifacts in the domain of digital marketing or electronic commerce that show a certain degree of technological liveliness, that is, not exhibiting relevance to all four qualitative variables. The reformed corpus can be very different from the current one, but may equivalently track down the landscape of technological liveliness in the corresponding domains. To researchers or educators, it shows the emergent trend of the digital media landscape. To design practitioners or technologists, it gives information on the promising areas for possible creative exploration and new orientations toward more experiential technologies.

What technological liveliness can also be

This book introduces new theoretical and design perspectives on what I call technological liveliness – the human experience of animated phenomena in today's digitally mediated environments. The discussion looks into the processes of how we see and perceive (being the observer), how we act and feel (via the body), how we interpret and imagine (with the mind), and how we improvise and create (being the performer) with computer-based systems. The four threads of human experience give rise to four principles with an array of qualitative variables. The variable values reflect the multidimensional inclinations toward technological liveliness. Hence, a digital media artifact can be articulated in a multi-threaded taxonomy by the four corresponding variable values. A corpus of works from one or more domains articulated in the taxonomy epitomizes how far technological liveliness pervades the areas.

To sum up, technological liveliness is a theoretical idea, a design stance, a multi-threaded taxonomy, and varied corpuses of artifacts. Broadly speaking, it symbolizes humans' enduring pursuit, with the computer as companion, of creating more 'human-familiar' and 'lifelike' dynamic phenomena, that is, an illusion of life. Technological liveliness in fact expands the meaning of 'illusion of life' in the digital media context. The expanded illusion includes self-movement, reaction, autonomous transformation, adaptation to changes, and contingency. These dynamic phenomena of life characterize animated phenomena. Echoing the very beginning of this book, technological liveliness is a convergence of animation (as an idea) and embodiment (in the phenomenological sense) in digital media.

Toward the end, I further sketch out the implications of technological liveliness, which resonate in the broad context of art, poetics, media, and culture.

Technological liveliness as an illusion of life in the age of computation

In his 1935 seminal essay 'The Work of Art in the Age of Mechanical Reproduction', Walter Benjamin marks the impact of reproduction technologies emerging at that time on the authenticity of the art object (Benjamin, 1968). Mechanical reproduction, he argued, replicates the original and negates its uniqueness in time and space. He eloquently described the phenomenon as 'the decay of the aura'. This decay reflects the emergent human desire to bring things 'closer', both 'spatially and humanly', including the art object once considered sacred. This view echoes with my proposal to bring computers and computer-based artifacts 'closer' to humans, while the art object moves further from the spiritual to the mortal and the computer transcends its mere mechanical existence. Initially the computer was a tool, an instrument, and a machine. Interactive multimedia and computer graphics technologies make it more 'human-familiar' by creating an expanded illusion of life in terms of animated phenomena.

To Benjamin, film was a new, celebrated form of art in that era, because the cinema allows the mass audience to be 'unconscious' critics of art by subsuming the cult value of the art object in public exhibition. Perception of film is a middle ground between the concentrated appreciation of painting and the distracted use of architecture. I would argue that animated phenomena in digital media today are comparable to films in the 1930s. They shift the original instrumental value of the computer to an evocative and imaginative value by immersing human users in enduring and everyday environments, presenting an inclusive sense of liveliness that draws their undivided and divided attention, triggering evocative material-based imagination in their minds, and turning them into performers or animators. Technological liveliness denotes this value-changing phenomenon of computing technology.

Technological liveliness as a simulacrum of life

While Benjamin asserted that copies eclipsed the aura of the original, Jean Baudrillard was interested in how simulacra displace or dismiss the original (Baudrillard, 1988). Simulacra are the signs in contemporary media context that have no original referents. These media objects seem to imitate something but actually bear no relation to any reality. In fact, a simulacrum is by itself a part of the real, not the imaginary. As Baudrillard's well-known example of Disneyland reveals, the theme park is not an imaginary world for kids, but instead a simulacrum of the 'real' adult world, because the same stereotypical 'childishness' is increasingly prevalent everywhere as we experience it first-hand. A cultural critic might say that the ideology of the park is an integral part of the hegemony of the American culture. In short, simulacra blur the distinction between the real and the imaginary, and even become part of the real.

In this regard, technological liveliness is not just an illusion of life, but also a simulacrum of life. As I have argued, animated phenomena in digital media provoke material-based imagination and destabilize the opposition between material images (the real) and mental images (the imaginary). People engaging in animated phenomena of today see the animated images as 'real' phenomena, because the associated sensorimotor experiences are so embodied and evocative. Moreover, this expanded illusion of life is so pervasive in today's digitally mediated contexts that it becomes an integral part of everyday life. The multimedia artifacts mentioned in this book apparently imitate people's everyday experiences through all-round liveliness and constantly changing environments. However, they actually engender unprecedented behaviors and habits; for example, Web users of SnowDays may email virtual snowflakes with greetings as well as print and mail paper copies of the flakes as Christmas cards (a feature provided by the website). Similarly, parents may buy their kids *Angry Birds* birthday cakes that come with physically playable and edible slingshots and birds for launching. These new human behaviors not only embody the simulation of life supported by animated phenomena in digital media but also make it part of everyday life. Hence, technological liveliness is embodied and realized as a simulacrum.

Technological liveliness as a huge co-performance of humans and technologies

Animated phenomena transcend the instrumental value of the computer, giving rise to an imaginative value. Through provoking material-based imagination, digital media artifacts give rise to a simulacrum of life. At the heart of this embodiment lies the motor–sensory feedback loop mobilized by computational systems. Hence, there exists a nuanced interplay between animated phenomena and computers. On one hand, animated phenomena instill computers with soul and spirit by creating a holistic illusion of life and constantly changing environments. On the other, computing and related technologies enable various dynamic functions, for example metamorphosis, in animated phenomena. As I argued in a separate paper (Chow, 2009), this interplay short-circuits the notions of spirituality and functionality. The two seemingly contrasting terms 'spirit' and 'function' actually share a subtle and unnoticed link both etymologically and phenomenologically. The Latin origin of 'spirit' literally means 'breath', which is a physiological process of inhaling and exhaling, and the ability to breathe is a phenomenal function of living things. Hence, spirituality and functionality jointly describe a phenomenon of life. Obviously computers and digital media artifacts cannot 'breathe' literally, yet as this book has shown, they do perform many other dynamic functions, such as moving in response to stimuli. These animated phenomena are part of the modern life and they are 'real' to human users in the simulacrum of life, and they revitalize the original connection between the spiritual and the functional.

So, technological liveliness can be regarded as the technology-enabled spiritual–functional connection that 'animates' the computer and brings it closer to humans. One can perceive and sense the phenomenon of life in today's computer-based systems. With animated phenomena, designers conceal the complexity and abstraction of the computer, and wrap it in a 'skin', which is very much like the costumes for marionettes, the lifelike shells of automata, the decorative cement of fountains, or the silk screen in shadow puppet theaters. These pre-digital systems embody the human pursuit of 'staging' technology, but 'veiling' it along the way, in order to create spectacles, suspense, and surprise for audiences. In this sense, animated phenomena help popularize and proliferate computing and related technologies in cultural and economical context. Their increasing accessibility and pervasiveness can potentially help adapt every technology-challenged novice into a tinkering hacker. Today many people are masters of configuring and customizing their smartphones. Users or consumers are invited to be animators, puppeteers, or even wizards in a kind of co-performance. It is a persistent and pervasive co-performance between humans and technologies in everyday life. Hence, technological liveliness, as a phenomenon, is not only technological but also cultural, economical, and personal.

Today, technological liveliness is becoming omnipresent. The huge co-performance continues to engross, assimilate, and shape our perception and psychology. It confronts us with a new uncanny valley, in which we negotiate familiarity and strangeness based on how we situate ourselves relative to those ubiquitous human-familiar digital media artifacts. One day we might see and 'believe' animated simulacra in digital media as natural as the dynamic phenomena in physical reality.

Consider the third animated case mentioned in Chapter 1 in which the baby flicks the paper magazine as if operating a tablet device. Our capacity to hunt or flee in physical space, which is believed to be a major training for human action and perception development in some primordial past (Arnheim, 1974, p. 372), would likely be shifted to techniques enabling us to 'crawl' or 'surf' in cyberspace.

References

Texts

Aarseth, E. J. (1997). *Cybertext: Perspectives on Ergodic Literature*. Baltimore, MD: Johns Hopkins University Press.

Aarseth, E. J. (2004). Genre Trouble: Narrativism and the Art of Simulation. In N. Wardrip-Fruin & P. Harrigan (Eds.), *First Person: New Media as Story, Performance, and Game* (pp. 45–55). Cambridge, MA: MIT Press.

Arnheim, R. (1969). *Visual Thinking*. Berkeley, CA: University of California Press.

Arnheim, R. (1974). *Art and Visual Perception: A Psychology of the Creative Eye* (New version, expanded and rev. ed.). Berkeley, CA: University of California Press.

Auslander, P. (1999). *Liveness: Performance in a Mediatized Culture*. London and New York: Routledge.

Barthes, R. (1973a). *Elements of Semiology*. New York: Hill and Wang.

Barthes, R. (1973b). *Mythologies*. London: Paladin.

Barthes, R. (1977a). The Death of the Author. In R. Barthes (Ed.), *Image, Music, Text* (S. Heath, Trans.) (pp. 142–148). London: Fontana.

Barthes, R. (1977b). From Work to Text. In R. Barthes (Ed.), *Image, Music, Text* (S. Heath, Trans.) (pp. 155–164). London: Fontana.

Barthes, R. (1977c). Rhetoric of the Image In R. Barthes (Ed.), *Image, Music, Text* (S. Heath, Trans.) (pp. 32–51). London: Fontana.

Barthes, R. & Balzac, H. D. (1974). *S/Z*. New York: Noonday Press.

Baudrillard, J. (1988). Simulacra and Simulation. In M. Poster (Ed.), *Jean Baudrillard, Selected Writings* (pp. 166–184). Stanford, CA: Stanford University Press.

Benjamin, W. (1968). The Work of Art in the Age of Mechanical Reproduction (H. Zohn, Trans.) *Illuminations* (pp. 217–251). New York: Schocken Books.

Blair, P. (1994). *Cartoon Animation*. Laguna Hills, CA: Walter Foster Pub.

Bolter, J. D. & Gromala, D. (2003). *Windows and Mirrors: Interaction Design, Digital Art, and the Myth of Transparency*. Cambridge, MA: MIT Press.

Bowker, G. C. & Star, S. L. (1999). *Sorting Things Out: Classification and its Consequences*. Cambridge, MA: MIT Press.

Brentano, F. C. (1995). *Psychology from an Empirical Standpoint* (Paperback ed.). London and New York: Routledge.

Cavallaro, D. (2006). *The Cinema of Mamoru Oshii: Fantasy, Technology, and Politics*. Jefferson, NC: McFarland & Co.

Cholodenko, A. (Ed.) (1991). *The Illusion of Life: Essays on Animation*. Sydney, NSW: Power Publications in Association with the Australian Film Commission.

Cholodenko, A. (Ed.) (2007). *The Illusion of Life II: More Essays on Animation*. Sydney, NSW: Power Pub.

Chow, K. K. N. (2009). The Spiritual-Functional Loop: Animation Redefined in the Digital Age. *Animation: An Interdisciplinary Journal, 4*(1), 77–89.

Chow, K. K. N. (2012). *Toward Intimacy in User Experience: Enduring Interaction in the Use of Computational Objects.* Paper presented at the 8th International Design and Emotion Conference, London.

Chow, K. K. N. & Harrell, D. F. (2011). *Enduring Interaction: An Approach to Analysis and Design of Animated Gestural Interfaces in Creative Computing Systems.* Paper presented at the 8th ACM Conference on Creativity and Cognition, Atlanta, USA.

Chow, K. K. N. & Harrell, D. F. (2012). Understanding Material-Based Imagination: Cognitive Coupling of Animation and User Action in Interactive Digital Artworks. *Leonardo Electronic Almanac, 17*(2), 50–65.

Colebrook, C. (2002). *Understanding Deleuze.* Crows Nest, NSW: Allen & Unwin.

Crawford, C. (2005). *Chris Crawford on Interactive Storytelling.* Berkeley, CA: New Riders.

Deleuze, G. (1986). *Cinema.* Minneapolis, MN: University of Minnesota.

Dennett, D. C. (1987). *The Intentional Stance.* Cambridge, MA: MIT Press.

Dewey, J. (1980). *Art as Experience.* New York: Perigee Books.

Dittrich, W. & Lea, S. (1994). Visual Perception of Intentional Motion. *Perception, 23*(3), 253–268.

Dixon, S. (2007). *Digital Performance: A History of New Media in Theater, Dance, Performance Art, and Installation.* Cambridge, MA: MIT Press.

Dourish, P. (2001). *Where the Action Is: The Foundations of Embedded Interaction.* Cambridge, MA: MIT Press.

Dreyfus, H. L. (1996). The Current Relevance of Merleau-Ponty's Phenomenology of Embodiment. *The Electronic Journal of Analytic Philosophy, 4*(Spring).

Eco, U. (1976). *A Theory of Semiotics.* Bloomington, IN: Indiana University Press.

Eco, U. (1989). *The Open Work.* Cambridge, MA: Harvard University Press.

Ekman, P. (1992). An Argument for Basic Emotions. *Cognition and Emotion, 6*(3), 169–200.

Ekman, P. (1994). All Emotions Are Basic. In P. Ekman & R. J. Davidson (Eds.), *The Nature of Emotion: Fundamental Questions* (pp. 15–19). New York: Oxford University Press, Ltd.

Eskelinen, M. (2004). Towards Computer Game Studies. In N. Wardrip-Fruin & P. Harrigan (Eds.), *First Person: New Media as Story, Performance, and Game* (pp. 36–44). Cambridge, MA: MIT Press.

Fagone, J. (2008). The Video-Game Programmer Saving Our 21st-Century Souls. *Esquire.* Features: Best and Brightest 2008. Retrieved March 28, 2013, from http://www.esquire.com/features/best-and-brightest-2008/future-of-video-game-design-1208

Fauconnier, G. (1985). *Mental Spaces: Aspects of Meaning Construction in Natural Language.* Cambridge, MA: MIT Press.

Fauconnier, G. (2001). Conceptual Blending and Analogy. In D. Gentner, K. J. Holyoak & B. N. Kokinov (Eds.), *The Analogical Mind: Perspectives from Cognitive Science* (pp. 255–285). Cambridge, MA: MIT Press.

Fauconnier, G. & Turner, M. (2002). *The Way We Think: Conceptual Blending and the Mind's Hidden Complexities.* New York: Basic Books.

Feng, Y. & Bodde, D. (1948). *A Short History of Chinese Philosophy.* New York: Macmillan Co.

Furniss, M. (1998). *Art in Motion: Animation Aesthetics.* Sydney, NSW: John Libbey.

Gibson, J. J. (1986). *The Ecological Approach to Visual Perception*. Hillsdale, NJ: L. Erlbaum.

Glenberg, A. M. (1997). What Memory is For. *Behavioral and Brain Sciences, 20*(1), 1–55.

Gombrich, E. H. (2002). *Art and Illusion: A Study in the Psychology of Pictorial Representation* (6th ed.). London: Phaidon Press.

Goodman, N. (1976). *Languages of Art: An Approach to a Theory of Symbols* (2nd ed.). Indianapolis, IN: Hakett Publications.

Gregory, R. L. (1997). *Eye and Brain: The Psychology of Seeing* (5th ed.). Princeton, NJ: Princeton University Press.

Hallnäs, L. (2011). On the Foundations of Interaction Design Aesthetics: Revisiting the Notions of Form and Expression. *International Journal of Design, 5*(1), 73–84.

Hayles, N. K. (2002). *Writing Machines*. Cambridge, MA: MIT Press.

Hayles, N. K. (2005). *My Mother was a Computer: Digital Subjects and Literary Texts*. Chicago, IL: University of Chicago Press.

Heider, F. & Simmel, M. (1944). An Experimental Study of Apparent Behavior. *American Journal of Psychology, 57*(2), 243–259.

Henricks, R. G. (1999). Re-exploring the Analogy of the *Dao* and the Field. In M. Csikszentmihalyi & P. J. Ivanhoe (Eds.), *Religious and Philosophical Aspects of the Laozi* (pp. 161–174). Albany, NY: State University of New York Press.

Hiraga, M. (2005). *Metaphor and Iconicity: A Cognitive Approach to Analysing Texts*. Houndmills, Basingstoke, Hampshire and New York: Palgrave Macmillan.

Hu, T. Y. G. (2010). *Frames of Anime: Culture and Image-building*. Hong Kong: Hong Kong University Press.

Hutchins, E. (2005). Material Anchors for Conceptual Blends. *Journal of Pragmatics, 37*(10), 1555–1577.

Jenkins, H. (2004). Game Design as Narrative Architecture. In N. Wardrip-Fruin & P. Harrigan (Eds.), *First Person: New Media as Story, Performance, and Game* (pp. 118–130). Cambridge, MA: MIT Press.

Johnson, M. (2008). *The Meaning of the Body: Aesthetics of Human Understanding*. Chicago, IL: University of Chicago Press.

Kaplin, S. (2001). A Puppet Tree: A Model for the Field of Puppet Theatre. In J. Bell (Ed.), *Puppets, Masks, and Performing Objects* (pp. 18–25). Cambridge, MA and London: MIT Press.

Kent, S. L. (2001). *The Ultimate History of Video Games: From Pong to Pokémon and Beyond, the Story Behind the Craze That Touched Our Lives and Changed the World*. Roseville, CA: Prima.

Kittler, F. A. (1997). There is No Software. In J. Johnston (Ed.), *Literature, Media, Information Systems: Essays* (pp. 147–155). Amsterdam: G+B Arts International.

Klein, N. M. (1993). *Seven Minutes: The Life and Death of the American Animated Cartoon*. London and New York: Verso.

Kleist, H. V. & Neumiller, T. G. (1972). On the Marionette Theatre. *The Drama Review: TDR, 16*(3), 22–26.

Knoespel, K. J. & Zhu, J. (2008). Continuous Materiality: Through a Hierarchy of Computational Codes. *The Fibreculture Journal* (11).

Koshland, D. E., Jr. (2002). The Seven Pillars of Life. *Science, 295*, 2215–2216.

Lakoff, G. (1987). *Women, Fire, and Dangerous Things: What Categories Reveal about the Mind*. Chicago, IL: University of Chicago Press.

Lakoff, G. & Johnson, M. (1999). *Philosophy in the Flesh: The Embodied Mind and its Challenge to Western Thought.* New York: Basic Books.

Lakoff, G. & Johnson, M. (2003). *Metaphors We Live By.* Chicago, IL: University of Chicago Press.

Lakoff, G. & Turner, M. (1989). *More than Cool Reason: A Field Guide to Poetic Metaphor.* Chicago, IL: University of Chicago Press.

Lamarre, T. (2009). *The Anime Machine: A Media Theory of Animation.* Minneapolis, MN: University of Minnesota Press.

Lewis, G. E. (2000). Too Many Notes: Computers, Complexity and Culture in Voyager. *Leonardo Music Journal, 10,* 33–39.

Lunenfeld, P. (1999). Unfinished Business. In P. Lunenfeld (Ed.), *The Digital Dialectic: New Essays on New Media* (pp. 6–23). Cambridge, MA: MIT Press.

Maeda, J. (2000). *Maeda@media.* London: Thames & Hudson.

Maiese, M. (2011). *Embodiment, Emotion, and Cognition.* Basingstoke, Hampshire and New York, NY: Palgrave Macmillan.

Mandler, J. M. (1992). How to Build a Baby: II. Conceptual Primitives. *Psychological Review, 99*(4), 587–604.

Manovich, L. (2001). *The Language of New Media.* Cambridge, MA: MIT Press.

Mateas, M. (2003). *Expressive AI: Games and Artificial Intelligence.* Paper presented at the Level Up: Digital Games Research Conference, Utrecht, The Netherlands.

Mazé, R. & Redström, J. (2005). Form and the Computational Object. *Digital Creativity, 16*(1), 7–18.

McCarthy, J. & Wright, P. (2004). *Technology as Experience.* Cambridge, MA: MIT Press.

McCloud, S. (1994). *Understanding Comics* (1st Harper Perennial ed.). New York, NY: Harper Perennial.

Merleau-Ponty, M. (1962). *Phenomenology of Perception.* London: Routledge & Kegan Paul.

Mitchell, W. J. T. (1986). *Iconology: Image, Text, Ideology.* Chicago, IL: University of Chicago Press.

Montfort, N. & Bogost, I. (2009). *Racing the Beam: The Atari Video Computer System.* Cambridge, MA: MIT Press.

Monticelli, R. D. (2006). The Feeling of Values: For a Phenomenological Theory of Affectivity. In S. Bagnara & G. C. Smith (Eds.), *Theories and Practice in Interaction Design* (pp. 57–76). Ivrea, Italy: Interaction Design Institute Ivrea and Mahwah, NJ: Lawrence Erlbaum.

Murray, J. H. (1997). *Hamlet on the Holodeck.* Cambridge, MA: MIT Press.

Murray, J. H. (2004). From Game-Story to Cyberdrama. In N. Wardrip-Fruin & P. Harrigan (Eds.), *First Person: New Media as Story, Performance, and Game* (pp. 2–11). Cambridge, MA: MIT Press.

Murray, J. H. (2012). *Inventing the Medium: Principles of Interaction Design as a Cultural Practice.* Cambridge, MA: MIT Press.

Needham, J. (1956). *Science and Civilisation in China* (Volume 2). Cambridge, UK: Cambridge University Press.

Needham, J. (1962). *Science and Civilisation in China* (Volume 4, Part 1). Cambridge, UK: Cambridge University Press.

Nielsen, J. (1993). *Usability Engineering.* Boston, MA: AP Professional.

Norman, D. A. (1988). *The Psychology of Everyday Things.* New York: Basic Books Inc.

Reiniger, L. (1970). *Shadow Theatres and Shadow Films*. London: Batsford and New York: Watson-Guptill Publications.

Reynolds, C. (1986). Boids (Flocks, Herds, and Schools: a Distributed Behavioral Model). Retrieved March 28, 2013, from http://www.red3d.com/cwr/boids/

Riskin, J. (2007). *Genesis Redux: Essays in the History and Philosophy of Artificial Life*. Chicago, IL: University of Chicago Press.

Rizzolatti, G. & Craighero, L. (2004). The Mirror-Neuron System. *Annual Review of Neuroscience, 27*, 169–192.

Rizzolatti, G., Fadiga, L., Gallese, V. & Fogassi, L. (1996). Premotor Cortex and the Recognition of Motor Actions. *Cognitive Brain Research, 3*, 131–141.

Rizzolatti, G. & Sinigaglia, C. (2008). *Mirrors in the Brain: How Our Minds Share Actions and Emotions*. Oxford and New York: Oxford University Press.

Rohrer, J. (2007). What I Was Trying to Do with Passage. Retrieved March 28, 2013, from http://hcsoftware.sourceforge.net/passage/statement.html

Russon, J. E. (2003). *Human Experience: Philosophy, Neurosis, and the Elements of Everyday Life*. Albany, NY: State University of New York Press.

Saussure, F. D. (1983). *Course in General Linguistics* (R. Harris, Trans.). London: Duckworth.

Scholl, B. J. & Tremoulet, P. D. (2000). Perceptual Causality and Animacy. *Trends in Cognitive Sciences, 4*(8), 299–309.

Shimohara, K. & Langton, C. (1996). *Preface of Artificial Life V*. Paper presented at the Fifth International Workshop on Artificial Life, Nara, Japan.

Shneiderman, B. (2003 [1983]). Direct Manipulation: A Step beyond Programming Languages. In N. Wardrip-Fruin & N. Montfort (Eds.), *The New Media Reader* (pp. 486–498). Cambridge, MA and London: MIT Press.

Shneiderman, B. & Maes, P. (1997). Direct Manipulation versus Interface Agents. *Interactions, 4*(6), 42–61.

Sobchack, V. C. (1992). *The Address of the Eye: A Phenomenology of Film Experience*. Princeton, NJ: Princeton University Press.

Sobchack, V. C. (2000). *Meta-morphing: Visual Transformation and the Culture of Quick-change*. Minneapolis, MN: University of Minnesota Press.

Sobchack, V. C. (2004). *Carnal Thoughts: Embodiment and Moving Image Culture*. Berkeley, CA: University of California Press.

Stafford, B. M. (2007). *Echo Objects: The Cognitive Work of Images*. Chicago, IL: University of Chicago Press.

Stafford, B. M. & Terpak, F. (2001). *Devices of Wonder: From the World in a Box to Images on a Screen*. Los Angeles, CA: Getty Research Institute.

Stewart, J. A. (1982). *The Perception of Animacy* (Ph.D. thesis), University of Pennsylvania.

Terpak, F. (2001). Automata (Batteries Not Included). In B. M. Stafford, F. Terpak & I. Poggi (Eds.), *Devices of Wonder: From the World in a Box to Images on a Screen* (pp. 266–274). Los Angeles, CA: Getty Research Institute.

Thelen, E. (1995). Time-Scale Dynamics and the Development of an Embodied Cognition. In R. F. Port & T. Van Gelder (Eds.), *Mind as Motion: Explorations in the Dynamics of Cognition*. Cambridge, MA: MIT Press.

Thomas, F. & Johnston, O. (1984). *Disney Animation: The Illusion of Life* (Popular ed.). New York: Abbeville Press.

Tillis, S. (2001). The Art of Puppetry in the Age of Media Production. In J. Bell (Ed.), *Puppets, Masks, and Performing Objects* (pp. 172–185). Cambridge, MA and London: MIT Press.

Tremoulet, P. D. & Feldman, J. (2000). Perception of Animacy from the Motion of a Single Object. *Perception, 29*(8), 943–951.

Turkle, S. (1984). *The Second Self: Computers and the Human Spirit.* New York: Simon and Schuster.

Turner, M. (1996). *The Literary Mind.* New York: Oxford University Press.

Utterback, C. (2004). Unusual Positions – Embodied Interaction with Symbolic Spaces. In N. Wardrip-Fruin & P. Harrigan (Eds.), *First Person: New Media as Story, Performance, and Game* (pp. 218–226). Cambridge, MA: MIT Press.

Varela, F. J., Thompson, E. & Rosch, E. (1991). *The Embodied Mind: Cognitive Science and Human Experience.* Cambridge, MA: MIT Press.

Wargo, R. J. J. (1990). Japanese Ethics: Beyond Good and Evil. *Philosophy East and West, 40*(4), 499–509.

Wells, P. (1998). *Understanding Animation.* London and New York: Routledge.

Wiener, N. (1961). *Cybernetics: Or, Control and Communication in the Animal and the Machine* (2nd ed.). New York: MIT Press.

Williams, R. (2001). *The Animator's Survival Kit.* London: Faber and Faber.

Wittgenstein, L. (1953). *Philosophical Investigations* (G. E. M. Anscombe, Trans.). Oxford: Blackwell.

Woolford, E. (1999). Animacy Hierarchy Effects on Object Agreement. In P. A. Kotey (Ed.), *New Dimensions in African Linguistics and Languages* (pp. 203–216). Trenton, NJ: Africa World Press.

Wu, H. (1996). *The Double Screen: Medium and Representation in Chinese Painting.* London: Reaktion Books.

Yamaguchi, M. (2002). Karakuri: The Ludic Relationship between Man and Machine in Tokugawa Japan. In J. Hendry & M. Raveri (Eds.), *Japan at Play: The Ludic and Logic of Power* (pp. 72–83). London and New York: Routledge.

Yusuke, S. (2011). *Concept of Kami in Japanese Animation and Comic: Late 20th Century Japanese Thought and Popular Culture.* Paper presented at the Joint Conference of the Association for Asian Studies and the International Convention of Asia Scholars, Honolulu, Hawaii, USA.

Film and TV

Aladdin. (1992). Directed by Ron Clements & John Musker. Walt Disney Pictures. Film.

Dark City. (1998). Directed by Alex Proyas. New Line Cinema. Film.

Dragon Ball. (1985–1995). Written by Akira Toriyama. Produced by Toei Animation. Television program.

Ghost in the Shell. (1995). Directed by Mamoru Oshii. Internationally distributed by Manga Entertainment. Film.

Jurassic Park. (1993). Directed by Steven Spielberg. Universal Studios. Film.

Luxo Jr. (1986). Directed and written by John Lasseter. Pixar. Short film.

Monsters, Inc. (2001). Directed by Pete Docter. Walt Disney Pictures. Film.

Princess Mononoke. (1997). Directed by Hayao Miyazaki. Internationally distributed by Miramax Films. Film.

Starship Troopers. (1997). Directed by Paul Verhoeven. Touchstone Pictures. Film.

Terminator 2: Judgment Day. (1991). Directed by James Cameron. TriStar Pictures. Film.

The Adventures of Prince Achmed. (1926). Directed and written by Lotte Reiniger. Milestone Films. Film.

The Perfect Storm. (2000). Directed by Wolfgang Petersen. Warner Bros. Pictures. Film.

Vertigo. (1958). Directed by Alfred Hitchcock. Originally distributed by Paramount Pictures. Film.

Digital Works

Angry Birds. (first released in 2009). Rovio Entertainment. Video game.

Animata. (circa 2008). Kitchen Budapest. Software system.

Breakout. (1976). Atari Inc. Video game.

Ecotonoha. (2003–circa 2010). Designed by Yugo Nakamura. NEC. Website.

Electroplankton. (2005). Designed by Toshio Iwai. Nintendo. Video game.

flOw. (2006). Created by Jenova Chen. Video game.

Game of Life. (1970). Written by John Conway. First mentioned by Martin Gardner in *Scientific American* 223 (October 1970): 120–123. Computer program.

Gran Turismo. (first released in 1997). Sony Computer Entertainment. Video game.

Koi Pond. (2009). The Blimp Pilots. iOS app.

La Linea Interactive. (2008). Created by Patrick Boivin. Uploaded to YouTube on August 18, 2008. Interactive video.

Lode Runner. (1983). Brøderbund. Video game.

Modern Living / Neurotica series. (1998). Created by Han Hoogerbrugge. Interactive comics.

N702iS Water-level Interface. (2006). Designed by Oki Sato & Takaya Fukumoto. NEC. Flash software.

Ōkami. (first released in 2006). Capcom. Video game.

Out My Window. (2010). Directed by Katerina Cizek. National Film Board of Canada. Interactive documentary.

Passage. (2007). Created by Jason Rohrer. Video game.

Phoenix Wright: Ace Attorney. (first released in 2001). Capcom. Video game.

Phoenix. (1980). Centuri. Video game.

Pong. (1972). Designed by Nolan Bushnell. Engineered by Al Alcorn. Atari Inc. Video game.

Prince of Persia. (1989). Brøderbund. Video game.

Ruben & Lullaby. (2009). Created by Erik Loyer. iOS app.

Shadow Monsters. (2004). Created by Philip Worthington. Interactive installation.

SnowDays. (2002–ongoing). Always Snowing LLC. Website.

Sodaconstructor. (2000). Created by Ed Burton. Soda Creative. Software system.

Spawn. (2009). EODSoft. iOS app.
Super Mario Bros. (first released in 1985). Nintendo. Video game.
Tetris. (1984). Designed by Alexey Pajitnov. Video game.
Text Rain. (1999). Created by Camille Utterback & Romy Achituv. Interactive installation.
Wii Sports. (2006). Nintendo. Video game.

Index

Printed in the United States
by Baker & Taylor Publisher Services